# "HELLO BROTHER"

# "HELLO BROTHER"

## The world from a motor scooter

## 1964-1967

## Gerry Rooney

Library of Congress Control Number:     2008909383
ISBN:            Hardcover               978-1-4363-7902-1
                 Softcover               978-1-4363-7901-4

**To order additional copies of this book, contact:**
Xlibris Corporation
1-888-795-4274
www.Xlibris.com
Orders@Xlibris.com
54488

# *DEDICATION*

I wish to dedicate this book to the many citizens of various parts of the world who allowed me to enter their lives and learn so many profound lessons from their hospitality. They led me on a world journey to the most precious prize of the entire sojourn—meeting my wife, Ayako Miyata, whose love, support and inspiration have changed and enriched my life in countless, beautiful ways. She continues to bless our children, Monica and Mark, and our grandchildren, Haley and Jack, with the caring, gentleness and commitment I found in her native land of Japan long before she came into my life. She has become the exquisite, life-long answer to my intrigue with the "Land of the Rising Sun".

# *ACKNOWLEDGMENTS*

I wish to acknowledge the following friends for their assistance and guidance in the publication of this book:

Benjamin Baker
Irmgard Denault
Ralph Hickok
Myra Lopes

# FOREWORD

When I first met Gerry Rooney at a youth hostel in Port Said, Egypt in 1966, both of us were traveling around the world and communicating in German. We often joke about this episode as being quite international because one Japanese and one American had met in Egypt and spoke mostly German. Since then, for over 42 years we have been close friends which means we know what the other is thinking and feeling even though we may not have met for a long time.

This voluminous book on Gerry's around-the-the-world journey for over three years all alone by scooter is not simply an adventurous story, but is a human drama. You will find Gerry in so many countries with geographical/cultural differences, as if he has been living there for years. This is because Gerry accepts these differences quickly through his linguistic talent and his warm-heartedness to recognize others as his fellow human beings.

I still remember his letter after his accomplishment of this long journey, which told us we are all brothers as in his poem cited at the end of this book. Gerry wrote these letters in English, German, French and some other languages as follows: "At one time I was traveling around the world on a USAF B-52 with nuclear bombs and, thereafter, I traveled the world on my scooter with my guitar. I have found people in all locations are the same once we communicate." You will find the same lessons as Gerry obtained through his journey by reading this fantastic book on humanity.

Dr. Hiroshi Nishida
Tokyo, Japan

# *PROLOGUE*

After having received my officer's commission as a 2nd Lieutenant upon graduation from college, I spent almost five years in the Strategic Air Command of the U.S. Air Force. As a navigator/bombardier in a B-52 I completed 15 flights to Europe as part of our airborne readiness during the cold war. We would take off from Dow AFB in Bangor, Maine and cross the Atlantic to be refueled in the air by our KC-135 tanker planes from Spain as we crossed that country into the Mediterranean Sea area. After a loop in the western part of that body we would refuel again, make a smaller loop and head back across the Atlantic landing at Dow AFB 24 hours after take-off. During these flights I would have the opportunity to look down on Spain, Portugal, Mt.Etna, the Balaric Islands and the North African coast. However, 6-7 miles above was the closest I ever got to any of this intriguing land.

When it became obvious to me that I would not make the Air Force my career I started planning on what to do thereafter. My decision was to travel and see some of the places I had flown over and many more if possible. I was at one of those "break points" in life having acquired a college degree, completed my military obligation and being single. I determined to take advantage of the lack of future obligations and planned to see some of the world. My initial plan was to go around parts of Europe for eight months to a year. As you will read, my lack of commitment to a schedule extended my journey in time and distance to an extent I could not have predicted at the outset. What I launched as a vague interest in learning about other people's lives became a true education of the human element in greatly diverse areas of the globe. This was to be the most life-changing experience one could imagine. I now invite the reader to follow me through the events, highs, lows, revelations and discoveries as I visited so many fellow inhabitants of this planet in their own back yards. To them I owe a great deal of gratitude, respect and admiration.

# CHAPTER ONE

## "To leave or not to leave; that is . . ."

Confronting armed Bedouins in the middle of the remote Jordanian desert at night, driving my motor scooter through a snow storm in the Alps, being accepted as an Arab on the construction site of the Aswan Dam and feeling comfortable as the female attendant picked up nearby soap wrappers in a communal Japanese bath were certainly the possible subjects of intoxicating daydreams. But, as I looked down at gorgeous Sally I had none of these fantasies in mind. Yet they were only a few of the adventures I faced in my coming travels.

She was a vivacious dark-haired eye-catcher who plied her journalist trade here in London. We were grassing in London's Hyde Park on my new, much-to-be-used poncho. I had met Sally a few days before as I watched "The Sound of Music" at the London Palace Theater. She was undoubtedly the most attractive girl I had met in my week in London. I had been used to just drooling over such a beauty from afar. However, having overheard her mention to her mother a guitar she had acquired but didn't know how to play, I had done the "diplomatic" thing by offering to give her some lessons from an imported "Yank" tutor. To the amazement of Bill, a fellow American visitor who had attended the theater with me, I had Sally's name, telephone number and a date before we got to the exit. I had spent the prior evening with Sally in her apartment actually teaching her, at least a little, about chord structures and tuning among other things. On this beautiful spring day in May I was supposed to initiate my world travels and I was fighting the urge to spend my entire sojourn on my poncho serenading Sally with my new guitar. What a monumental challenge for a young, eager bachelor to have to make this choice.

London's tulips greeted me

I had already checked out of the Highgate Youth Hostel in which I had been getting my first taste of this low-budget, youth-oriented system of inns, which I intended to use often. Hostels are quite affordable although you sacrifice a bit of privacy for the rates. Coming from a family of seven children, often augmented in numbers by foster children, I had long since lost any significant concern for a great deal of privacy. The overnight fee for this hostel and all of those in England was 3 shillings 6 pence (the equivalent of 49 cents US). The English pound was worth $2.80 USA making a shilling (the twentieth part) worth 14 cents. In many hostels you could get an English breakfast for 2 shillings 6 pence (US 35 cents). The night before I had been late getting back from Sally's apartment (there was always a curfew at hostels) and had been fined 3 S 6 (49 cents). However, this morning I had volunteered to help wash all the breakfast dishes after those assigned had run out on the chore (another requirement of hostel living) and my "fine" had been reimbursed by the warden, as the person in charge is known. He had allowed me to stay four days beyond the normal 3-day limit in big city hostels.

I had arrived in London on Whitsun Holiday weekend (Saturday, May 16, 1964) with one military style B-4 bag and a sleeping bag, the sum total of my luggage for a trip I thought could take me around the world. BOAC flight 562 had settled onto the firmament of its homeland in a sea of warm sunshine after a short six hour flight from Boston. My first encounter with foreign customs and immigration proved to be uneventful. I was given a visa good for two months, two big white "X's" on my unopened bags and I was on my way. I headed for the Highgate Youth Hostel and along the way decided to carry my B-4 bag on my shoulder. As I swung it up to that position and bent down to accommodate it my prescription sunglasses fell out of my pocket and smashed on the sidewalk. I spent the week seeing the sites of this historic capital and preparing for the first part of my journey which included leaving my sunglasses for repair and forwarding to my pen-pal's house in Ireland. I had learned how to get around by the "tube" (subway) quite well and I found it quite convenient. I also had to search for an acoustic guitar and a bicycle on which I would see the countryside. I ended up buying a 3-speed Triumph bicycle for 9 pounds ($25.20) and modifying it so I could mount two second-hand army back-packs on the back fender as panniers. Realizing that I would not be able to accommodate my B-4 bag on the Triumph, I had removed all the essentials I could fit into the panniers and also sent this bag on by surface carrier to the home of my Irish pen pal. I managed to mount my sleeping bag across the rear carrier and strapped my new German-made Framus guitar upside down on it. I had bought it for $42 with $11 more for a case that might withstand the bumpy trip ahead as well as the expected rains. Now I was ready for the road.

When I first loaded my bike to start my peddling around the hills of Britain it was on a beautiful clear day and I couldn't help but check on the possibility of spending a few more precious hours with Sally. We met at Hyde Park, which led to my current dilemma. Before I knew it the time was 7:15 PM and I had to force myself to part with this elegant example of charming English womanhood. I headed down the 23 miles of road leading to Windsor singing the songs from the musical, which had been the stage for my first meeting with this fair young maiden from Birmingham.

# CHAPTER TWO

## On the road

When I awoke the following morning in the hostel my legs made it plain that I was fortunate in having come only 23 miles on the cycle the previous day. Not only were the leg muscles sore but, another part of my anatomy reminded me that it would not hurt matters if I decided to lose a few extra pounds which had been carried by the all-too-narrow seat the day before.

As I was leaving church that morning Mother Nature decided that it was time to water the lawn and I donned my faithful poncho earning myself many disbelieving glances from the local populace; a reaction, which was to follow me in many lands. It was made of dark green nylon with a hood and snaps down the sides allowing it to be opened into a rectangle approximately 7' x 4'. It would turn out to be the best $2 investment I would make for the trip. I had no idea as to the number of uses I would make of it in so many different countries I was to visit.

On this day I spent some time visiting Windsor Castle, which had been the home of royalty for 800 years and, thereafter, treated myself to a real English lunch of steak and kidney pie. I quite enjoyed it and was to be pleased on many occasions that I was never a finicky eater. I crossed the bridge over the Thames River and found myself within a few minutes walk of the most famous school in the world, Eton College, founded by Henry VI in 1440. I found the young students' attire, tuxedos, in great contrast to the gang of "Rockers" who were causing concern on the other side of the bridge. They were probably cruising around on their motorcycles looking for a smaller number of their better-dressed rivals, the "Mods", who move about on motor scooters. Together they represented a more modern version of what the British remember as the "Teddy Boys".

On the next day I pushed my tired legs a bit more and covered the 45 miles to the former capital of England, Winchester. As I cycled through the countryside I became aware of another popular and practical habit of the British, roadside picnics around the boot (trunk) of the car at noon. I found that a car was not always necessary for this event as I observed whole families touring on motorcycles with side-cars. Almost always this ritual was accompanied by a small fire over which to heat water for the ever-present cup of tea. When chatting with different individuals along the way I found that they were generally awestruck that a "Yank" would consider travel by bicycle. This was probably due to the foreign perception that all Americans travel in the equivalent of a Cadillac.

Due to the heat of the day and my efforts in this relatively longer trip, I decided that a cool dip in a pool would be the finest thing I could do for my tired body and my sagging spirits. As of the first plunge I learned that the pool was built over a stream, which was spring-fed from only 6 miles away. Once I got over the initial shock I headed for the diving board and did a reasonable "jack-knife". Having been pre-assured by the manager regarding the depth, I was more than surprised when I stabbed both arms into the loose mucky riverbed up to my elbows. Thereafter, I had to be content with simply relaxing in the frigid bath.

The hostel in Winchester was rather charming showing evidence of its original purpose as a gristmill. Most of the decor consisted of rough planking from former days. At wash-up time the visitors would descend through a trap door in the main room to the area of the waterwheel beside the stream. Several washbasins were located on a rough shelf along with small mirrors. Close by was a bucket with a rope attached which would be lowered into the stream to obtain water for washing. This was reportedly (and believably) the oldest hostel in England. However, this did not detract from the charm of the environment as attested to by the large number of hostellers present.

For supper I tried another typical British standard, fish and chips. Of course chips are French fried potatoes. What we called potato chips are known as crisps in England. Being a fish lover this dish was to provide many a meal for me in my tour of Britain at only 19 cents US, a low-budget traveler's dream.

Before heading for Southampton I splurged on a polyethylene water bottle and a life-saving padded seat cover. I found that I did much less stand-up peddling during the 55-mile ride to the city from which the Mayflower left to carry the Pilgrims to the New World in 1620. A large monument in memory of one of the youngest men on that ship, John Alden, stands in a prominent place facing the port from which he departed. As I scanned the harbor I noticed that a much more modern vessel, the Queen Elizabeth, was tied up there.

Not far on the road to Blanford I crossed a stock grid and found myself in close proximity to various un-penned animals as I continued through the New Forest. The relatively slow pace of a bicycle through such a beautiful area almost defies a person to ignore the wonders of nature. I was quickly brought back to the realities of our mechanical age when I passed within four feet of a three-car collision as it happened. With my heart doing an Anglo-Saxon version of the cha-cha, I carried on to become involved again with what nature had provided.

Milton Abbas Hostel was listed as being in Blanford, but after many hours I realized that it was actually located eight miles beyond the town in the hills. After considerable effort I ended up at about 10:30 PM on the top of a small mountain, pushing the bike through waist-high grass, which was already soaked with dew. I was convinced that, if there was a hostel there, it had to be the most remote one in the world. Having waded around for another half hour, I followed a slight flicker of light and came upon the elusive building. I quickly realized why the light was so dim; there was no electricity. This plus the lack of running water and the condition of the premises might discourage some visitors but, to real genuine hostellers, it provided the basic physical shell around which to build a sincere, if short, friendship. I'd always been a believer in people and their worth as compared to fancy surroundings and sophisticated facilities. I'm anything but a stylish dresser which supports my outlook that, "clothes certainly do not make the man". These and other such basic premises were to be continually confirmed by even more obvious examples among the various peoples I would meet who are really not so different under the surface.

The following day was very warm and would have been ideal if I had not had to strain in low gear to top many of the rolling hills, which compensated with green panoramas to please the eye and lens. I should mention that I had bought a Zeiss Ikon Contessa (German-made camera) from a colonel in the Air Force prior to my leaving. It **was** a uniquely small camera with a folding lens and all of the functions had to be manually set. This took some getting used to for me having done all my limited photography with a Kodak Brownie Hawkeye "aim and shoot" model prior to this. I had made a decision to take colored slides so I could later show them to many people at a time. This camera was a steal for $150.

Having stopped to chat with some wondering Gypsies of the more genuine variety, I decided that I would sacrifice sitting for progress and push the bike up the long steep hill ahead. I had almost succeeded in doing so when I was stopped by the sound of a pleasant greeting from a woman across the street. She had queried as to where I had come from with such a huge load on my "push bike". She chuckled at the answer of, "near Boston originally" and decided that if she did not offer me a cool drink, I might not make it to the top. Thus, I was ushered into the kitchen of Mrs. Agnes (Bunny) Newton and started the first in a long series of invaluable experiences with the families of the countries through which I was traveling. As we chatted about my background and current intentions, the cool drink extended to tea and sandwiches. As we swapped a number of common outlooks, it became quite obvious that she had a great liking for her "Yank" cousins across the Atlantic. I learned this was partly due to the fact that she had been a British nurse assigned with the U.S. Army Air Corps in North Africa during World War II. She still retained a contact with many of her former associates who had returned to their homes in the USA. When I mentioned that I had just finished five years of duty in her favorite branch of the service (now the USAF), it not only endeared me to her but prompted her to ask me to wait until her son, John, returned from school. He was in his early teens and, like many of that age, he had an insatiable curiosity regarding airplanes and flying. Sometime during the following hour "mom" decided that she was going to adopt me for the day. Excuses of having to make more progress not withstanding, she settled the matter quickly and started playing the hostess in earnest. She placed a chair in the back yard overlooking the beautiful rolling countryside, the town of Shaftesbury being the highest in England, and brought the local newspaper for me to read while I was waiting. Shortly thereafter all my soiled clothes had to be dug out of my rucksacks so she could wash them. Upon his arrival, John and I had a great chat, which ended with a guitar songfest, which was also witnessed by a number of close and curious neighbors.

I found Harry, the father, and Wendy, the daughter, equally as hospitable as the other family members. "Mom" had introduced me to her homemade curry and chutney in the afternoon and dinner was just as homey as I quickly integrated into the atmosphere of this typical English home. I had learned that curry is like a spicy stew and chutney reminded me of the piccalilli my mother made when I was younger. With our large family and both parents emigrating from Scotland, our usual meals were rather basic and seldom involved delving into any exotic dishes from other cultures.

"Bunny" and family

The evening was spent in exchanging ideas regarding life in our respective countries and the consistent sadness at the news of the assassination of Pres. John F. Kennedy just six months prior. This was a subject to be brought up with consistent grief throughout my travels.

The day was topped off with a soothing hot bath after which I was tucked into an extremely comfortable bed to contemplate the close bond I had formed with this fine family in such a short time. I had no way of knowing how far into the future this relationship would last.

Morning brought a church holyday and we attended Mass together, the Newtons being one of the few Roman Catholic families in the area. At the end of Mass "mom" had to introduce me to the priest and her friends at the town teahouse where we all partook of their after-church ritual of coffee. I was paraded through the town as if I were some dignitary with proud introductions at every stop including the local grocery store. As I finally packed my bike for departure, my hostess was preparing lunch and we chatted our way to a last warm good-by but, not before I had signed and left my copy of "Profiles in Courage" for this warm-hearted bundle of hospitality. We had discussed the book the prior evening and she had mentioned that it was not available there. I thought that by leaving it I could convey a small amount of appreciation for the open warmth and basic humane concern I had found in the home of absolute strangers. The expression on her face as I peddled away from Sabratha (the name of her home) told me that she well understood my intentions.

This had been the first of many fascinating experiences which would bolster my faith in people to the point where I would travel anywhere among any type of people with confidence in finding the heterogeneous distribution of personalities present in my home town. I later determined that the most significant factor in confirming this idea was to be the manner in which I presented my aim and purpose in being present among the local populace.

The Roman Baths of the Town of Bath were amazingly well preserved considering that they had been started in 863 B.C. They adjoin the Abbey, which had been the site of the crowning of the first King of England, Edgar, in 973 A.D. The road through Oxford to Stratford-on-Avon gleamed its reflection of all due to the continual presence of fallen rain. During that journey I had had the occasion of using my poncho for its prime purpose of rain repellent. I felt quite comfortable when I first donned it and headed down the slick highway. However, I was to become aware of several aspects of this arrangement, which I had not considered. First, as I gained speed along the well-traveled road, I found the front of the poncho becoming filled with air, which would lift it to the point where I could hardly see over the top. I ended up fighting to keep it down with one hand as I used the other in my struggle to retain control of the bicycle at high speed amidst traffic. A length of half inch elastic tied around my waist eventually took care of the situation. Next the air stream filled the hood of my "old faithful" and elevated the rear portion of the hood resulting in the front part coming down over my eyes to obscure my vision. This was adjusted by threading a piece of nylon cord through some holes I punched around the face area of the hood. This allowed me to tie it under my chin after I had put on my long-billed cap. I found that problems, taken one at a time without the pressure of time limits set by "modern" society, could usually be solved quite simply using materials and tools on hand. In the case of complex involvements, a bit of ingenuity can go a long way towards maintenance until the genuine material can be obtained.

I am not much interested in things of the past and I admit to a great void in my liberal education. I am more concerned with the present and the factors that govern the day-to-day lives of the masses. However, I could not help but be impressed as I visited the various areas of the town of Shakespeare. The Collegiate Church of the Holy Trinity in which he was buried in 1616 seemed to have retained the aura of his eternal presence. Therein are displayed the original recordings of his baptismal and burial ceremonies. The theatre, although of more modern design, sits on the edge of his beloved Avon, which flows its continuous tribute to the renowned author. Even though in honesty I must disclaim any useful acquaintanceship with his works, I cannot but recognize the talent of this great writer whose contribution to the literature of the world is widely hailed and universally applauded. When I saw his "King Henry V" in the theatre there was standing room only. But the time on my feet was well spent as I absorbed a fractional amount of the depth of his work. I had to agree that the four shillings (.56) admission was a mere token for the overall experience of witnessing the performance of his play in the actual surroundings of his homeland.

A statue of Lady Godiva is located in the central square of Coventry where she made her famous ride in protest to the heavy taxes her husband levied on the people there. Not far away stands the remains of Coventry Cathedral, which was almost totally destroyed in an air raid in 1940. Behind the alter (built in 1373) are found the only two remaining words of an inscription, "Father, forgive . . ." The new cathedral, for which Queen Elizabeth laid the corner stone in 1956, is physically attached to the old one and stands in great contrast to it. This was the only city in England, which at this time had the equivalent of the American shopping plaza with many diverse shops located along a central mall.

Continuing north I passed through Birmingham and Matlock Bath on my way into the Peak District. Castleton Youth Hostel being closed, I stayed at Edale Hostel, which was very large and beautifully situated on the side of a hill. I was amazed to find that in this area I could read a newspaper outside by natural light at 11:00 PM and it was not due to bright moon light. The following day I returned to the Castleton Hostel to pick up the first mail I received since I left home. I was thankful to see that this included the mailers for my film.

With the 1600-foot mountain (which I had crossed the night before) in front of me I decided to take the easy way out and caught a train for the ten-mile trip through the tunnel in the hill. I actually felt like a first-class tourist for about 25 minutes as I scanned the remains of Roman roads crossing this rugged area.

Although I was quite comfortable doing 55 to 65 miles a day by this time, I had to make a real effort to climb the hills through Oldham and Burnley on the way to Clitheroe. I believe that it was this particular stretch of cycling that caused the strain of my Achilles' tendon that was to bother me for several days to come. Later as I had supper in the Blackburn's Farmhouse Restaurant, I found out that my destination was another 11 miles up the hill. With my leg bothering me at that late hour, I got permission from the owners to use their barn loft for shelter and spread out my sleeping bag for its inauguration. At breakfast the next morning I learned that my hosts were great fans of my mother's famous cousin. Matt Busby was considered to be the

"Babe Ruth" of British soccer. He was a fine player and had greatly extended his fame as the Manager of the Manchester United Soccer Team. Having met him in California during his American tour, I felt a great deal of pride at the consistency of the expressions of admiration and affection for him, which I encountered throughout the British Empire. Young Roger Blackburn had missed getting Matt's autograph on his big day at the match so, I promised to try to get it for him when I would visit Matt a short while later. I can remember this young man being quite concerned that I was so far away from my home and my mother. I had to vow that I would send him a card when I had finally arrived within the protective walls of my home again.

My British transportation

From the 500-year old Blackburn farmhouse I headed through the Trough of Boland to enter Lancashire. As I peddled on to Kendal in the Lake District, it occurred to me that many English families seemed to use motorcycles with sidecars as a common means of transportation. The high price of petrol (gas), about .55 per gallon, helped to account for this as well as the abundance of small four-cylinder cars. Average sized American cars were considered to be over-powered monsters in the land where the Mini Minor was a favorite choice.

I was quite impressed with the discipline and respect I found in the Longlands School in Kendal where I was a guest teacher for a day thanks to the invitation from a new-found friend, Fred Atkinson. We had met in the hostel in London and I jumped at the chance to compare his school with those at which I had taught back home. I doubted that my ex-students would have been favorably impressed with the 9:00 AM to 4:00 PM schedule, which was common there. After school we took a ride through the Lake District which, in keeping with its reputation, was experiencing brutal, rainy weather. The road from the dock on the far side of Lake Windemere led us to many charming spots including Ambleside where we viewed the home and gravesite of William Wadsworth, the poet.

The next day 25 miles of cycling on the way to Manchester was enough to convince me that my left leg was not yet totally healed. Thus, I boarded a train for the remainder of the trip to Manchester Station. It was only a matter of a few miles from the train stop to 210 Kings Road, Chorlton where I had a joyous reunion with my mother's first cousin, Matt Busby, whose reputation as a beloved sportsman and personality had echoed along the roads that had led me to his door-step. My reception was, indeed, a royal one by the entire family including Jean (Matt's wife), Sandy and Irene (son and wife) and Don and Sheila (daughter and her husband). Four grandchildren completed Matt's close family in the immediate vicinity.

In the Busbys' garden

The beauty of Northern Wales

During my five days with the Busby's I was to spend much time with Matt and, thus, to acquire an understanding of how his popularity had spread so universally among soccer fans and others. Although his position often resulted in us associating with dignitaries of position or distinction, he never assumed any airs nor did he lose his down-to-earth humane outlook towards his fellow man regardless of the social place of the other individual. The esteem in which Matt was held by all had been emphasized by the reaction to a disastrous plane crash in Munich some years earlier which claimed the lives of a large percentage of those players known as "Busby's Babes". Matt, himself, had been seriously injured in that crash but had made a remarkable recovery to his present fit condition.

In Matt's office at Old Trafford, the United's stadium, I got his autograph for a couple of young fans including Roger Blackburn. As it was the off-season I couldn't get a chance to see the boys in action, but I had seen them in the USA when I first met their famous manager of whom I had heard so much in my younger days. The time spent with Matt and Jean was almost like stopping back home for a bit of more normal living during my hostel hopping. One understandable drawback to hostelling is that there are a number of rules, which do get quite restrictive at times. Because hostels were started primarily for hikers and cyclists who intend to spend the entire day taking advantage of the great outdoors, the policy of the hostels is usually "early to bed and early to rise" with lights out between 10 and 10:30 PM. I used to jokingly refer to the overall atmosphere as "compulsory health".

With panniers full of newly washed and mended clothes, and a great appreciation for a proudly proclaimed relative and his family, I headed out of Manchester and crossed the border into Wales. The northern beaches were fine but I decided to leave them in order to cut through the Snowdon Mountain area from Colwyn Bay to Bettsw-y-coed where Swallow Falls display their diverse patterns on the jagged rocks in the gorge. The hills certainly would have discouraged me on my southern journey from here had it not been for the majestic, uncluttered scenery which continually surrounded me. Thanks to the rest in Manchester I could at least count on my full strength in both ankles again. Just before reaching the sea again at Portmadoc, I passed through Tremadoc where stands the birthplace of Thomas Edward Lawrence, "Lawrence of Arabia".

As I continued south along the rugged and beautiful coast, I noticed that a number of local people would revert to their Welsh Gaelic tongue when a stranger would come into the area. Many of the people still work in the abundant coal mines. A relatively new product in the area had been produced

Harlech Castle on the coast

by extracting gas from the coal. What surprised me most was that this gas is piped the whole length of Wales to consumers.

The signs along the way often displayed some of the longest town names in the world, a fact for which the Welsh are well known. From Harlech to Barmouth, around enchanting Mawddach Estuary, to Aberdovey (where I had to pedal an additional 20 miles because the ferry operator was evidently not in the mood to make the short run), to Borth, to Aberystwyth and finally to Fishguard, I kept up a good pace doing 70 miles on the last day. I can well remember noting the beauty of this coast in my diary. Wales is generally very rugged land and is, therefore, not as extensively developed as the neighboring country.

In Fishguard I bought the tickets for my bicycle and me to cross St. George's Channel. It cost only a total of $5 for both for the three-hour trip. As the boat was not due to leave until 2:30 AM, I took some local advice and boarded early to catch a couple hours of sleep before the late train would come to fill the boat to capacity. As the "St. Andrew" put increasingly more distance between it and the dock at Fishguard, I thought ahead to the next land and the people I would find there. For reference I reflected on a statement that had been made to me by an Englishman two weeks prior. He had been to Ireland many times and spoke of the relaxed, unhurried pace of the citizens there. He maintained that it was the only place in the world where a person's reaction to seeing his home in flames would be to write a postcard to the fire brigade. There are countless humorous tales of the inhabitants of the Emerald Isle and now I was plowing through the Irish Sea on my way to becoming a willing recipient of the charm and hospitality so evenly spread around this land of Shamrocks and Leprechauns.

# CHAPTER THREE

## The "Irish Rover"

Dawn had not broken when our ship made its way into the relative calm of Rosslare Harbor, but the sun was dancing on the horizon before we were allowed to leave the ship at dockside. As they left a number of people were still chuckling at the shipboard antics of one returning Irishman. He had well "fortified" himself for the crossing long before departure and had been a center of amusement for the other passengers. He had climaxed his performance, when all were getting ready for arrival, by standing up in the middle of the large crowded lounge and walking smartly out the huge door. Considering his condition it would have been an unbelievable feat had he not missed the door by a yard or more, resulting in a resounding collision between himself and the solid wall. His efforts were rewarded with an overwhelming round of applause as his slightly more sober mate guided him through the opening.

Another item that tickled the funny bone of many waiting vehicle owners occurred when the huge crane lowered its mighty steel cable into the hold of the ship and came up with the sole burden of my bicycle and attached baggage including my guitar. Hoping not to have to unload my equipment for inspection, I had been carefully sizing up the customs inspectors. When my choice for "Mr. Jovial of the Year" was free of clients I wheeled my bicycle over with passport in hand and was directly on my way with white "X's" on my unopened luggage and a witty comment about me coming over to spread my music around the "sod". He had not even looked into my passport much less affixed an entry stamp. Although I didn't realize it at the time, this fact was to become much more significant in my future travels.

Breakfast took care of one of my two major needs at the time; sleep being the other. As a matter of coincidence, it seemed that I was destined to enter a new country always on a Sunday. This not being an exception I headed on my way looking for the first church, which in contrast to norm in England would almost assuredly be a Catholic church. After Mass in Wexford I was informed that there would be a *Fleadh Ceoil* in Enniscorthy and I headed there to take in this festival of music, dance and expositions. Although the step dancing competition was certainly notable, I found the most genuine spirit of the day along the streets and lanes where impromptu displays of song and dance occurred in wandering, never-ending patterns. In keeping with the reputation of the Irish, the entire get-together was punctuated with alcoholic incentive and after a few hours among the merry-makers, my appreciation of the musical aspect of the day was overcome by the certainty that, for the majority of the locals, the *Fleadh Ceoil* was only a slightly more official excuse for drinking themselves out of their senses. Somehow through it all they remained cheery and amiable to all including this stranger.

My first real destination in Ireland was the home of my pen-pal, Marie Needham. I had been introduced to her by her Aunt Mai whose other niece was married to one of my fellow SAC navigators at Dow Air Force Base in Bangor, Maine. Gerry and Eileen Monier were a warm and talented young couple with two charming daughters, Marlene and Jean. On several occasions when Aunt Mai (the Duchess) was with them, I would visit the Moniers and spend some of the time singing and playing songs from the "Old Country" which I had learned through my two Scottish immigrant parents. When I had decided to leave the Air force and travel, I had to promise that one of my stops would be at "Gurteen", the name of the family farm and home.

Knowing that the Needham family would be wondering as to the day of my arrival, I telephoned them and was surprised to find myself talking to Aunt Mai who had just arrived home only a few days prior. With my intention of traveling around the south on the way to her house, I found her a little bit surprised that I would not be there directly. I then chatted with my pen-pal, Marie, for the first time and assured her that I would see her within the week.

During the days that it took me to make my swing through the south, I started to absorb a bit of real Ireland. While taking bread and breakfast with the Whitemore's in Clonroche, I was introduced to the round loaves of brown soda bread the likes of which I was to find in no other country. With directions from them I pedaled to Dunganstown, outside of New Ross, and visited the one small remaining building of Kennedy Homestead. A Kennedy cousin, Josie Ryan, permitted me to enter the locked building to view photos of the late President during his visit here and to sign the registration book, which he had initiated. He had mingled freely with local citizens of all social positions and I was to find that throughout Ireland, more so than elsewhere, recollections of him consistently prompted involuntary expressions of disbelief and despair.

Josey Ryan, a cousin of JFK

Cycling was not very difficult in the first part of my southern journey but as I entered the small village of Killeagh, I got my first real puncture (flat tire) although I had been coping with slow leaks periodically up to that point. I decided it was time to buy a new inner tube and was told where I could do so by an old man sitting on a window ledge by the side of the road. My newfound friend indicated that he would watch the bicycle while I made the purchase and would, thereafter, help me to make the necessary repairs. Although it was easily a one-man job I accepted his enthusiastic offer. While unloading the bike he jokingly made a few comments to the effect that I should play a few tunes there and he would pass the hat for me. With the work completed I re-loaded the gear except for the guitar and offered to sing him a few tunes for his help. Despite his plea that it would be too much bother I insisted that it was the least I could do for his assistance. By this time, the lady of the house was at the front door and I asked if I might be allowed to wash my hands before handling the guitar. She ushered me in and quickly provided soap and towel for which I thanked her and returned to the sidewalk area. Unknown to me, while I was washing the old man had been summoning everyone within earshot and I stepped out the front door to be met by a ready-made audience. So, I sat on the window ledge beside my new "publicity agent" and proceeded to sing songs of several styles and rhythms. Soon people were coming from all directions, from shops and streets. The neighbors were hanging out the windows and motorists were stopping in the road. After about 30 minutes the local primary school was dismissed and the little tots came down the sidewalk (footpath) like a mini herd. They ended up sitting on their lunch pails in a semi circle in front of me. For almost two hours we ran the musical gauntlet from the old sing-a-longs to the more up-beat rock and roll songs of the day to the delight of the younger set present.

With twenty miles of cycling yet between me and the city of Cork, I finally decided that I would have to continue on. I packed my guitar, signed a few autographs for newfound fans, and headed out of the village with a large portion of the local populace waving a sad and sincere farewell. As I pedaled to Cork I reflected on how little it had taken to befriend a large part of a whole village. Of course, my instrument had been the means of accelerating the formation of this relationship, but I believe it could have been done in many other ways. I was to learn throughout my journey that it is this personal contact, this direct communication, which can so easily bring about understanding between peoples and, thus, greatly reduce the levels of suspicion and distrust.

Cork is one of the three "cities" in Ireland and boasts a bustling port. After an overnight stay in a local hostel, I pedaled the six miles to Blarney where I received the "gift of eloquence" as I kissed the stone embedded in the wall on the second story of the castle. A man who has worked there for many years holds the legs of the person wishing to kiss the stone. The visitor must lie on his/her back with head towards the wall and bend over backwards to reach the stone where it was put there below floor level in 1446.

Cycling became tougher as I went through Killarney, Tralee and on to meet the River Shannon at Glin. I noticed that there seemed to be more jaunting carts in this area, especially around Lough Leane. The mountains and lakes were beautiful and they somewhat reminded me of Northern Wales. Peat was still a very common fuel here and I often observed it being cut in the bogs along the roadside. To pass a country side thatched cottage in early evening and smell the smoke from the peat fire only emphasized the fact that I was, indeed, on the Emerald Isle. Seeing women in the fields doing work that normally would be done by men in the USA, also lent an air of authenticity to the surroundings.

WARNING.  I got the "gift"

In Limerick I visited Kyleglass House where Marie had lived while going to school there. I had written many letters to that address and it was a bit strange to see the place actually appear. After making myself known, I was given a grand reception by the Mother and Sisters with a tour of the chapel and tea to follow, all of which later took the Neddhams by surprise. After looking around Limerick's castle, etc. I cycled to Bansha and checked in at the hostel. That evening, as we had a songfest, I met a number of new friends. The outstanding one of this group was a Hungarian refugee who lived in Sweden at the time. Antal Ritzl had been touring around on a motor scooter and was the kind of out-going individual who makes friends easily. He spoke English quite well in addition to Swedish, German and his native Hungarian. He displayed the great zest for life and adventure for which his countrymen are well known. Before departing we exchanged addresses and promised to keep in touch in the future.

Having visited St. Patrick's Rock of Cashel where the Irish kings had been crowned, I headed north towards Rathcabbin on the home stretch of my cycle tour. As a result of being sent 10 miles out of my way, by a well-intended but uninformed local chap, I ended up covering over 70 miles that day before reaching the gates of Gurteen House. I met my pen-pal who had come out to make one of the many routine checks for my arrival which had been taking place all day long. As we entered the front hall of the house she yelled, "He's here", which by this time was a much over-used joke by all of the look-outs. With no response I verbally feigned a degree of disgust at the lack of reception and was immediately surrounded by the entire family led by Aunt Mai. I was introduced to all and they went directly outside to view this great pushbike that had made such a trip. They couldn't believe the amount of baggage I had taken along with me on the two-wheeler.

Needhams and Aunt Mai

Aunt Mai, as they say in Ireland, was "herself". Her brother, John Needham, was the father of the family and was one of the most progressive farmers in the Midlands. He had had a heart attack not long before and with hip problems, his running of the farm was done mostly in brainwork and bookwork. He had a shrewd and conservative manner to the point where he expected equipment to last forever and he would become completely disgusted if a vintage piece broke down. He had a great "gift of the gab" and was easily sidetracked during an errand to catch up on the local gossip or farm news. He was a great family man and could tell tales at the dinner table for hours. His specialty in this regard was the era of the "black and tans" who were British prisoners sent over as a policing force to crush the rebellion. They had a free hand to do as they pleased. Their uniforms were those of the prison with a special jacket on top. It was from the contrasting colors of these garments that they received their nickname. John's wife, Myra, was certainly the heart and soul of this family. With a rosy complexion and a ready smile, she would go about her daily chores with an endurance that would be the envy of many professional athletes. From the milking of the cows to the polishing of the brass, she could be seen in apparent continual motion. She would start her day long before the rest of us as she baked the day's supply of brown soda bread in the early morning. She showed an interest in everyone and everything and was as holy as the water that she spread around at the slightest provocation.

Marie, my pen pal, was a cross between what most Americans consider to be the typical Irish colleen and American girls of the same age. She was the oldest of the five children and was very intelligent although this did not prevent her from coming down to earth and enjoying a good laugh or event. She, as the rest of the children, was the product of a definitely religious and respectful Irish upbringing. She was as at home in doing housework as she was in doing office work and had ability and ambition in both. She was of average height and kept her dark hair cut short.

Richard, being the oldest son, actually did the running of the farm with the hired help on a day-to-day basis. He's quite progressive and when he differs with his father, some rare arguments occur. He was easygoing and quite accommodating. We got along well and he would go out of his way to be helpful. He was quite tall with red hair and a winning smile. I remember noting that he had some very definite ideas regarding the place of women in society.

Richard ran the farm with help

Pauline was a bundle of ambition who just couldn't keep busy enough. She blends in easily with the entire group and is a lot of fun. She would make a first-rate nurse as Aunt Mai often said. She always makes a point of defending her native land vs the USA with Aunt Mai or anyone else.

John seemed destined to live with the unbearable fact that his younger sister was taller than he. He looked far younger than his 12 years although he was an avid participant in football and hurling. He preferred either to work but did enjoy going to the sheep fairs with his father. The requirement that all school children must study the Irish language was being hotly disputed at the time. It had been so for many years and, due to this, John could read and write Irish better than he could English.

Gay, the youngest in the family, was recovering from pneumonia and was under close care and attention. She was a sharp-minded little girl and often surprised many adults with some of her answers.

Gurteen House was a large two-story stucco building set back from the road with two long drives leading in from the gates. Mr. Needham had defied the opinion of engineers and had successfully constructed a huge concrete rain catch-tank on the roof of the house at the back. The other farm buildings were attached to the house and formed a quadrangle with it. There were chickens, sheep, pigs, cows, 2 dogs and one large fearsome bull. Behind the farm buildings were huge fields of grain and vegetables as far as the eye could see. Other parts of the Needham farm were in more isolated sections of the area.

For three and a half weeks I became part of this fine family and couldn't have been more at home had I been in my own. At any time when I was visiting foreign friends in their homes, I tried to be useful if possible. Thanks to my interests and my engineering background, I had done most of the types of work associated with maintaining or improving a house. When I was allowed to do some work, it not only made me feel that I was returning the hospitality, but I also felt more like a member of the family pulling my weight. I was always happy to have the opportunity to acquire a feeling of accomplishment, having done something worthwhile and possibly rather technical.

One day I noticed that there were some assorted parts of a doorbell circuit around and yet there was no bell installed. Upon inquiry I found out that the parts had been there for some years in anticipation of someone completing the job. I took stock of the required parts and sized up a few other minor electric projects that had been waiting for some time. With the list in my pocket I headed down the back drive only to hit a loose stone in the gravel while turning the bend. I flew gracefully over the handlebars and left a deposit of skin on the road. Being that the family was timing this "great cyclist" on the trip to town, I idiotically jumped up, straightened out the bike, wiped the blood off my hands and sped the 8 miles to Birr in 25 minutes. They were none the wiser until I returned as the accident had occurred out of their view behind a clump of trees.

When I had the door-bell functioning properly it was considered like one of the wonders of the world. It even had a small light which illuminated the name-plate at all times. Thereafter everyone had to try it several times and if a friend came to visit and knocked on the inside door, s/he was promptly led outside and introduced to the latest addition to the outstanding features of Gurteen.

Some of the daily chores in which I was often involved were herding the sheep, chopping the wood and milking the cows. In the evening Mrs. Needham, Aunt Mai and I would bring the milking cows in and drain them dry. Although I caught on pretty fast I must admit that either of them could milk faster than I could. One time I had Pauline take a flash picture of me milking. The cow received a direct message from the flash and almost knocked me over.

Startled cow and me

We would take the milk into the house where about a half gallon would be kept as whole milk while the rest was separated with a hand-crank machine. The skim milk was used to feed the young animals and the cream was used

for cooking and table purposes. Any cream that was not consumed would
be allowed to turn and would subsequently be turned into rich fresh butter.
With jams made from local berries and almost all other food products coming
from the farm, the meals were an absolute menace to any weight-watcher.
Not doing my daily cycling, as when I was traveling, I started to put on some
unnecessary pounds. The meals that came from that wood-fired stove would
have pleased anyone from a gourmet to a starving lumber-jack. The big meal
of the day was eaten at noon and a light supper (tea) was eaten in the early
evening. Prior to going to bed, and usually just after saying the family rosary,
we'd have a late night snack of brown bread spread with home-churned butter
and homemade jam. Either a cup of tea or a glass of fresh milk would help
to wash this down.

There were many memorable experiences during my stay and it seemed
that, in many cases, the particular occurrence was not outstanding in itself, but
the people involved made it memorable because there seemed to be something
extra derived from the fact that it was a mutually shared experience. Thus, the
little things became big due to the relish with which each detail was repeated
in the later telling. It seemed strange in contrast to think of the extent to
which some maladjusted people back in the USA had to go in order to "get
their kicks". I truly believe that it is a case of becoming too materialistic and,
therefore, not being able to find value nor satisfaction in intangibles such as
humor, friendship and sharing.

One episode which was remembered with delight weeks thereafter
occurred when Mr. and Mrs. Needham, Aunt Mai, Marie and I drove to the
home of the their relatives, the Ryan's. We chatted, had some refreshments,
sang some songs and finally headed home with Mr. Needham at the wheel.
About half way down the road I thought I detected a slight odor of smoke
in the car. Thinking that it might have come from something we passed
I said nothing. A little further along Marie calmly indicated she thought
something was burning. Nobody got very upset about it, especially Mr.
Needham who was slightly hard of hearing. Not long thereafter Aunt Mai
decided that something was definitely wrong and let everyone know of her
thought on the matter. At that time Mr. Needham shook it all off as some
sissified feminine reaction to discomfort or some such silly thing. Being a
guest I didn't feel like speaking out too boldly and soon John Needham was
bounding intently across the countryside with, what amounted to, a small
cloud in the back seat. Aunt Mai oscillated between trying to gulp in fresh
air from the open window and yelling at her brother to bring the car to a
halt before we were all asphyxiated. When our driver finally got the message

he braked to a stop and we all piled out like tear-gassed rats in a hole. The majority of the smoke was in the rear portion of the car, so I opened the trunk (boot) sending out a ripple of smoke signals. As Mr. Needham made sure the motor and all lights were turned off, I reached into the trunk and snatched out my constant companion (my guitar). Upon inspection I found out that one wire of the tail lights had become grounded on the metal frame and the wire covering was melting away from the excessive heat. With the problem wire disconnected and isolated the vehicle was fully aired out. Only then could we once again climb aboard to finish the homeward journey in a much more cautious atmosphere. As might be expected, our roadside "fire drill" was the main topic of conversation for weeks thereafter.

Our pilgrimage to the holy town of Knock was, likewise, a memorable event. Aunt Mai, Marie, Pauline and I joined a local church group for the 90-mile bus ride to the town where the Blessed Mother had appeared to 15 people in 1879. The passengers were mostly housewives and children with a half dozen men including the man in charge. The bus driver had obviously never been to Knock before and didn't have clue as to the route leading there. It may possibly been that he was not a Catholic, in which case I'm sure he would never care to be one due to the amount of verbal abuse he had to take from 30+ back-seat drivers who had been over the road a number of times. I couldn't count the number of times we passed an intersection only to realize that we had taken the wrong road. Then the man in charge would have to get out and stop the traffic so the bus could be turned around amidst flowing comments regarding the possible ancestry of the driver. At Knock the bus was parked in a designated area and all passengers were told to return to it by 6:00 PM.

The spirit of the pilgrims at the site from all parts of Ireland was truly inspiring when I realized that, in my local experiences to date, the people didn't save their religious fervor for occasions like this, but actually made it part of their everyday lives. Realistically I couldn't say that this was universal throughout the Irish population, but it seemed to form a significant part of the outlooks of the majority of people. I believe that goodness is brought out in people in many different ways, but I would strongly submit that, in the case of the inhabitants of the Emerald Isle, it can be attributed to their overwhelming faith.

The largest percent of the group had satisfied themselves long before 6:00 PM and had wearily returned to the bus. However, at 7:20 PM we were still waiting for stragglers. It seemed that a few of the men were trying to calm their nerves (at the pub) for the return trip and each time a fellow was sent to retrieve them, he became involved with his nerves. The last to climb aboard were a lady and her daughter who had decided to add to the bargain of the day by saying an extra rosary with another group they had met while heading for the exit. What surprised me was the reaction of our group to their arrival an hour and half late. Rather than one of indignation, it was one of congratulations and almost envy of their good fortune. I remember thinking at the time that if we had been back in the USA, we would have most likely been an hour's journey down the road with a slightly less crowded bus

Knowing how fond the Irish are of joking I collaborated one day with Gay to fool the rest of the family. She had come to the front room of the house where I was playing a few tunes on the piano. She had with her a harmonica, which she had recently acquired and was trying to figure out which she demonstrated. Knowing that the others were in the adjacent rooms I winked at Gay and in a very loud voice said, "That's a wonderful instrument you have there. Please play me a tune.". With that I took up the harmonica and played a lively version of "Oh Susanna", the only song I knew on that instrument. Within a few bars the others came rushing into the room to see how she had progressed so rapidly. Of course they were greeted by Gay's big laughing grin after which we all had a good laugh.

Since I had arrived at Gurteen House I had been on the look-out for some motorized means of continuing my travels. I had totaled just under 1200 miles of cycling from London to the Neadham's doorstep and I thought, for the sake of making better time, I would switch modes of transportation. Another consideration was the fact that my huge B-4 bag was waiting at Gurteen when I arrived, as were my sunglasses and a set of developed slides. The results of my photographic efforts were very satisfying and I continued to use the camera with great faith, knowing that any missed shots could not be re-taken.

Upon asking in Birr I found out that a young local schoolteacher had a motor scooter which she no longer used. She had it brought to a local gas station where I viewed it and arranged to meet her for a chat. The cycle was a 1960 yellow and black NSU Prima D of 150 cc displacement. She had bought it new but hadn't used it for some time. It had only been driven 2500 miles, but needed some work due to inattention. She said that she would have the garage man, who was an NSU dealer, put it in good operating condition if I wished to buy it. When we came to dealing in regard to the price, Richard went with me and beforehand briefed me on the local customs regarding such bargaining. I would inquire as to the asking price and then offer something significantly lower. After the two major parties had offered a significant number of reasons for our different conceptions of a just price, Richard would settle it half way between the two. As if it were a movie script, it happened exactly that way. Mary Conway was asking 60 pounds and I offered her 50. Richard intervened with the suggestion that we consider 55 pounds which was quickly agreed by both parties. Thus, for the equivalent of $154 US I became the owner of an intricate combination of nuts and bolts, metal and wire, glass and rubber, which was to become my faithful and constant companion (and means of transportation) for the rest of my journey.

On the day that I obtained my scooter, with some reluctance, I sold my bicycle to a local dealer for 8 pounds. I agreed to take the scooter with the speedometer inoperative, as the local "experts" claimed that it would have to be sent to Dublin for repair or replacement. So, my first somewhat erratic attempt at piloting a 2-wheeled motorized vehicle came as I haltingly drove my NSU the 8 miles back to Rathcabbin. Later, upon taking apart the speedometer, I found out why it was not functioning. The chamber containing the rather delicate, magnetically driven bell-shaped receptor was completely filled with fresh grease. This confirmed many of my suspicions regarding the relative worth of many of the company-trained experts to whom the motor manuals always refer the layman for technical problems. A complete washing of all parts with gasoline and re-assembly proved to be sufficient to return the mechanism to its original functioning state.

Obtaining insurance from a local agent was due to prove difficult if not impossible, so I took a bus ride to Dublin where I readily got the insurance at the company office. While there I, likewise, registered the scooter in the AA, the national Automobile Association. The bus ride to and from Dublin was an experience in itself. There were all manner of things picked up a various stops to be delivered further down the route. As we stopped on a countryside road to allow the crossing of a herd of sheep, the shepherd struck up a lengthy conversation with the driver and all waited patiently to continue the trip. This bus had a regular run each day going to Dublin in the morning and retracing the route in the early evening. Thus, the bus remained in the capital city during the part of the day when the local race track was at the height of its activity. This accounted for the extra amount of bookkeeping that the conductor seemed to be doing at most stops along the way. Of course, the good or bad news as to the outcome was related during the return trip.

With the tax paid on the scooter I registered it for a 3-month period not knowing what re-registration requirements I might run into in other countries. The three letters of the *BIE265* number indicated that it was registered in

County Claire. Having completed the legal formalities, I started to make plans for my departure. Before leaving Gurteen I took a short ride to Lorrha one day in order to view and photograph the O'Kennedy tomb and coat-of-arms located in the ruins of the Dominican Priory. The inscription on the tomb dates from 1692 and reads: "The Lord is the portion of my inheritance. Here lies a man of ancient lineage, brilliantly distinguished for justice, hospitality, piety and faith. Those qualities, however, could not resist the fates. To each person the limits of life are assigned. Nevertheless, those gifts could do this for him, that everlasting glory will remain to him on earth while he himself is in heaven." (From: History of Ancient Ormond). I couldn't help but think of how applicable this last sentence was to one of the descendants whose glory echoed around the world although his life had been taken almost a year before.

I won the everlasting respect and admiration of Mr. Needham by building and installing, what he referred to as, a "right door". It was a barn door, which I made of sturdy planking with diagonal cross-braces for support. He proudly demonstrated that portal to all who came near Gurteen. Just inside this building was a set of scales used for weighing grain and products. However, I noticed that the members of the family used it to weigh themselves also. Therefore, when I was trying to think of what I could leave the family as a gift of appreciation to everyone, I decided that a bathroom scale would fill the intention well, they being as practical as I. It was received with delight and all had to queue up to be checked. I remember that a special mark was put on the indicator at my weight reading which, by that time was many pounds more than when I had arrived. I used the 14 pounds/stone equivalent to convert from the British system to ours. Although Ireland had broken away from England, it still retained the system of weights, measures and currency then common throughout the British Empire.

It was with deep-felt reluctance that I loaded my scooter for the first time with all of my baggage on July 24th. Once it and myself had been sprinkled with Mrs. Needham's holy water I said a round of gloomy farewells and seated myself on the "Irish Rover" (so named by the Needhams after a popular local song), to head down the first of so many thousands of miles I was to cover from that perch. I went east through the magnificence of the Wicklow Valley with the mountains sloping up on each side. This road eventually led to the fabled village of Glendalock. It was easy to see why the Irish Airlines used the picture of this hamlet with its seven churches in advertising posters. The combination of setting and structure makes this a favorite spot for visitors be they from near or far.

Loaded scooter at Glendalock

Beauty of the Irish countryside

My day's journey ended in Dublin where I re-met Marie who was visiting a family friend, Babs Scanlon, while she made application for work there. The following day, my birthday, and the next few were spent with my pen pal playing guide to the capital city. We saw the National War Memorial, the Book of Kells and attended the Abbey Theatre performance of "The Plough and the Stars". We had some rare adventure together including a scooter trip with my guitar to DunLaoghaire for an evening of song and conversation at a friend's home. With heavy traffic and driving rain, the return trip was a treacherous and wet one. It didn't really bother us as we joked about our predicament the whole way home.

Upon leaving Dublin I headed north along the coast to Dundalk and then west through Cavan to Sligo. I must admit that I observed this area being on a par with any in Ireland as regards scenery. The low hills covered with cocks (or trams which are piles) of hay seemed like continuous ocean swells in between which could be seen lakes of clear blue. This panorama was as typical of "The Sod" as the Irish nod of salute which, at first, reminded me of a reactive gesture of disgust or disbelief back home.

As I approached the border of Northern Ireland, I was thankful that I had purchased a windshield for the scooter in Dublin because the weather was overcast and quite miserable with mist. On such days I would accuse the locals of having super-sensitive thermostats. They would be complaining of being chilled to the bone and twenty minutes after the sun came out it would be "shokin' hot".

The River Foyle forms the frontier between Lifford in the South and Strabane in the North. When I arrived at the bridge between the two I received the shocking news that the Queen's men would not allow me to cross until I paid them a 25 pound sterling import duty on the scooter. This was actually a bond, which would be returned sometime in the future after I had proven that I had taken the vehicle out of the British Isles. This wasn't definite enough for me and, besides, this $72 US comprised almost all of the money I had with me then. So, upon inquiry, I was told that there was another small bridge a few miles away that was rarely patrolled by the officials. It was used by locals who lived on one side of the border and worked on the other side. I was warned that anything taken over that bridge could be confiscated by border officials. With the possibility of a little intrigue in the air, I scooted across the little bridge and up through the small village only to learn that the only road out of it led right back to within a hundred yards of the main bridge at Strabane. Feeling like "The Fugitive" I thought that at any moment the long arm of the law might interrupt my plans. However, I went through the town and headed for Belfast with no problem and very little regret that I had taken a short-cut of convenience on the Queen's men.

My last night on the Emerald Isle was spent at the Gortin Gap Youth Hostel which had been known to the US 28th Division as Lislap Forest when they were there during WW II. The elderly woman in charge had kept in touch with many of "her boys" and spoke of them with nostalgia. With continuing bad weather I limited my touring to Lough Neagh and Belfast Castle. From there I carried on to Larne to catch the steamer to Stranrar. Lough Neagh was supposed to have been formed by a mythical giant who scooped up the land and through it out to sea where it became the Isle of Man.

Leaving Ireland after a stay of any appreciable length, leaves one with the feeling that he has exchanged something. He has left an irretrievable part of himself there and replaced it with a bit of the "stuff" of the Sod. This bit is bound to show through occasionally in the future just to remind him that he has spread a part of himself through a land of warm-hearted, easy-going folks who balk at the fierce pace of "modern" world societies. They were always ready to take time out for the more important things in life such as being truly neighborly to all who fall within the Biblical description of the word "neighbor".

# CHAPTER FOUR

## "Home" at last

On August 1st I left the ship at Stranrar and touched the land of both parents for the first time. Their families had immigrated separately to the USA when they were teenagers. They only became acquainted when my two grandfathers worked in the same foundry. Eventually my parents had met and married in Boston. Many of the other members of both families also immigrated to the USA. I was to find that it was a blessing that I had been brought up with relatives who still had a heavy Scottish brogue. If not, I'm afraid I would not have understood half of what I was listening to in Scotland. My mother was Annie Bridget Paterson from a family of 8 children. Her mother was Mary Greer and her father was Robert Paterson.

I got a rather cold reception in the "old country", as my parents would refer to it. Given that it was the height of the vacation season in Europe, the Youth Hostel at Stranrar was "packed out" and I joined several other travelers who slept on the floor that night. The following day in the drizzle I went to church and stopped at the U.S. Air Force Base at Prestwick to have lunch. On these occasions I would have to change some money back to US dollars as that was all that was used on the base. I noted that it seemed quite familiar to be in these surroundings again as would happen in many locations as I traveled.

When I arrived in Paisley I looked up my mother's Aunt Nellie Smythe who was not a blood relative, as I remember, but a wonderful acquaintance who had been like an aunt to my mother. I was warmly welcomed and quickly introduced to Aunt Nellie's entire family.

Aunt Nellie at home with family

She had a small apartment of her own and I became her house guest while I searched out the areas I had heard about for so many years. Of course, I took many photos in order to record the current status of these places, which had been so familiar to my mother. Aunt Nellie's granddaughter, Kathy, became my guide as we three discussed the places of concern. The former home site of my mother's family at Underwood Lane in Glenburn had been torn down but I took a picture of the area with the observatory dome in the background. My mother and her siblings used to pass the dome on their way to school. They often passed the home of their grandparents on their father's side but without ever being allowed to visit. My grandfather had been ostracized from his family when he married a Catholic girl, he being from a family of staunch Presbyterians. At that time there was a strict distinction made between the majority Protestant population and the minority Catholic segment. My mother often recounted the fear of going outside the house when the celebration of the "Orangemen's Walk" was scheduled. It celebrated the coronation of William of Orange who took over the reign in 1689. These discriminatory feelings ran deep in the local population. As an example of this I well remember my mother recounting an incident in her young days when she and her sisters entertained with their Scottish Highland dancing. They were booked to perform at a Grange Hall party in their area one week. A few days prior to the event a gentleman from the club knocked on the door one evening and inquired of my grandmother as to whether, or not, they were Catholic. When she replied in the affirmative she was told that the booking was canceled. This made a lasting impression on my mother who was a young teen-ager at the time.

The gate Mom entered to work

As was the case with most young girls from common families, my mother finished schooling at the age of 15 and went to work in the Coates Thread Mill. I took a photo of the gate she used to pass through each day, as I was sure that she would easily recall the familiar location. Other places I photographed were Paisley Abbey, Coates Memorial Church, the City Hall, the war memorial at the Cross, St. Mary's School and Church both of which my mother had attended. I took a photo inside the church and was to be surprised years later at my mother's accurate memory of it. She mentioned to me that she thought the pulpit was on the other side of the altar. Sure enough I had inserted my slide into the projector backwards. This was after 45 years

St. Mary's church with lectern

of absence without having returned to her hometown. I took several day and night photos of Paisley from the Glennifer Braes (hills) including a photo of the "Bonnie Wee Well" made famous by Robert Burns' poem.

During my stay with Aunt Nellie I took a side trip to Largs where I met Annie "Ma" MaGuire who, with her daughter Kathy, runs St. Anne's Boarding House on the waterfront. They are friends of our former neighbors, the Orlando's, in Wilmington. Annie's husband had just died three weeks prior. I had some long talks with Kathy and she talked me into being their guest overnight so I could go sailing on the River (Firth of) Clyde the next day. After dinner I tried to "earn my supper" by using the piano to entertain the older houseguests with many of the old songs I had heard in my youth. Kathy later mentioned that my visit had truly lifted her mother's spirits during a trying time for the family.

The next morning I sailed with Eric MacKenzie up the Clyde to Dunoon and the Holy Lock where the US Polaris nuclear submarines were stationed. There had been demonstrations there recently by those who would oppose all means of war. I was to find that there was not always a positive reaction to the presence of US forces in many parts of the world. In general I found very few people who disliked the citizens of the USA but they often disagreed with our government policies.

A more personal emotion hit me as I recalled the fact that my mother had sailed the Clyde in the opposite direction as she headed for the "new world" as a young teen-ager. I had asked her before what her thoughts were as she left her native country behind for a new life in a world she hardly knew. Her reply was that her prime and only thought for most of the journey was to get over the sea-sickness that kept her company for the entire trip.

One of the side trips I took was to visit Matt Busby's mother in Bellshill. She was in England but I was able to catch up on the family news with his two sisters, Maggie and Doakes. From the surroundings of his hometown I was even more convinced that he was from a very common background but used his athletic gifts to make his name a household word in the British Isles and the soccer world. I also took a trip to the capital at Edinburgh on the scooter and parked on Princess Street. It was as if this avenue was a line between two eras of history. On one side I was looking at the most modern of shops not unlike 5th Avenue in New York. As I turned to face the other side of the street I looked up in awe at Edinburgh Castle, which could have been a photograph from hundreds of years before. With the immediate surroundings unchanged it must have looked the same as in the days of the Scottish Kings. I toured the castle viewing the crown and the crown jewels.

Edinburgh Castle—never changed

With my initial look at Edinburgh behind me I headed for Mussellburgh and Newcraighall, my father's hometown. I stopped and visited my father's Aunt Jenny who was a spry 86 years old. Her son, Eddie, still lived with her and her daughter, Elsie, and husband, Joe Muir, lived next door. Aunt Jenny and her family gave me a huge amount of information about my father's upbringing including some photos of him and my mother that I had never seen. I couldn't get over how one of the photos of my father looked like me when I was younger. I had always been told that I resembled my mother's side of our family. Aunt Jenny's grandson, Tom, was home on vacation from working in Saudi Arabia and he became my guide to the localities, which would have been familiar to my father. He drove me to my father's old house in Miller Hill where I had him take a photo of me standing in the doorway. I well remember a sepia photo of my father standing in that same doorway holding his dog prior to his coming to the USA. Prior to that, like all boys at 15 years of age, he had worked in the local coal mines.

Posing for Dad's old photo

Newcraighall was a mining community of very hard-working common folks in his day. There was no running water in the houses and people would gather around the central water trough outside to wash up in the morning in any weather. Of course houses were heated by coal burners. Coal came in large chunks and was smashed with a hammer to accommodate the size of the stove. I noticed that this method was still used in many houses at the time of my visiting. I also met my grandfather's brother, Garrett Rooney, and his wife. He was able to tell me a lot about my father's early days and he added some new photos to my growing collection. Heading back to Paisley I stopped to photograph one of the "Seven Wonders of the World", the Firth of Forth Bridge from the Queensferry side. I was to see it from a different vantage point in the future.

One of the day trips I took from Aunt Nellie's house was a 1½-hour train and bus ride to go bowling with Susan and Robert. This was one of the three bowling alleys in Scotland. It had six lanes. I later joined the entire family in a mini-bus to attend the Tattoo, a festival of music from around the world held on the esplanade of Edinburgh Castle, There were various bands and groups from everywhere. They varied from Highland dancers to steel drum bands from the West Indies. Most were quite spectacular and the evening finished with a lone piper spotlighted on the castle wall playing the "Piper's Lament". I could have easily pictured my mother and her sisters joining the Highland dancers. I felt something stirring within me as I toured Scotland and was saturated by the atmosphere, which had been hinted to me throughout my upbringing.

At this time I checked on the insurance coverage of my scooter and found that the extension of coverage to the continent (green card) would have cost me half of the annual premium per month. I canceled the policy as of the end of August this being the 22$^{nd}$ of the month. This was in preparation to my leaving Aunt Nellie and heading for the Highlands which I did on August 24$^{th}$. In the often-present rain known as Scottish mist, I made my way to the Highlands passing Loch Lomond of song fame. Despite the rain there were a couple of kilted locals to meet the tour busses that frequented the area. As I put miles behind me the terrain got much steeper as exemplified by Glen Coe and Glen Falloch, which became subjects of my Zeiss Ikon. Most of the mountaintops were shrouded in mist and fog. My photo of Glen Falloch attests to the fact that the sun does come out in the Highlands as I caught the spectacle of a brilliant rainbow. I noted that the mountains reminded me of the Sierra Nevadas in California.

At the Glen Nevis Youth Hostel I ended up sleeping on the floor with a number of Germans who were there to climb the highest peak in Scotland, Ben Nevis at 4406 feet. As I traveled I got to long for the non-vacation periods as all facilities seemed to get over-run when the students were free from school. The next day I took a photo of Ben Nevis and headed for the ferry to the Isle of Skye. This was one of the most depressing days of the trip thus far as it poured driving rain all day long. The roads were in ill-repair and the strong wind caused me to have to gear down even going *down-hill* at times. Despite my extensive rain gear everything (including myself) got wet. Having left the Isle I checked into the hostel at Kyles of Lochalsh where I spread my wet belongings wherever someone else had not.

Although I periodically called for him/her I failed to get any response from Nessie (the Loch Ness Monster) as I toured along the side of this huge lake. With Nessie not posing I decided to take a photo of Urquhart Castle on the shore. In the area of Glen Moriston I found a typical highland vista where a white homestead was surrounded by a fence with fields of heather all around. My camera captured the shot for the future. The custom for a visitor is to pick some heather and attach it to the outside of the vehicle for luck in the journey. Not to be outdone I managed to mount a sprig or two of heather on the windshield of the scooter.

Having passed through Inverness I proceeded to the most elegant Youth Hostel I was to encounter in my journey. Carbisdale Castle was the newest castle in the British Isles having been built for the Dower Duchess of Sutherland between 1900 and 1912. As might be expected it had two art galleries including sculptured works, a ballroom, library, music room, juke box and many dorms. All of this elegance had its price as I climbed the 71 steps to my dorm on several trips. It was a bit trying on one of my fellow *youth* hostellers who was 83 years old. The window of our dorm looked out onto the Sutherland River where I caught a gorgeous photo of the sunset there. This was indeed rugged country. For some reason the Duchess decided that she didn't really care for her castle and sold it to a millionaire whose son later donated it to the Youth Hostel Association. What a find at 3 shillings 6 pence (.49 US)a night.

My road to the south now took me past Balmoral Castle, which is the Queen's summer residence. In Aberdeen I almost got a trip to Norway on a Norwegian merchant boat. I was told I'd have to speak to the captain who was due back in a couple of hours. I had been making my first try at growing a beard and it was getting to the soft stage but still a bit messy. A well-meaning man who was a foreman at the dock advised me to get a shave before meeting the captain so I would make the right impression. So went my most extensive attempt to become bearded. By the time I actually met the captain of the Caribia he indicated that he would have to contact his headquarters in Norway to get permission and there was not enough time to do so. Thus, cleanly shaven I checked into the local youth hostel where I met, and spent some time with, a beautiful young French girl by the name of Viviane whom I was to meet again much later.

The Highlands at its most scenic

The elegant Carbisdale Youth Hostel

I met a young American at the hostel who had just finished a paper-back book which he offered to me. It was an intriguing adventure of a British secret service man who used a combination of technology and incredible skill (with great luck included) to catch and/or outwit all kinds of demonic characters. This was the first time I had ever heard of James Bond. I had no idea how widespread his fame was even at that time.

As I journeyed south along the coast I checked at the ports of Dundee and Leith for possible passage to Norway but with no results. I finally arrived at the home of my father's aunt, Jenny Burns, where I had had an earlier visit. In the following days his cousin, Elsie, and her husband, Joe Muir, took care of many of my needs inasmuch as I was sorely needing the money I was expecting to receive from home at this point. Through several mix-ups the money didn't arrive for 11 more days during which my assets in hand were reduced to 1 shilling (.12 US). I was really getting down during this period as I was anxious to get to Norway before it got too cold. My spirits were temporarily lifted one day in Edinburgh when a little girl asked me to take her hand to cross the street. Ah, the feeling of being needed!!!

During my time with the Muir's I was thrilled to visit the local coal mines from which Joe was now retired. He described in detail the differences between the mining conditions of my father's time and the present. Workers had showers available and actually went home clean versus the coated images of mankind that trudged home in past days. We also took a drive to Burtisland where we had the novel opportunity to swim in a saltwater swimming pool fed from the sea. The water stung my eyes quite smartly and I didn't last too long in the water. On the way home I was given the privilege of driving the car across the brand new Forth Road Bridge that the Queen had dedicated only two days earlier. When I finally received a check that American Express would cash I bought some gifts for Aunt Jenny, Elsie and Joe. I had done a number of odd jobs for them to show my appreciation. They had taken great care of me and it was truly like leaving family again. As I left them for the last time I stopped at a railroad workstation to try to find my father's boyhood buddy, John Douglas. He was not at that station but his co-worker was able to contact him by telephone and I had a chat about his younger days with my father.

As I waited for the opportunity to leave Scotland I made a list of words, which were commonly used there which we don't use in the USA. Some are typical from all of the British Isles. My list was as follows:

| Scottish | American | Scottish | American |
|---|---|---|---|
| ken | know, understand | press | closet |
| bairn | baby | lorry | truck |
| aye | yes | spanner | wrench |
| chock-o-block | full | queue | line |
| sort | fix, repair | right! | To draw attention |
| pram | baby carriage | valve | radio tube |
| wireless | radio | to cry | to call |
| yens | ones | | |

There may have been many more that didn't catch my notice due to the fact that I had been brought up with the Scottish brogue and had little difficulty in understanding most local conversations

Crossing back into England I arrived at Newcastle-on-Tyne where I was to take the Leda to Norway. I bought the tickets for myself and my scooter which were approx. $28 US for me and $5.50 US for it. As I headed through British customs/immigration on the way to the ship I was warned about the fact that my visa was good for two months and I had stayed in England for almost four months. I offered some lame excuse about being so taken with the charm of the country that I lost track of time. Immediately I silently gave thanks that the Irish port officer had not stamped my passport when I entered Ireland. Otherwise, this officer would want to know how I returned to England without an entry stamp. Another bullet dodged.

# CHAPTER FIVE

## "Tack så mycket"

It was a rough trip across the North Sea as we made our way towards Bergen. I met several Americans on the ship. They were traveling to all parts of Europe. We arrived in the rain and we were to find out that Bergen has its share of rainy days because it was on the up-wind side of the mountains, which parallel the coast to the east. Most of us checked into the local youth hostel that was at the upper end of a funicular (mountain cable car). I noted that the Norwegian girls were very attractive and that the boys actually looked like boys again after witnessing the English hairstyles for the past 4 months. Several of us went to an evening Mass at a convent and I felt a familiarity as the German ex-altar boy next to me said the Latin dialogue Mass just as I did. This was to be true in many countries and languages, as the Church had not gone to Mass in the vernacular yet. I had no trouble buying insurance for the scooter, which cost 4 kroner (.56 US) per day.

I next headed for Kvandal where I got the ferry across the fjord. The road ends at the dock and you cannot proceed without using the ferry. This country is very rugged and rocky and reminded me of the Highlands of Scotland. However, the roads were less developed and much of the surface between towns was unpaved. At each town I would find 1-2 kilometers of asphalt before and after the cut-off to the center. There were quite a few mountain tunnels of various lengths along the edges of the fjords. I stayed in a hostel near the Eidfjord Mountains and took photos of that rugged area. As my journey took me over the peak of the mountains I had my first accident on the scooter. Due to the crushed stone on the unpaved road the scooter went out of control at about 25 miles per hour and threw me into the ditch landing on my left knee, elbow, shoulder and head. It felt as if I

Norway's driving challenge

had re-injured my shoulder, which I put out of commission while playing rag-tag football for the Bomb Squadron in the Air Force. At that time I had separated my left clavicle.

With a lack of spectators there was nothing to do but right the scooter (which was in good shape) and drive the other 7 miles (10 kilometers) to Geilo. The snow in the surrounding hills testified to the popularity of this area in the ski season. Due to the heat of the day and the melt, the amount and speed of rushing water seemed to be in every direction. I headed directly to the doctor's office and after examining me he declared that I had just strained the shoulder and should rest. This medical reassurance cost me the great sum of $4.06 US and I gladly paid it. In order to follow his advice I checked into the huge hostel at Geilo and relaxed in the absence of many other visitors.

On the following day I was fit enough to head for Oslo, the capital. In the town of Torpo I took a photo of an 11$^{th}$ century *stave* church. The staves are the vertical boards which hold up the roof structure, in this case for over 1,000 years. A small suspension bridge near Nesbuyen caught my eye and resulted in a prized photo. I found these latitudes in Norway and Sweden very similar in foliage to our New England. I would see many of the same autumn colors decorating the landscape I traveled through. The houses were very neat and well taken care of.

The Oslo hostel was more like a hotel as compared to the rural ones I had been staying in up to this point. Again I found many of my countrymen among those who were seeking new things beyond the horizon. The following day was filled with visiting the notable sites of this modern city. One item that caught my eye and camera was the Viking ship built in 800 AD. It took a bit of imagination to realize the bravery of these ancient sailors who had to brave the open ocean on this vessel where all were on deck at all times. Only supplies were stored below. A more modern feat was accomplished by Thor Hyerdahl who captained the Kon Tiki raft which took 6 men on a 101-day trip from Peru to Polynesia in 1947.

Frogner Park proved to be another wonder given that, all of the extensive sculptural work had been done by a local artist over a 30 year period for mere sustenance from the city. One piece known as "Towering Humanity" was truly amazing for its scope and intricacy. Our last night in Oslo was spent having a great jam session at the hostel with several musicians who had brought instruments from all over. I was to frequently reiterate, "Music is the universal language".

Viking ship from 800 A.D.

I had a bit of awakening as I crossed the unguarded border from Norway to Sweden. As I continued on my scooter up a strange ramp the lanes switched at the top resulting in my driving on the left side of the road in Sweden. It was the only Scandinavian country I visited which used the same road rules as the British. (Note: In the late 60's Sweden changed to right-side driving to match its neighbors). The roads were in much better condition than in Norway. As I headed for Stockholm I stopped for the night in Kristinehamn and tried to find a hostel. The local one was closed for the season, as were many others in this area. Even the local KFUM (YMCA) was full. Upon asking a woman (who happened to have a beautiful daughter with her) about possible lodging I was referred to a guesthouse and got a room for the night for 10 kroner ($1.70). I had the privilege of spending some evening hours with them and learned a bit about this progressive, yet quaint, country.

On the following day the clutch cable of the scooter broke as I approached the town of Örebro and I had to stop to make repairs with a new cable I had

Örebro's water tower/restaurant

with me. After the work I strolled the outdoor market and had some lunch. I was quite impressed with the local water tower, which looked like a World's Fair project. It had a restaurant and observation platform on the top, which I just had to record with my camera. This unique combination of utility and pleasure was not uncommon in Sweden.

When I finally arrived in the thriving capital of Stockholm I was set back as the "new" clutch cable broke when I was some distance from the Youth Hostel located on the other side of the harbor. The city is built over the ocean inlets and there are many bridges connecting the various sections. The steel inner cable of the clutch had pulled out of its solder in the plug that is inserted in the clutch handle. In order to make a usable clutch arrangement I pulled the steel inner cable out of its housing and brought it up through the hole in the flooring which is for the brake pedal. I fastened the end of the cable to the utility hook, which was just below the instrument panel. Now by pushing my foot against the middle of the cable it was distorted enough to exert pressure to release the clutch and it got me across the city to "Alf Chapman", a beautiful three-masted schooner that was permanently anchored in the bay in a section of the city. This was one of the most unique hostels I had seen in my travels. I was assigned to a cabin and met some of the many other travelers visiting this gorgeous setting.

The following day I took in some of the sites of the capital city including the changing of the guards at the palace. The military uniforms of those involved looked more like those of our ROTC unit at college and I was immediately reminded of the contrast to the genuine pomp and pageantry of the British. Skansen Park is a favorite with the locals and I had to admire a wooden water tower that was very well preserved. I joined some other "yanks" for a visit to see the "Vasa ship" built in 1628. It was to be the unsinkable addition to the Swedish fleet having been built by imported craftsmen from several countries. With sailors and families aboard it was launched with great fanfare and sank within the first two miles of sailing. It was later speculated that, various parts of the ship were built by different foreigners and their measurements were not consistent. Thus, it listed to one side and took in huge amounts of water ending its short reign as the pride of the fleet. It was discovered buried in silt at the bottom of the bay in the mid 1900's and brought to the surface for preservation. Due to its need to be in a constantly humid environment, it was located in a special building where the humidity made it seem like we were touring a locker room after a rigorous NFL game.

Alf Chapman hostel-central Stockholm

I used the remainder of the day to get the scooter into decent travel condition. A new small condenser I had bought made a great difference. I was able to re-build the clutch cable and after cleaning up I joined an impromptu jam session on the deck of the ship. It was truly a special moment with the lights of Stockholm all around us as we joined our musical forces to produce an international concert for all there.

The next day I was headed for Göteborg to visit Antal Ritzl whom I had met in an Irish youth hostel. On the way I ran out of gas and stopped at a BP (British Petroleum) distribution center. Not only did I get free gas but coffee, sweet rolls and hospitality. Traveling alone it is a great boost to the morale to encounter common fellow beings who open themselves to you with absolutely nothing to gain for themselves. I felt quite at home as I viewed the autumn leaves in the area of Bogsta where I took a photo of a church and a lake in a setting that quite reminded me of my New England fall surroundings. When I arrived at the Omberg youth hostel I found it closed. Given that it was in a forest I opted to sleep out under the clear skies. My sleeping bag kept me quite warm and I had fashioned a lean-to on the side of the scooter with my ever-useful poncho.

The increase in the wind speed woke me in the morning and I got an early start. I arrived in Göteborg in mid-afternoon and re-met Antal, the energetic and enthusiastic Hungarian immigrant I well remembered from our time together in Ireland. He quickly introduced me to his Swedish host family of David, Judit and Dick Sjölander. Antal had escaped with his father and brother from Hungary before the "curtain" came down trapping his mother and other family members in a land where he could not even visit them until he became a Swedish citizen. We in the US certainly take our freedom of movement for granted. I did note that, because I was going to stay more than one day here, I had to go to the local police station and register my visit with the Sjölanders.

Antal & the Sjölander's

In the following week and a half I shared Antal's room, his friends and his lifestyle. We had many a great session with his friends and neighbors one of whom was a gorgeous model named Monika. He had talked me into serenading her below her window one evening. It was not my idea to do this but I was not reluctant. The zest for life of this likeable Hungarian initiated this and many other adventures. I noted in my diary that most Swedish girls were ardent churchgoers in contract to the traditional looseness passed out by the American media.

The Sjölander's became my host family and somewhat adopted me for the stay. We had long talks at delicious meals cooked by Judit in her neat kitchen. We'd have tasty pulverized coffee on the terrace, which had a beautiful view of Savedalen being that the house was high on a hill. I noted that Judit would take a 7-hour rail trip to Denmark to buy food, which was noticeably cheaper there. She got a kick out of it when I insisted on going to the local store by myself to buy the ingredients for a spaghetti dinner I wanted to cook for them. I was proud to be able to come home with the required groceries given the great limitations of my Swedish. The whole family seemed to enjoy the meal and Antal said he hadn't had anything like it in 7 years in Sweden. Again I wanted always to contribute something to those who had enriched my world adventure by allowing me to be part of their family for even a short time. They took the time to teach me the blessing after meals that is something like, "*Tacks för moten, den var gut, vi är alla matt*" (Thanks for the food, it was good, we are all full).

I finally left the comfort of the Sjölanders' home and the joyful company of Antal and drove to Hälsingborg to take the ferryboat to Halsingör (the first city in Denmark). After going through customs and immigration I came out the dock road and turned onto the main boulevard. I almost panicked as I found myself facing three lanes of oncoming traffic. I quickly remembered that Sweden was the only country of Scandinavia where they drove on the left. Thanks to driving a 2-wheeled vehicle I was able to make an instant adjustment to the right side after which I took a few moments to swap my rear-view mirror to the other side of the windshield.

Welcome to Copenhagen Harbor

Copenhagen was my first real stop in Denmark. It was a truly modern city with much to see and do. One of my trips was to the harbor where I met the "Little Mermaid" who had literally lost her head over some college boys not long before. However, she had been repaired and sat on the rock where she greeted many eager visitors to the city. The Youth Hostel here was more like a hotel. It was huge and many visitors were in residence from all over the world.

I soon met Neils Christian Rasmussen, a young medical student who spoke very good English. (Note: I was to be progressively embarrassed by the number of European people who spoke several languages including mine). Neils provided my first introduction to Frank Buchman who originated the "moral rearmament" movement in youth. I was not familiar at all with this movement but was encouraged to find out that someone had taken it on as a priority. Neils became my guide and in the following days we had lunch at his beautiful home and visited the countryside including Erimetagen, the Kings hunting grounds.

Roaming around with the king's deer

I later toured the center of the city and photographed many buildings and sights. I noted that the Danes love to eat hot dogs at little kiosks in public squares. More often than not there is no bread involved or, if there is, it is eaten on the side. The hot dogs are eaten by hand and dipped into a pile of ketchup or mustard. Another favorite for the Danes seemed to be American made cars, which I saw in many locations.

On October 9th I was having some serious trouble with the scooter and I spent a most discouraging, rainy day pushing it all around the city to several NSU dealers who couldn't or wouldn't repair it. Finally I found the right one and got it fixed for 71 kroner ($14), a very reasonable price. Just 3 days before I had blown the head gasket and replaced it myself for a total cost of 2 kroner. However, this later problem was something that I didn't have the equipment nor experience to deal with. Once all was set I left for Germany crossing Denmark through Korser, Nybro and Odense. In Odense I stayed in a nearly deserted youth hostel and had an opportunity to visit the Hans Christian Anderson museum containing many of his original manuscripts. I also took a photo of his house, which was bordered by cobble-stoned streets. I went to church and had the novel experience of going to confession to a priest who could not speak my language, nor I his. This system involves multi-language cards with both languages side by side and a bit of hand expression. I was to find it in other parts of the world as well.

H.K.A house—source of so many beautiful stories

# CHAPTER SIX

## On the Continent

Now heading south towards Hamburg I came to the German border for the first time. At the crossing I met Peter Brardt of Cincinnati. He was on a BMW 250 motorcycle and had taken an over-seas discharge from the US Army after 2.5 years in Stuttgart. He was returning from a solo trip to Hammerfest, Norway (within the Arctic Circle). He had been born in Germany and spoke very good German. He had been in an airborne unit, which made him a *fallschirmspringer* in German. We decided to travel together for a few days as we were both heading south. Of course, his cycle was much more powerful and faster than mine. I bought insurance for my scooter and noted that is was quite a bit cheaper than in Scandinavia.

Our first night we stopped at the Schleswig Youth Hostel and continued on to Hamburg. I was hoping to get to Munich soon as I was down to my last $25. Luckily for me we stayed with Peter's grandparents who still lived in Hamburg. They were from Prussia and were typically strict. His grandmother was a bit concerned when we went out on the town to see the sights and didn't get back until late. The sights of Hamburg had included the St. Pauli district (red light) where prostitution is legal and the offerings are boldly displayed in the alley windows. Of course, those who are obvious foreigners have to dodge the street version of the same. We ended up at a dance club and met some very nice local girls, which resulted in us getting in late at Pete's grandparents house. Despite her being upset a bit, his grandmother had prepared the usual plate of *smor brod* (small, single slice sandwiches with a variety of topping including liverwurst) and a pot of dark, rich coffee.

Finally we had to say farewell to these very warm and caring people. We had a song fest with the guitar and then headed for Bremen. On the way

Peter's motorcycle broke down and I ended up towing him 60 kilometers (40 miles) at night in the rain on the autobahn. We used parachute shroud line, which he always kept with him. At our slow pace we were considered a nuisance on the highway. However, we had no other options. At one point a huge, empty, flatbed trailer truck passed us and pulled over ahead of us. As we approached we stopped the cycles and Peter went to talk to the driver. In my incurable optimism I assumed that the driver would allow us to put the cycles on the truck and ride inside the empty cab. After a couple of minutes Peter returned to convey to me that the driver considered us a hazard for others and said we should get off the road. So much for my optimism.

Later as we entered Bremen we got involved in traffic and when the rope went slack at one stop light, it wrapped around the axle of Pete's front wheel. As I continued his cycle flipped over in the middle of the intersection and I stopped and rushed back to see if he was hurt. He was lying on the ground and when I asked if he was okay, his only concern was that he might have damaged the newly purchased Norwegian sweater he was wearing. Finally we got to the youth hostel, which was very modern. There were people from many countries including a car full of girls from California. While Peter was fixing his cycle the next morning these girls were loading their car nearby and we decided to have a little fun with them. We both greeted them in German and then I went on to have a 20-minute conversation with them in German-accented English. When I mentioned that I had a sister in Sepulveda (purposely miss-pronounced), California one of them went wild because she lived near there. They could have all shot me as they were pulling out and I announced that I was born, brought up and lived in the Boston area. Thank God they were good sports.

As we traveled from north to south on the west side of Germany we met and stayed with other relatives of Peter. Although they would go out of their way to be accommodating, Peter resented the formality of it all. He would be content to throw his sleeping bag on someone's carpet, but they would insist on him (and me) having a comfortable room even if they rented it at a hotel (which they did on one occasion). By contrast we met a Scottish couple at a coffee house one day and they invited us to lunch at their near-by home. Jim Welsh (and Margaret) were stationed in Germany with the British Army. Peter was totally at ease with them given their relaxed outlook and manner.

Our next notable stop was in Cologne (*Köln*) where we stayed at the youth hostel. While there we encountered three "too cool" young citizens of the USA who were obnoxious and making a bad reputation for all of us. Unfortunately

there would be several notable times when I would apologize to foreigners for
the outlooks and/or actions of my fellow citizens. This incident was quickly
forgotten as we viewed the beautiful Cathedral of Cologne that was purposely
spared from the WW II bombings. I photographed this treasure as it peered
down through some fog. We went on to the capital at Bonn and had lunch
in the parliament building. From here we followed the Rhine River south to
Wiesbaden enjoying the gorgeous scenery along the way. The hills on both
sides of the river are dotted with beautiful old castles and vineyards. One of
the hostels we stayed in was one of these old castles. Other sites along the
way included Lorelei Rock (which lured sailors to their death), *Die Pfalz* (a
small castle in the middle of the river) and the bridge at Ramagen near Bad
Honnef (the site of a vicious battle where the allies crossed the Rhine). I noted
that when we were visiting a German paratrooper friend of Peter I observed
another incident that indicated some evidence of regimentation, which was
unusual to me. His friend rather cautiously played his radio even though it
was not "registered".

With a quick stop at Wiesbaden Air Force Base we continued to Pete's
old army camp (Nellingen Army Post) at Stuttgart. We ended up sleeping
overnight on our sleeping bags in the aisle of the barracks. We were only
slightly disturbed in the early morning when the sergeant came in calling for
an early inspection. When he recognized Pete on the floor he instructed both
of us to sleep in. After breakfast I said farewell to one of the few travel mates
I had met and headed for Munich. As I headed along the highway about
30 kilometers east of Stuttgart I pulled over to take in (and photograph)
the beautiful autumn scene of the village of Nürtingen cradled in the valley
between huge mountains.

Because it was the third week in October and we had seen the sun for
only about four hours in the past three weeks, it was getting quite chilly to
ride an open vehicle. By this time I was improving my German through total
immersion. I continued to find that "necessity was the mother of invention".
I wanted to try to speak to all of the people of any country, so I would have
to make a decent attempt at learning their language.

In a way I was glad to be on my own again because Pete had been fond
of traveling for an hour or so and then stopping for coffee. This meant we
didn't make much progress and I was getting low on funds. I would normally
get additional cash by having my mother withdraw from my bank account
(which I had put in her name also) and forward it by international money
order to a future destination. This is the manner in which I would also receive
mail as I traveled. Common destinations would be youth hostels, American

Hostel overlooking the River Rhine

Storybook Bavarian village—Nürtigen

Embassies, American Express offices and the General Delivery department of any post office. As for my writing, I found the most convenient method was to use aerogrammes, which were stamped, airmail sheets, which could be written on several surfaces, then folded and dropped into any mailbox. They could be sent to any country in the world.

I passed through Munich and headed for Ebersburg and the home of Gusti Ehrl and her family. She was a close pen-pal of Marie Needham and I was instructed to make sure and visit with the Ehrl's along my route. Before arriving I decided I had better make myself more presentable and I invested 2 marks (50 cents) in a haircut after 6 weeks of travel. I was soon being introduced to Gusti's entire family. Mr. and Mrs. Ehrl were the hard-working parents of 8 children. Gusti was the oldest followed by Zita, Josef, Hildegard. Peter, Felix, Lucia and Moritz. The three oldest children spoke good English and I improved my German somewhat by helping Hildegard (Hiddi) with her English homework. Their house was quite large with two small shops in the front. One was like a small general food store and the other was solely for selling meat (many varieties of *wurst*). The mother ran these shops most of the time with some help from the older children. Mr. Ehrl worked at his brother's *wurst* processing shop where he commuted by bicycle each day. All worked long hours and did so with a smile.

My Bavarian family—Ehrls

The uncle with whom the father worked had been a POW in the USA during WW II. The word among his fellow soldiers was that, if you were going to get captured, get captured by the Americans not the French or Russians who gave out harsh treatment. He said in the POW camp in the USA, if you really were a goof-up, they would make you do grounds duty that amounted to using a pointed stick to pick up the papers from the surrounding yard.

The Ehrls' house had a rather large back yard in which I would sometimes find Josef (Seppi) practicing the zither under a tree. With the Alps clearly visible in the background the atmosphere couldn't have been more complete. All of the children played some instrument and we would have some lively "jam sessions" with my guitar. It turned out that their favorite sing-a-long song from the USA was "Rudolph the Red-nosed Reindeer" which had to be sung several times at every opportunity. They all marveled at the motor scooter, which had carried me so far from Marie Needham's home. I often gave Lucia a ride to her Kindergarten class on it. On one occasion Mrs. Ehrl was late for church and I offered to take her quickly on the scooter. With her substantial girth leaning against me all the way she punctuated the trip with a series of gasps and screams. I'm sure she said a prayer of thanksgiving when she arrived. I did note that she never asked for a ride on the scooter again.

I had received a check with my funds when I arrived at Ehrls' house and I was finally able to do some shopping in Munich. Gusti went with me to see how much it would be to repair my ailing scooter. The first shop wanted 650 marks, which we got down to 300 by checking other repair shops. Later after I picked it up for 265 marks (about $65) with the engine supposedly like new I noticed on the way home that the generator light was on. By the time we arrived the batteries were dead again. The following day I adjusted the voltage regulator and all was well. I continued to have electrical problems, which found me at the Bosch repair shop. At first they tested and announced that the batteries were both good. When I later took the scooter for them to do repair work they stated that both batteries had to be replaced, costing me another 100 DM. I later noted that the repair shop had stated that, had I needed a voltage generator, I would be out of luck because they did not have one. That's why I was taken by surprise later when I received a statement from Bosch saying that I owed them an additional 31.8 DM for a voltage regulator. I called them to protest on the basis that they had indicated that they didn't even have on for my scooter. They insisted and I hung up resolving to let Bosch chase me around the world before I would pay for something they did not do for me.

As time went on I truly enjoyed being a temporary part of this typical Bavarian family. People in this southeastern part of the country are known to be very friendly and quite religious. The typical greeting is "*Grüsse Gott*" (I greet you with God). The autumn colors were spectacular as we took a long walk together and climbed the local fire look-out tower for a superb panoramic view of the valley. We often visited their relatives and friends giving me a broader insight to the local culture.

When the sun finally came out after two weeks of clouds, I decided to head for Munich as a more typical tourist and take some photos. I quietly took a side trip on that day to view the extermination camp at Dachau where Hitler had had millions of Jews and others killed. It was a bit eerie to see the actual false shower rooms in which victims were gassed as well as the ovens in which the corpses were reduced to ashes. Over the door of the crematorium there was a sign, which would convey the hopes of all rational beings, "Nimmer noch mal" (never again).

Having taught high school in the USA I was quite surprised to learn that in Germany the class schedule was like college at home with each days schedule being different including classes on Saturday. Also when there was a class dance the boys could only invite the girls from their class. A truly unique item was the "*foehn*" winds which came off the Alps at certain times of the year. They were reported to affect individuals in many ways. They were an acceptable excuse for not taking an examination in school.

Frau Ehrl was a hard-working mother who had a digestive system like a vacuum cleaner. She never wasted food having lived through the lean days of WW II. Having been from a family of 7 children, I could easily agree with this philosophy. I noted that when she ate an apple the only thing left was the stem. She was always very positive and easy going. When I had a chance I went to Munich to do some shopping and bought her a new power can-opener. She thought that was the greatest thing in the world. As well as giving small gifts to show my appreciation, when a houseguest, I would also try to do some work around the house especially if it required some skill with which I had experience. In my travels I was to do a great amount of electrical work including appliance repairs

In the middle of November I started to feel weak and sick with a loss of appetite. I stayed in bed for a couple of days but later was talked into visiting the local doctor with Hiddi as my guide. After examination he stated that I had "*Gelbsucht*" which is yellow jaundice or hepatitis. He recommended two weeks in the hospital as a minimum. It was at the hospital that I found out that they would not accept my "Universal Prudential" health insurance. When I spoke to the family about this they indicated that *Gelbsucht* was not uncommon in this area and the only things they would do at the hospital for me was allow rest and give lots of liquids and food when my system would accept them. They said that they could do the same for me at their home. And so, Hiddi (with the beautiful blue eyes, dimples and blond pony-tail) became my nurse. She was very sweet and attentive and exchanged English-for-German lessons with me very often. With her good care and the support of all the Ehrl's I was fit and ready for the road in 6 days. At this time of year I was trying to head south due to the on-coming cold winter weather.

# CHAPTER SEVEN

## Good-by Ehrl's (once)

On November 26th I said the round of sad good-by's and drove the cold 370 kilometers (240 miles) to Zug, Switzerland where I found the local Youth Hostel closed. While inquiring about the hostel at Brandenburg Guest House I was invited by Frau Brandenburg to use her son's bedroom as he was away. Again, as would happen so often, I was kindly "adopted" as a family member for the day. As I ate a great meal that was quickly prepared for me, I had to relate my background and motivations for making such a trip. Young people on the continent freely travel to other European countries even on weekends but it was unusual to see an American travel for such a long time. The atmosphere of the guesthouse was greatly enhanced for me by the presence of two very attractive teen-age daughters. The following morning I had breakfast and got a tour of the surroundings. One item that got my attention was that there was a still for making liquor in the back shed. What hit me was that the leftover mash from the still was thrown onto the ground and eaten by the many chickens they kept. I had never seen a "high" chicken before but it was obvious and I chocked it up to another of the world's lessons for me. As suspected the Brandenburg's would not consider taking any payment for the care I had received at their guesthouse. I headed for Lucern, Bern and Lausanne where I stayed in the local hostel.

As I headed south in Switzerland I found it a challenge to change from German to French having gotten quite conversant with the former. I arrived in Geneva in the rain and met Dick Atkinson, the brother of Fred whom I had visited in the Lake District of England. He was teaching chemistry and physics at the Internationale Ecole which caters to those of significant means from all over the world. Dick hosted me for a couple of days during which he showed me the school and around Geneva which is very international with the Red Cross, United Nations and many well-known companies located there. Although Switzerland was a very popular tourist destination, I found the locals generally not very hospitable. This may come from the sense of outsiders taking over the desirable surroundings of their beautiful country.

On December 1st I left on a sunny morning for Lyon, France through the French Alps. My determination would be put to the test in the last 50 kilometers in which I was driving in a snowstorm. With little traction for a scooter the speed of travel is cut drastically. I finally found the hostel at Lyon, which was not very impressive for a large city hostel. I was to find a great variety of facilities in the Youth Hostel system as well as in the Maison des Jeunes system that I found only in France. The next day I located the hostel at Avignon, which was very nice but closed. I had to call the warden as I had my mail forwarded there. I was pleased to find two letters one of which contained an international check from my account at home. At this point I was down to change in my pocket. With my new financial resources I continued on to Tarascone and checked into the hostel there. The young warden was quite helpful and allowed me to stay (I was the only one visiting) and to pay for my lodging the next day when I would cash the check. That night I was resigned to having no supper until a young man who worked there invited me to share his potatoes which he was "French frying". I found out that he was like a permanent resident there because he worked in the area but home was some distance away. The next morning I traveled to banks in three towns and could not find one, which would cash my check. I was told that the only sure way to get it cashed was to go to Marseilles, a popular tourist center. I drove the 100 kilometers there and had no trouble cashing the check for a fee. On my return I snapped a photo of some land that looked very much like Arizona. By the time I got back I had to stay another night at the same hostel and I treated the warden and the other resident to some fine pastries for their kindness. The next day I drove to Narbonne where I stayed at the Maison des Jeunes as there were no hostels in the city. It was the same price and I found some very friendly people working there. My attempts at conversational French were obviously appreciated even though they were quite rudimentary.

I continued on the winding coastal road to Spain and appreciated the beauty of the Costa Brava. I had taken the time to review my Basic Spanish in order to say, "Yo quiero comprar seguro" (I wish to buy insurance). I had gotten used to the idea that each country would require me to part with some cash at the border in order to enter. After memorizing these words for many hours of travel I was surprised (and almost put out) that the border guard didn't want to hear anything about insurance. So, I entered the land of sun and sand and remember the feeling of the strong rays on my cold body, which prompted me to yell, "OK big orange eye, scald my ass and get it warm for a change". I headed for Barcelona and checked in at the Youth Hostel there. It was an elegant villa with great potential but obviously had not been taken care off. The balmy weather of the next two days saw me visiting the city after church. In a central park people had gathered and piled their coats and wraps on the grass and were doing a slow, elegant dance to some live music. I was later told that this was Sardana dancing that was a traditional dance very popular with many locals. Not being bashful at all I joined in the dance and later chatted a bit with some of the other participants. The hospitality was as warm as the weather. At night I went out with two other travelers and we visited Pan Ams Club, which was typical in the red-light district. There were many US sailors around the area looking for comfort/pleasure. What I saw of the offerings were not very impressive.

# CHAPTER EIGHT

## The "Scandinavian Florida"

After having my first adventure with the Spanish postal service I bought boat tickets to Mallorca (the largest of the Balaric Islands) that I had heard so much about. After driving through the snowstorm in the French Alps I was resigned to the idea of going south and "planting" for the winter. From what I had heard, Mallorca would be an ideal place to do so. I had looked down on these islands many times from our B-52 when I was a navigator/bombardier on SAC crew E-22. In 1962 our crew was the "Crew of the Year" in 8th Air Force and we won a trip to Mallorca for 10 days. However, as things would go in the military, the trip was postponed multiple times and we never did get it.

Now on December 7th I was boarding a ship for the 10 hour crossing to this beautiful location of so many "escapes" by those from northern Europe. I later got to refer to Mallorca as the "Scandinavian Florida". It was quite a bargain at that time as the tickets for the scooter and me were a total of 337 pesetas ($5.50). On the ship I met Tony and Pete, two American GI's who were on leave from their base in Germany. We hit it off well and hung around together for the next few days. When the boat docked in the morning we got a ride to a pension and got rooms for 35 pesetas (.55) per night. The exchange rate was 64 pesetas to the dollar. In the European countries the exchange rates were generally fixed which was quite in contrast to what I would later find as I moved further east. Tony and Pete rented motor scooters and we got our first look at the beaches of this popular resort. We took in some rays at Palma Nova beach and toured a large part of the island. At night with Tony on my back seat I had a minor accident as the back wheel slowly skidded out from under us on a watered-down street. I was to find that the streets were cleaned at night by hosing them down. As well, the sidewalks were usually cleaned by the workers of the stores or pensions bordering the roads. You had to be careful not to be included in the sweep of washing water that issued forth from many doorways.

During the following week I got settled in Mallorca and met many new friends both visitors and natives. One day I met Diane Tipper of Australia who was going around the world in the opposite direction. She was from the Melbourne area and we swapped addresses with the promise to look up each other (or our families) if we got close to the areas involved. Soon Tony, Pete and Diane moved on to their own plans and I moved to Pension Aglaya in the old Spanish area of Palma. The price was still 35 pesetas with hot and cold water in my room and a shared shower across the hallway. This pension, like most, was operated by a family and almost all members played some part in the services rendered. Nobody spoke English, which was as I preferred. I was only starting to learn Spanish but used French with the niece of the owner who ran the reception desk. Another great feature of this pension was that they had one of the two self-service cafeterias on the island. So, when I saw what looked like a delicious beef stew, I could ask for it by pointing and later learn that it was *estefado*.

Friends at Pension Aglaya coffee bar

As it was mid December I spent some time sending over 70 Christmas cards to family and recently found friends. I had an experience when I tried to phone my mother for Christmas. I had to book the call and then wait 45 minutes for the operator to try to place it. My call of 5 minutes cost me $23.50. I had had no response to an ad I put in the local paper to tutor English. As well, I had several leads for entertainment work but no real offers.

As I started to get familiar with my new surroundings I noted that military guards were everywhere in order to insure the peace. Generalissimo Franco kept the populace in a surrounding that insured the lack of rebellion. The ordinary soldiers were a raggedy-looking lot. I was told that when they reported for duty the next person in line got the next uniform regardless of size. This seemed to be borne out one day as I tried to take a photo of a guard at a government building and he scurried around a corner so I could not include him and his ill-fitting uniform in the picture. Franco seemed to rule with an iron hand. If a person put a Franco stamp on a letter upside down, his name was recorded in Madrid. Soldiers were paid 15 pesetas per month and had to serve for 1.5 years.

Palma's Gothic cathedral from the harbor

I had bought a small paperback book, Hugo's "Spanish in Three Months without a Master", to learn Spanish. It was quite straightforward and I started using a fair amount of the local language especially around the pension. I had a unique experience when I went to church in the cathedral and decided to go to confession. I wasn't sure how I'd do this given that there were no English-speaking priests around at the time. However, the whole process was facilitated by a series of flip charts, which had Spanish on one side of the page and the comparable English across from it on the other side. By pointing out the most obvious lines and waiting for the response I found that I could get through it quite easily. Presumably this could be done for any other foreign language as well. This was similar to the system I had used in Denmark. One other thing that brought me a bit of comfort in the church occurred when I went to a small local church one Sunday. I sat beside a middle-aged man with whom I could not have much of a conversation. Yet, we both said the Latin of the Mass together having been altar boys in our younger years. Although this was due to change in time, I remember getting a feeling of the universality of the church in this situation.

Christmas Day was a "rags to riches" emotional roller coaster for me. In the morning I had gone to church and returned to my pension, which was almost deserted. I re-read the 5 Christmas cards I had received and went to bed a bit "down in the dumps". Later I went back to the Hotel de Mar (Club Orfeo) where I had been getting promises for a tryout as a foreign singer. This had been postponed several times. On this night there were some more changes in the plan, but I finally was allowed to sing with the band to the very high-class audience. Everything went over very well with the clientele and the Club Director, Sr. Orloff, asked me how much I would work for so he could contact the Directors to OK a contract for me for the next three months. I told him that it would be 400 pesetas a night, which was $6.50 for 7 hours of work. It doesn't sound like much, but in Spain, that would have been a very comfortable salary for me. I left the club floating on air at the prospect of this work after trying so many ways to earn my keep in this beautiful island location until the spring would beckon me to travel again. Christmas had, indeed, brought its own special spirit.

I had to get used to the idea that children did not get presents on Christmas Day but on Epiphany, January 5th when they leave grain in their shoes on the balconies for the horses of the Three Kings, the Magi. On this day *Los Tres Reis* arrived at the dock by boat and led a procession of horses and mules from the dock up the main street to an orphanage where they distributed presents and food. All of the children and their parents come out to greet the Kings. Everyone gets involved in the day. On special holidays the countryside people would make unique food products and sell them from little stalls along the city streets. One type of sweet was *torrones* and my favorite became *jijona* which was made from hazel nuts and tasted a bit like peanut butter.

Another thing I had to get used to was the hours of the average daily schedule. Generally meals are moved back 2-4 hours. For me, breakfast was usually in mid-morning and consisted of a cup of *cafe con leche* (strong coffee with heated milk added) and two *ensaimadas* (light swirled rolls with powdered sugar sprinkled on top). Most people had lunch at 3:00 PM and dinner about 10:00 PM. Siesta time was 1:30-4:00 PM during which time all the shops closed and people met friends and ate together. At night when the shops closed for the day the staff would wash the floors inside the entrances and display additional items in that area so strollers could do late window-shopping—a very popular pastime.

During the time I was seeking work I had quite a number of hours (days) in which I could explore this very scenic island. In time I traveled completely around the island on various day trips. On one of these I visited the Cueves de Drach (caves), which were very impressive. They contained an underground river on which we were barged to a theater carved out of the rocks. As we sat in the theater seats the absolute silence was incredible. Then we could hear the soft strains of classical music. As the volume became louder we witnessed the orchestral barge floating slowly by us with a full complement of professional musicians. They created the purest musical tones I had ever heard.

Later on this day I headed for San Salvador, a monastery of hermit monks, located on the peak of a 1600-foot mountain. The winding road to the top was a picturesque challenge to the clutch of my scooter. The original building dates from 1313, but the present building was erected in 1788. After ringing an old doorbell I was greeted by a bearded monk who was very hospitable and showed me around. Having been told I could do so by others, I made arrangements to stay there for the night for a small donation. It turned out that I was the only visitor on this day to stay over. I was shown my room and then went to the chapel for the saying of the Rosary. There was not electricity in the entire building and all illumination was by candles and gaslights. As you might expect there were many candles in the chapel. I was told that this monastery is often used for retreats for which it would be ideal.

For dinner I went to the small restaurant, which is run by the family who live there and take care of the needs of the monks. After eating I was invited to sit with the family and a couple of the monks as they chatted about all manner of things. Of course they were curious about me and my travels.

Despite the warmth of most days the altitude of this location made it extremely cold at night. As we sat around a large table we were warmed by the pan of coals from the fire which was inserted into a rack under the middle of the table. The long, thick tablecloth was then pulled up over our legs providing a cozy table atmosphere. I later found that I had no such source of warmth in my room and I spent the majority of the night trying to get my bed warm enough to fall asleep.

The women of the house did some very fine needlework (like embroidery) in extremely poor lighting. However, their work was exquisite. The following morning while having breakfast I watched the women iron their products from the night before. They used a very tall iron into which coals from the fireplace were inserted and brought up to temperature. I remember noting that the pillowcases and other items when finished looked like they had been done with the most modern techniques and equipment. It showed what we can do when we understand the essence of the process and become innovative as regards the means of getting the job done.

As it was lightly raining I decided to wait a while for it to clear so that I could take some photos of the monastery and the beautiful panoramic views of the plains in all directions. After satisfying my need for photographic documentation I said a reluctant farewell to San Salvador, an ideal place for thought and meditation. I returned to Palma by way of several other picturesque villages.

Having been disappointed by Sr. Orloff and the Hotel de Mar I pursued other means of work. When I visited a shop called Alba I met the staff, Nurry, Delores, Margarita and Tony. Nurry was an absolute ball of fire. She spoke several languages and had traveled extensively. After getting acquainted she recommended that I try for work at the Tagomago Nightclub. When I checked at the club they said there was nothing available at the time but there was a benefit show being put on for charity, which would give me exposure even though not paid. I sang in the show at the Teatro Lirico and was followed by "Los Valldemosas" who indicated they wanted to talk to me after their performance. They owned half share in the Tagomago Club and wanted me to sing at the club while they were away for the next two weeks. Two days later I went to the club and rehearsed with the house orchestra (Los Tagos) and sang that night. There were two shows each night and I sang in them as well as with the band for dancing. I was paid 250 pesetas per night working from 10:00 PM to 3:00 AM. Given that my room was 35 pesetas a night and I could get a full meal for the same price, I was doing quite well for myself at this point.

View from San Salvador Monastery

Nurry, Margarita & Delores

After Los Valldemosas returned they kept me on to sing for dancing with the house orchestra. The guest band was a young group called Los Quartro Platinos who were contracted for a specific period of time. I became disturbed by Los Tagos who would all play cards while Los Quatros Plantinos were on stage. I often wanted to take just a few minutes to talk over musical arrangements so that our numbers would be polished. However, they were always content with things as they were and "playing it by ear" while on stage. In our nightly routine we would start playing for dancing as soon as the doorman (Mateo Alberti) announced that clients were coming. We would play for the small crowd until Los Quatros Platinos did their set. When they finished there was the first floor show which I was not part of after Los Valldemosas returned. Los Tagos provided the show music minus me. After the floor show Los Quatros Platinos played their second set (the house would be pretty full by this time) until time for the second floor show. After this show the house orchestra (with me) would continue to play for dancing as most of the guests departed. When all had left we would quit for the night. The result of this schedule got me very frustrated because I never got to sing for a large audience. After complaining to the artistic director he delayed the change of orchestras between shows so I could do a couple of numbers for the larger audience. At one point I got some drumming experience when the drummer of the house orchestra was drafted into Franco's army although he was in his forties, married and had children. I filled in sometimes until they got a replacement.

I mentioned Mateo, the doorman, who became a good friend as I spent much time chatting with him before the first clients would show up. He usually worked only for tips and had a regular day job on tour boats in order to support his family. On one night he was trying to be his most courteous self to accommodate the guests when his foot got run over by a taxi. He continued to work 1.5 hours until closing time before he would get any aid. Such was the worth of having a job in Spain. He was paid a small percentage and tips, which amounted to about 1,000 pesetas a month. At that I realized that the club was fairly expensive for the customers. The first drink of the night cost 250 pesetas (my salary for the night). After that they were 50 pesetas.

I spent the days meeting many new friends and exploring the surroundings. There were many English people visiting and I would get a particular kick out of their being so relieved to be able to "let their hair down" here which they would not think of doing in Britain. On one trip I visited Valldemosa (home town of "Los Valldemosas") and was able to tour Cartuja, a monastery where Chopin had written some of his works while residing there from 1838-1839. The piano that he used was there on display. As I traveled I was enchanted by the many old *molinos* (windmills) which were still operating and performing useful tasks.

As a few articles and advertising appeared in the local newspapers about my singing at Tagomago, my hosts at Aglaya started to consider me like a celebrity living at their pension. They were so kind and genuine that I really began to feel a part of the family. The son-in-law, Carlos, would see me coming to the bar in the morning and automatically prepare my *cafe-con-leche* and two *ensaimadas*. On one occasion I was eating in the cafeteria on the lower level when I noticed that one of the working daughters would load dishes into the small dumbwaiter, press the button and then smack the unit on the side to get it going. The poor girl was developing a significant bruise on her right hand as a result. The next day I offered to take a look at the mechanism for the father of the family. He was all too eager to have me do so and was totally elated when I repaired the switch inside. He later showed me a second complete control panel that had been totally replaced when the same problem had occurred before. I also remember a profound "*gracias*" from the working daughter. Thereafter, I was considered the "great guru of electricity".

I had sent some of my exposed slide film to France for developing and when I received them I was not too pleased. However, I was able to show them to my Spanish family at the pension so they could get an idea of where I had been before I arrived at their door. I would use pre-paid mailers for my films and usually I would put my home address in the USA as the return address. But on occasion I would want to check on my Zeiss Ikon Contessa to make sure that there were no major problems. In this case I would use a return address of a location, which I would definitely visit in several weeks. I would use the address of the Youth Hostel I intended to visit, the local American Express office or the General Delivery of the local post office. This was also how my mother would forward to me funds I requested from my savings account when I was short of finances. One of the friendly local regulars at the pension cafeteria was Miguel, a veteran who had been through a lot and had an opinion on everything. He roamed around selling trinkets and lottery tickets on the street. The selling of all lottery tickets in Spain was reserved for veterans. I remember that the periodic grand prize was referred to as "*El Gordo*" (the fat one).

I watched a local sport on TV, which was called "*ballomano*". It was similar to basketball but the goals were more like ice-hockey goals. I also noticed that one of the popular dances being done by young people was called *La yenka* which was the "bunny hop" we had been doing eleven years earlier. One way in which I got occasional relief from my struggling Spanish was to go to an English language movie when available. Once I watched "Counterfeit Traitor" with William Holden and was surprised to see scenes of places I had visited. In one scene he was moving around the city of Stockholm and passed the site of the Grand Hotel. You could easily see nearby Alf Chapman, the youth hostel I had stayed in on the edge of the harbor. On another night I went to a small theater and watched Peter Sellers in "The Pink Panther", which I thoroughly enjoyed not knowing that it was the beginning of a smash series of films.

I was a bit frustrated when I tried to send money out of the country to pay a doctor's bill in the USA. The only official way I could do so was to bring the bill, my passport and the money in US dollars to the main bank. They would review everything and then send it to Madrid for processing. In about a week I would find out if it were OK. Being an extremely practical person I sent the well-wrapped dollars in a regular letter envelope (which was illegal). Although I intended to learn the culture of each country I visited and to live

on their standards while I was there, certain rules, etc just got on my nerves
to the point that I decided to take shortcuts of convenience. The result never
offended anyone but might have angered locals had I made it known.

One local small club I got to enjoy was the Indigo Jazz Club owned by
Ramon who was engaged to Lucia Graves, daughter of Robert Graves, the
English poet. Ramon had originally intended to use me at the club but it
did not work out. However, I met many likable characters there and passed
many hours with them. It was about this time that, after over 6,000 miles
of travel, I got the first flat tire of the trip. Because my scooter was quite
unique for the locals (electric starter) it was often the object of scrutiny and
comment. One evening, as I left the Indigo, I noticed that someone had
carried the scrutiny a bit far; the scooter was missing. I frantically searched
the surrounding streets and was greatly relieved to find it parked about a
half mile away on the side of the road. The thief apparently couldn't figure
out how to get it started and pushed it to this location. The only damage
was that it was out of gas because he/she had pulled out the choke and left
it out. A quick fresh supply of gas mixture solved the problem easily. I also
was subject to the scooter being hit while it was parked. At this point it had
happened four times. Usually the damage was minor and I was able to correct
it with some owner "TLC".

One day I was walking along the main Paseo Maritimo when I noticed
a US sailor standing by a jeep and looking very perplexed. He was from the
flagship Valcouver docked in the harbor. I asked if I could help him at all.
It turned out that he was out of gas, had no money and couldn't speak any
Spanish. I bought him 2 liters of gas and pushed the jeep to get it started.
Then he asked me to go back to the ship with him to confirm his story. When
we got there I related the story for the young man. I identified myself with
my papers as a reserve Air Force officer and was invited aboard and offered
funds for the gas. I refused the pesetas but accepted a tour of the ship. An
officer was assigned for this task and we spent quite a time together ending
up in the stateroom for coffee. It put me in touch with a style of life that I
hadn't experienced for a year.

As spring came around I let the directors of the club know that I intended
to leave in March. They wanted me to stay on for the summer season when
they go outside to the terraced club location. I noted for myself that a few
things would have to change if I were to remain. I made plans to visit the
island of Ibiza before I continued my journey. It was known as an art colony.
On April 4th I finally left Tagomago and took a plane to Ibiza. It was a bit
strange to fly again having not been in the air since I arrived in England more

than one year prior. Ibiza was quite a bit smaller and less commercial than Mallorca. It definitely had the feel of an art colony. It seemed that there were more visitors than natives here. I stayed at a decent pension and found the food here quite good and varied. One dish I remember savoring greatly was a truly authentic *paella*. This is a rice dish with vegetables and seafood with many select spices.

Moorish style church—Ibiza

I visited the fortress on the hill, which gave a beautiful view of the harbor which it had protected in former times. Most of the houses were white and were built in the Moorish style. The roads were exceptionally straight which was deceiving when I decided to walk to a Moorish church I saw "just down the road". A half hour later I was still walking towards that church in San Rafael. I took a photo of it when I arrived and one of the very straight road leading to it. I found out that I walked 7 kilometers (about 4.5 miles). I returned to the city to purchase my return ticket on the boat. It was only 70 pesetas (about $2). I walked through the hilly streets of the city at night until my boat left at midnight.

I spent the next few days in Mallorca getting packed, preparing the scooter and saying good-by's to many good friends like Nurry and the staff of Capucine, her most recent shop. During this visit I was embarrassed again by one of my fellow Americans. The shop custom tailored leather and suede clothing which was first class and very reasonable for foreigners. While I was waiting to say farewell to Nurry I went into the back room to see Tony, the presser. While we were chatting I could not help but overhear a woman from New York who was visiting on a tour boat for a number of hours. She wanted a great variety of products and was bargaining with Nurry for a huge discount. Nurry got permission to offer her a 10% discount, which is the most they give to anyone including the staff. The lady was not satisfied with this and said, "We are here from a large cruise ship and when I return with these products I will refer a number of other customers to you. So, whatever extra discount you give me, you can make up on them.". I turned to Tony and said, "*Hoy yo soy espanol*" (Today I am Spanish)

I noted that the scooter mileage was 10,250 miles when I left Mallorca. I also repaired the dumbwaiter at the pension again just before I left. After a frustrating loading of the scooter onto the boat we left at 8:40 PM for Valencia. I was forced to buy a first class ticket as it was the only one available. It cost me 513 pesetas with 200 more for the scooter, a mere $11, which I couldn't complain about even though I would never opt to travel first class. This part of my philosophy relates to the idea that I can learn the average life of the natives from the common person who would travel common class. In first class I actually shared a cabin with an 80-year old man who wanted to ride to Sevilla on the back seat of my scooter.

# CHAPTER NINE

## Surrounded by citrus

The following morning we docked in Valencia harbor and after another delay in unloading because of a car accident on the ramp, I got my scooter and headed into the city. I took the road to Alicante and was pleasantly surprised as I traveled south along the coast through the orange groves famous in this part of the country. The weather was beautiful and the fragrance of the orange blossoms surrounded me as I proceeded south through Alicante to Murcia. As I continued towards Granada I started to see the Sierra Nevada Mountains in the distance with snow on the peaks. This was quite unique inasmuch as I was traveling in the hottest climate I had encountered to date. To protect myself from the strong sun I had kept a nylon outer ski jacket with me, which was light in weight but an adequate protection from the sun and wind, I thought. During one typical day of travel I stopped at lunchtime at a roadside cafe. I ordered a sandwich (*bocadillo*) and a drink and stood near the bar waiting. All of a sudden the room started to turn slowly and I became quite dizzy. I had to force myself to control my movements as I made my way to a table and chair near the wall. After I had drunk quite a bit of water and relaxed my head cleared. I took my time to finish my sandwich and dug into my pack to find my old visor cap, which I made sure to wear thereafter not wanting another incident of what might have been mild sunstroke. I stayed that night in the small town of Cullar de Baza where I found the usually inexpensive pension. After settling and having dinner I joined the locals in the *paseo* strolling with their friends. I made a host of instant friends by bringing out the guitar and having a song session for the young people. I later ended up serenading a beautiful young lady. I would probably never see these people again, but I had the privilege of sharing a few hours of human interaction with them all of which continued to validate the reason for my travels.

Local laborer with Sierra Nevadas

Granada is a storied old city in Spain and the home of Alhambra, the famous Moorish Castle. I visited this fabulous example of Moorish architecture but was more intrigued by the fact that poorer people still lived in hollowed-out caves in the surrounding hills. I was to find the contrast between the "have's" and the "have not's" to be quite distinct in most countries through which I traveled. Unfortunately the disparity between the two groups can be a source of envy, anger and conflict leading to riots and wars in many cases. It seems to me that the priorities of all countries should include the availability of opportunities for all citizens to live in a decent life style.

As I continued south through the Costa Del Sol, I was well aware that the scooter was running very poorly and needed some attention. The plus side of this part of the trip was that, because the scooter was so slow, I had more time to take in the beautiful scenery on the way to Motril and Malaga on the Med. Sea. The latter was a large city with many visiting tourists taking advantage of all the area had to offer in the way of climate, beaches and scenery. I headed for Gibraltar, which is a small peninsula jutting into the Med. Sea and owned by Britain. As I approached it I was reminded of the small three-wheeled delivery trucks found throughout Spain. One of my Spanish friends in Mallorca had

Gibralta, reminder of my insurance company

told me that these ugly little noisy machines were referred to as "Gibs", short for Gibraltar, the shame of Spain. It did seem strange to cross international borders to visit an area famous for its "rock" while I still considered myself to be in Spain. I left my scooter at the border in order not to go through another hassle with the Queen's men regarding its registration and insurance. Through some advice I made my way to "Toch H", a shantytown run by Jock, a Scot who had been greeting low-budget travelers for 14 years. I made this my home base while I explored the Rock. I stayed overnight with Jock and many others and returned to Spain the next morning.

As I continued towards Seville I found the scooter so weak that I sometimes had to gear down to go down hills. I decided to stop at a town of Los Barrios to try to deal with this problem. I found a pension and the owners directed me to a local motorcycle shop where the owner took a test ride and decided that the whole exhaust system had to be de-coked (due to carbon from the exhaust blocking up all of the passages for air flow). This mechanic owned a shop, which was the front portion of his house. He went directly to work and removed all of the parts of the exhaust system while his assistant used a hand bellows to bring the coals of the open burn tray to a red-hot condition. All parts were inserted into the inferno and the resulting smoke accumulated at the ceiling level until it was so deep that it started to enter the living quarters. This didn't apparently faze the owner and he continued to burn out all of the residue until the parts were totally cleaned out. He then re-assembled all and gave it a test run. To me it was like new. It had never run this well since I got it. The bill for the entire procedure was a mere 210 pesetas ($3.23). At the pension I reported my good luck to the owners as we shared coffee in the evening. I slept well and the following morning I had coffee and bread with them after which they presented me with my entire B and B bill of 25 pesetas (.40 US). I dropped by the repair shop on my way out of town and Pepe wanted to buy my guitar. We had a session after which I hit the road for Seville.

In Seville I looked up a pen pal, Maruja who had been waiting to show me the sights of the area. Her family welcomed me and let me stay with them for several days until I later moved to a pension. Maruja and her friends were great guides for the activities which were taking place at this time. It was *Semana Santa* (Holy Week) and we saw two of the processions, which take place all day and night. *Pasos* (holy floats) are built at local churches and carried through the streets by up to 40 men to the Cathedral where they are blessed and then returned to their home churches. Sometimes this takes 12-14 hours. Two of the popular floats contain statues of the Virgin Mary. One is named *La Triana* and the other is *La Macarena*. The latter was worth one half million pesetas. The honor guards who lead the processions are garbed in hoods and robes that reminded me of the KKK. However, the colors of their robes were unique to their parish churches. The chanting of the crowds seemed almost like a football rivalry.

Near Maruja's house was the Philippine Embassy, which had a small public bar. Mr. Mills, a retired US Army sergeant, who boarded with Maruja's family helped to keep this mini-bar in business. I visited there and met four Australian girls, including Nola Burns, who had been working to finance their travels. As usual we exchanged addresses and promised to look each other up if we ever got close. At that time I didn't realize what a significant role this exchange would play in my future travels.

Given that it was Easter time I went to church at the Cathedral on Easter Sunday and was pleasantly surprised to meet my Massachusetts Senator, Ted Kennedy, at the door. He was on crutches, being in the last stage of recovery from a near-fatal plane crash, but was in good spirits He was with his wife, Joan, to whom he introduced me. We chatted for a few minutes about home and what I intended to do on my trip. He was familiar with my hometown of Wilmington and knew several of the local politicians there. I later learned that many of the Kennedy family members (including Jackie) were in town for *"La Feria"*, the spring festival. This event follows Holy Week by a week and the whole of the festival grounds was covered with semi-permanent nightclubs or *casetas*. These were sponsored by local civic groups and others including the NCO and Officers Clubs of the nearby US Moron AFB. People of the surrounding villages made home-crafted goods and brought them for sale to the area of *La Feria*. They would set up on the sidewalks and sleep there beside their little stands for the whole week. I was lucky to find that a number of them offered *turones* including my favorite *jijona*. A visit to La Feria usually consisted of spending the entire evening meeting friends and visiting the many *casetas* into the sunrise hours. At that time we would visit a Feria bar, have a cup of strong coffee and a shot of *aguardiente* (strong anise-type licorice liquor). That would shock us into awakening to participate in anything desirable during the day such as viewing the festive and beautiful *Feria* Parade.

In search of some work to pay my way I went to Moron AFB and inquired regarding entertainment work at the Officers Club and the NCO Club. I was told that not much was going on in either because all efforts were being made to prepare the *casetas* at the *Feria* grounds. I was told that the Club Officer of the Officers Club was at the *caseta*. When I went there and asked for him I

*La Feria* parade in Seville

was directed to Captain Dave Seering who had been our Club Officer at Dow AFB in Bangor, Maine when I was assigned there. We had a bit of a re-union and Dave was able to line up some part-time entertainment work for me at the *caseta* during that week. The work was great but it also gave me an opportunity to meet some wonderful new friends, most of them in the military. One evening I met Major Leslie Bridges who had been one of my AFROTC instructors at U/Mass-Amherst 10 years prior.

During the abundant free time I had I toured around this beautiful capital of the southern region of Spain. Aside from the Cathedral I visited the Giraldi Tower, the Santa Cruz area (old Jewish Quarter) and the Archives of Indies where I was able to view letters and maps of Columbus, Cortez and many other adventurers who had launched their sojourns from this area. Of course, I recorded the splendor with my faithful Zeiss Ikon camera.

One of my most homesick days came with the arrival of a letter from Diane Tipper which she had written in my home in the USA. She had looked up my family and stayed with my mother as she prepared to drive across the whole country by herself. One of our neighbors, Frank Kasynski, who designed and built recreation campers outfitted the back of her car with a bed and other conveniences. Her goal was to drive to the Pacific Ocean and then return to Australia where she would wait for me to arrive at some future time.

One of the nicest "non-ugly American" families I found in Seville was that of John and Anel Taylor from Texas. He and his family (including mother-in-law, Annabel) had come to Spain with the idea of getting totally involved in the culture of a different country. They had looked forward to the different life style, food and language. However, when they arrived they were escorted to the "All American" housing area on the base where they could live almost the same way as they did in the States. It was not long until they rebelled against this type of restriction and moved off base to a villa, which had everything including a swimming pool for them and their six young kids. They quickly learned the language to a useful degree and became part of the local community. The children picked up the language quickly as the live-in maid was a warm, animated version of "Aunt Jemima" who spoke no English. (Day-work maids were available for 25-40 pesetas per day.) I was extremely happy to see that some of our American personnel were giving an appropriate impression to the Spanish community in which they lived. Others who clung to the air base would hardly consider going into town for lunch. I thought that this was such a pity given that most travelers, like myself, were willing to spend a fair amount of effort and funds to be in exactly this situation. I had also witnessed several off-duty GI's at the bar of my pension loudly denouncing Spain and proclaiming that they couldn't wait to get back to the USA. Of course the effect was lessened by the fact that it was said in English due to their idea that it was not worthwhile to try to learn Spanish. However, enough words and the facial expressions used gave the owners a good idea of what was being said. Afterwards I would have a chat to let them know that all Americans were not the same. Thank God they had also met fine American visitors. As was not uncommon, the mother of the owner-family wanted me to find a nice local girl and settle down there.

Prior to, and during my travels, many people had asked me if I had any concerns for my well being as I traveled through so many diverse areas of the globe. Generally my answer was that I trusted people to be humane and considerate. It was at about this time in my journey that it struck me that all people in all locations; regardless of race, sex, ethnicity, class or education have the ability to detect sincerity in another person. This will make the difference no matter where you go. Show people that you are human and have the same concerns and needs as they do, and they will open their lives to you. This is what made my trip so genuine and something that would re-confirm for me the universality of humanity.

One of the nicest "gigs" I had while in Seville was entertaining the American Women's Club for their monthly meeting. As would be expected, the majority of the members were the wives of military personnel stationed in the area. I had met many of them at the *Feria* ground in the *casetas* and I was warmly received. It happened that a number of the husbands involved had received transfer orders, which were to be effective before the following meeting. Thus, this was the last meeting for quite a few of the long-time members. Taking this cue I ended my set with "Vaya con Dios" which I did in English and Spanish. There was hardly a dry eye in the house by the finish. I'm sure I could have spent quite a few months in this area living on these types of gigs and the generous invitations of the many military personnel I came across. I was truly lucky and blessed throughout my journey.

On May 15th I noted that I had been on the road for one year. I was still not sure how long the entire journey would be. The next day I had my last lunch at the pension garden for which "Mama" refused to take any payment. She saw me off on my journey with tears in her eyes still hoping that I would settle down locally. I headed for Portugal passing through Huelva and crossed the river/border in a small ferry to enter this other occupant of the Iberian Peninsula. On the small boat I met Anselmo Damaio who was returning to Portugal with his wife and family from a vacation in Spain. They lived in Almada facing across the river from Lisbon. They were very kind and hospitable to me and invited me to visit them when I got into the Lisbon area. Anselmo spoke Spanish and that made things easier for me.

Adopted by Anselmo's family

I made some quick observations of the Portuguese people as I traveled the southern part of their country. For one I found the young men more respectful of the young girls than I had found in Spain. There young men would call out all sorts of derogatory or suggestive remarks to passing Spanish girls with no thought of it. Also I found that Portugal was not cheaper than Spain as I had been told. I noticed that more Portuguese spoke French than Spanish. There was also a smaller percentage of Catholics as compared to Spain where the whole country had been made Catholic during the reign of Jaime I of France after he drove out the Moors. I was amazed at the huge loads Portuguese women could carry on their heads. On one day I saw a young lady ahead on the road carrying something on her head. When I got close enough I realized she was quite small and young and was carrying a cast iron pump of significant weight.

As I passed through Faro and headed for Portimao I noticed that the countryside was quite dry and dusty. There didn't seem to be much vegetation in the southern part of Portugal. In Portimao I looked up Tony and Grace Grady whom I had met at the *caseta* during the *Feria* in Seville. He was an artist and writer and they had re-located from England. In fact I found many Englishmen living in southern Portugal especially those who had retired. Tony was a huge fellow who reminded me of Sebastian Cabot with a full flowing beard. He and Grace showed me many beautiful and interesting sites in the area including the "Three Brothers" beach, which was so isolated and slightly used. Another popular beach we visited was *"Praia de Rocha"* which has since become totally over-run with developments. Tony had become a regular man-about-town and a stroll with him always involved meeting friends and stopping at the *bodega* for a glass of wine (often local *vino verde*). I noted that while visiting in his household for a few days I had to register with the police as I had been required to do in Sweden.

One family that Tony introduced me to was the Barley's who owned *"Os Arcos"* pub in Lagos. They were also from England and ran a very popular business. During my stay with Tony and Grace the Barley's asked me to play for Mr. Barley's birthday party that was held at their pub. I did so and was paid 300 escudos for my efforts. This equated to about $9.00, a great pay for a couple of hours work. They asked me to stay on and perform during the summer season with steady work. However, I had to move ahead with my journey and thanked them for their generous offer.

One day Tony and Grace took me to Monchique mountains where we could see the great western coastline of the country. With so much coastline, I could understand why so many of the Portuguese immigrants to the USA had been fishermen at home. The altitude was about 3000 feet and the wind was truly incredible. In fact it was these same winds, which knocked over my scooter while it was parked in town and broke the windshield. As we stopped for lunch, along with the usual abundant wine, we tried *"presunto"*, naturally cured ham. It is an always-popular treat in Portugal. The average *bodega* had huge wooden casks of wine that were cooled by draping large sheets of wet burlap over them. The vaporization of the water from the burlap would cool the wine.

I found that the products of Portugal were almonds, olives, rice, wood, cork, fish and wine (Port, Madera and Mateus). Much of the wine came from the north where, I presume, the climate and soil are much more suitable for growing grapes. Of course, fresh fish could be found anywhere along the extensive coastline.

When I finally left the Grady's I headed north along the coast to some beautiful and unique areas. I passed through Aljizur, Odemira, Soa Torpes, Sines, Sesimbra and continued to Almada where I stopped to visit Anselmo and his family. They were Mrs. Damaio, Isabel, Anselmo Jr. and Anna Maria (the maid). They were happy to see me and were very generous in their hospitality. It was May 26th. They introduced me to *bacalhau* which is a dried cooked fish like cod but with the color of salmon. They loved music and we had many sessions with the guitar many of which they insisted on recording. They took me to many places including their summerhouse near Caparica Beach. During the days I explored some of the Lisbon area on my own. This included the beaches at Estoril, Sintra (the National Palace of Pena) and the Torre de Belem (beautiful little castle on the banks of the Tagos River). I visited the statue of Christo Rei in Almada where I could clearly see the shore of Lisbon across the river and look down on the Salazar Bridge, which was under construction. For now we had to board the frequent ferries that plied between the two shores. The return trip price for my scooter was 6 escudos (.18 US). I was amazed at the huge bags of produce carried on the heads of women as we rode the ferry to Lisbon.

On June 4th I said my final farewell to the family and went down to the ferry dock to make my last crossing to Lisbon. I was sent off with big *"embrasos"* from Anselmo and the local mayor. As I traveled across the river I met two American couples who had just 3 weeks to see a good part of Europe. They were envious of my freedom and journey. One of the men asked to take my picture and get my address so he could send the picture to my mother when he got back to the states and let her know that I was doing fine. This was very touching to me as it was the first time I was aware of anyone being personally concerned about my mother worrying about me.

Little-used beach at St. Torpes

As I headed for Fatima I noticed the more solid vegetation in the area. The countryside is hardly developed and is probably about the same as it was in 1917 when *"Nosso Senorha"* (Our Lady) appeared to three peasant children in Fatima. The basilica is quite large and is the destination of many Catholic pilgrims who come to be present in this holy ground. Our Lady appeared several times to the two girls and one boy over a period. There is a special presence here.

After my usual photos I continued on to Coimbra, which is reportedly the most romantic town in Portugal. It is a university town with many college students. As is said in the song "Coimbra", *"Coimbra do Chopal ainda es capital do amor in Portugal ainda"*. (Coimbra of the Chopal is still the capital of love in Portugal, yet). The Chopal is a tree-lined walkway along the river where many lovers stroll. As well there is a park called *"Dos Pequenitos"* where there is an arboreal display as well as a mini-city with beautiful buildings of children proportion through which all are invited to stroll. I took photos of some Portuguese Girl Scouts and Boy Scouts on a field trip there.

Coimbra's "Dos pequenitos' park

The road now took me to Guarda and Vila Formosa, which was at the Spanish border. I had decided not to take the long detour to see the northern part of Portugal. I opted to make better time on my trip back to the major part of France. I stayed in a pension in Vila Formosa and the next day crossed

Just a post office in Madrid

back into Spain with no incidents. I drove through Salamanca, Avila and into Madrid. With stops along the way it took me into the evening to cover the 328 kilometers (about 220 miles). Because there was a festival in town it was very difficult to find a room. Finally I was clued in to an alternative method. I drove along the well-populated areas of Madrid until I found a night watchman. I had been told they knew which private citizens would rent out a room in their apartments for a night or more. He hooked me up with a couple whose room I rented for 70 pesetas (considered expensive at $1.15). The next day I was able to check into the YHA at *Casa de Campo* where on two occasions I was embarrassed by "ugly Americans" who wanted to skip paying part of their bill. It really grated me because they had more money as travelers than most of the others staying there. I ended up getting somewhat involved because I had to translate for them. I shamed them into paying what they owed and did some damage control with the warden. Luckily they had met all kinds of people from all countries and were quite understanding.

During the six days I spent in Madrid I was able to visit some extremely interesting sites around this charming capital city. I attended my first bullfight here and found much of it uninteresting. I did appreciate the matador who fought the bull from the backs of several superb horses. He controlled his mounts mostly with his knees. I did notice that General Franco was present with a bodyguard the equivalent of a small army.

As mentioned before I made frequent use of local post offices wherever I went. In the case of Madrid the main post office was in the *Plaza de Cibeles* and it looked like a beautiful castle-like building. Here I would check with *postal restante,* the Spanish version of general delivery. I recorded this unique edifice with my camera as I proceeded to the university for dinner. I had found that good food and reasonable prices was often found at college campuses or truck stops. On this occasion I had the rare pleasure of trying octopus cooked in its own juice (ink black). It was served over rice and I rated it as quite tasty.

Although I admit to being quite deficient in my liberal education I had to make a visit to the Prado Museum to view the many world-known treasures. I often thought how much more this opportunity could be enjoyed by someone who was schooled in art. However, I had to go according to the adage that "beauty is in the eye of the beholder".

On a clear day I headed out of Madrid and drove north toward the French border. I stopped for the night in a pension in San Mateo where I ended up having another music session with the guitar. As well, I watched a Portuguese bullfight on TV and was astounded at the courage of those who would line up to take the full charge of this huge beast. The horns of the bull were padded and the object of the action was to try to immobilize the bull. *El toro* was not killed in this type of fight. The next day would take me into France by a route I had not planned on. I had thought of visiting Andorra, a small country in the Pyrenees, but it was too far out of my intended path. As I cut through these stately mountains I ran out of gas and had to search to find some I could buy. The gas was useless without the oil I needed for the 2-stroke mixture and I was relieved to find that I still had retained the remains of a quart of oil I had bought in Norway the previous year. (Note: I've always been known to "hold onto things"—thank God.)

# CHAPTER TEN

## "S'il vous plait"

When I entered France, as I had done many times, I changed my Spanish pesetas for French francs at the rate of 5 francs for the equivalent of 1 US dollar. I was to get used to France in a more thorough way this time given that I had much more pleasant weather than my last encounter through the French Alps in a snowstorm. I found the roads better but things were more expensive than in Spain.

Now in southern France I drove to the area of Lourdes where I hoped to visit the basilica and grotto. I searched my Youth Hostel directory and found one in the surrounding countryside. It was a farm setting and the female warden was a roly-poly middle-aged lady with a jolly disposition. I greeted her in French and asked if she had space for me that night. She said there was plenty of space and proceeded to have me make out the registration form. This process usually requires some means of identification beyond having the YHA member card. I took out my passport to show her and she queried, "*Vous etes American?*" (You are American?). When I answered in the affirmative she gave me one of the biggest language compliments I received in my journey. She said. "*Vous ne parlez pas en francais comme les American, mais comme nous*".(You do not speak French like the Americans, but like us). Although I suspected she was being very kind my confidence in French got a huge boost from this delightful lady. The following day I traveled the road to Lourdes where I found many things commercialized and I had to do some deep reflections in order to comprehend the significance of this holy site, which had been the scene of so many miracles. I found Bernadette's home and could hardly see it for all the souvenir shops that surrounded it. I continued along the winding roads north and noted that the restaurants at which I stopped for a sandwich seemed to serve only complete meals. This was not in keeping with my food budget so I would buy items in a local grocery store and make my own picnic along the way.

On my road to Paris I intended to stop in Sens to visit Viviane Hauquelin, a beautiful young French girl I had first met in the Youth Hostel in Aberdeen, Scotland. She spoke English quite well and was a charming example of young womanhood. When I arrived at her home she was very happy to see me and her family were extremely welcoming. I was invited to stay overnight and I became a temporary part of the family. Viviane had a younger sister, Francine, and an older married brother. I enjoyed very much chatting with her father who was a mechanic and had a garage/gas station on his property. At dinner that evening he gave me a lesson in appreciation of food and family. He said, "For the Americans a meal is a habit. For the French, it is a celebration". I could detect what he meant as each person at the table seemed to relish each course and the togetherness even with this foreigner in their midst.

The next day I recorded some of Viviane's favorite American songs for her, "Lemon Tree" and "Everybody Loves Somebody Sometime" (thank God for my ever-present guitar). She went on to her grandmother's house between Sens and Paris and I stopped there to say good-by once again. We were both quite sad that we were going to leave each other with little prospects of getting together in the future. We promised to write and I headed for Paris by way of Versailles where I witnessed the grandeur of the palace. As I had in Sens I took a number of photos to visually record the surroundings of my journey.

From a great distance on the highway I could see the Eiffel Tower as I approached the city of Paris. The famous sights were as spectacular as imagined. I was brought down to earth by the sputtering of my scooter, which was a little sick. So, I looked forward to another of the many repair sessions, which would keep my steed in running condition. However, after much checking I was able to relax as I found a room for 12 francs ($2.40) per night including breakfast at #53 Blvd. St. Germain on the Left Bank. The atmosphere was much like a Youth Hostel with the privacy of individual rooms. The staff were very kind and friendly to all who stopped there. I say this in contrast to the many impressions that foreigners have that Paris is full of unfriendly, stuck-up people. On one occasion I met a girl from Iowa whom I helped with translation, as she knew no French. She was very thankful and indicated that I was the first person who had been kind to her in her five days in Paris.

I had had my own experience with boilerplate Parisians when I first tried to look up the half-sister of my Portuguese friend, Anselmo, and her stepmother. He had given me the address at which they worked for a rich family. When I went to the house I rang the bell at the front door to be greeted by an older woman who had very little patience with my level of French. After I made it clear to her that I wished to speak to Odete she motioned that I would have to ring at the door on the lower level. I thanked her and went to the other indicated door and rang that bell. I was taken aback when the same woman appeared at this door and told me that she would see if Odete could greet me at this time. It finally struck me that Odete, being a servant, was not allowed to greet people of her social level at the normal entrance to the house. Although this irritated me quite a bit, I could understand that a similar scene might play out in the "ritzy" section of any large city in the world. So, I continued my visit to Paris and France with the intention of trying to meet those who are more typical of the country and my commoner background. I was sure that my overall impression would be more justified, as I would later look back on those who had accepted me as a sincere friend from afar.

Of course I was an avid sight-seer as well as a traveler and I spent a lot of time touring the famous locations in Paris and recording them with my ever-present Zeiss Icon. Some of the most visually stunning photos were taken at night including one with a tripod in the middle of the Champs Elysee. After having visited the Eiffel Tower, Sacre Coeur, Montmart, Arc de Triomphe and many other areas, I went to #140 Rue de Bac to visit a location which had been introduced to me by my home town pastor, Father Leahy. This was the chapel in which the Blessed Mother had appeared to St. Catherine Laboure in 1830. The Virgin Mary initiated the Miraculous Medal there in November of 1830. The unpreserved body of the nun is there to be viewed intact.

As I would usually do, I considered how I might make some travel funds while visiting this fascinating world capital. I had been given the address of a small intimate club, which might be able to use me but, it did not work out. So, I decided that I should be a street-side troubadour as is common in many cities of Europe. I took my guitar and headed for the left bank (*la rive gauche*) where most foreigners consider being there a must so they can say they've seen the "real Paris". I was soon joined by a couple of young fans who wanted me to entertain on any street corner. They would attract passers-by and encourage them to drop a few coins in the guitar case. I noted that there were many other musicians in the area with similar intentions often in "hootenanny groups". After a while I started to learn the ropes of this troubadouring and I would go to side-walk cafe tables where "Ralph and Hilda" from Des Moines were taking in the true Paris atmosphere. In order to add to the authenticity of their experience I would approach them with my best French-accented English and always speak directly to the female partner. This often resulted in a flush of excitement as Hilda informed Ralph that they were going to be serenaded by a real roving troubadour. Poor Ralph didn't have a chance of refusing. One very popular song I had learned in French was "I Left my Heart In San Francisco" and it was my #1 weapon in my tour of tables.

In two hours of entertaining I was able to earn 45 francs ($9) and was very satisfied with the results. Being an optimist I went out to do the same the following night and ended up getting arrested. I couldn't believe that a plain-clothes detective had nothing better to do than to check whether, or not, I had a permit for entertaining. He apparently was not bothered by the several groups who were doing the same along the boulevard in very loud tones. I had to escort the officer to the local police station and he really got suspicious when he learned that I didn't have my passport on me. I had purposely left it at the hotel in case I should misplace it while running around with my guitar. I was asked by the detective how much I had received from the last couple I entertained. When I told him it was 7 francs he said I must be good. Getting a little bolder, I responded that I was very good. I was required to pass over the 7 francs for his evidence. I was made to wait on a bench in the squad room while they supposedly checked my hotel for the confirmation of the information I had given them. Unfortunately I could only remember the name I had for the place and it was a former name which they didn't understand. As time went by it appeared that they were doing nothing about my case. I went over to the desk officer and asked in clear French if there was an officer there who spoke English and could explain what was being done regarding my predicament. This officer used my request as a source of amusement to the other officers who bantered back and forth having a great laugh and I was told to just sit and wait. I guess I should have felt well-treated when I saw some young Algerians who were found not to have any identifying papers on them resulting in them being tossed directly into the cell. At that time the French were having many problems with their Algerian colony.

After 3 hours I was called to the service window, received the 7 francs back and was admonished not to commit this heinous crime again. This episode convinced me that I had done enough troubadouring in Paris and I decided to take a tour of the city the following night on the scooter. As luck would have it I met Marge, an American teacher of Spanish, who was going to spend a year in Spain. I invited her along and we toured the old section of Paris including a visit to the site of the Bastille.

The following day, as I prepared to leave, I met Priscilla from New York who was checking out because she just didn't know which way to turn. She was totally lost which was unfortunate given that she was driving a car. She had no clue as to where to go, how to get there and found the people very unfriendly. We had breakfast together and I convinced her that she was in a good location and that there were many English-speaking people around this hotel and she should give it another chance. After our chat and a word from me to the hostess she decided to stay another week. I never heard from her again but I hope she was able to fulfill a few of the dreams she had when she approached Paris on her own with no plan.

# CHAPTER ELEVEN

## Benelux

I finally headed for Luxembourg through beautiful rolling hills dotted by cemeteries of American, Italian and other soldiers who had lost their lives in WW II. The local people I met were quite down-to-earth and I was soon at the border. Here I had to buy vehicle insurance, which was good both there and in Belgium. The money was in francs and was printed under both names. It was equal and valid in both. I checked into the Luxembourg Youth Hostel and could not find my friend, Antal, from Sweden. We had made a plan to meet here but a note from him indicated that he was at the hostel at Borglinster (18 kilometers away). Thanks to a phone call he came to this hostel the next day and we had an enthusiastic reunion. We immediately went into town where Antal had met some girls who worked in a restaurant the day before. With my pal's passionate urging we ended up having quite a jam session with my guitar at the restaurant. The language spoken seemed to be a mixture of German and French which was fine with Antal who speaks Hungarian, Swedish, German and English.

The following day we decided to take a day trip around the country and were rewarded with beautiful scenery and great weather. By this time we had developed a noon tradition of buying some local bread, sausage, fruit, wine, etc. and making a picnic in some beautiful surroundings on my ever-useful poncho. On occasion, depending on how much sleep we had gotten the night before, we might also take a nap after lunch. During this day we stopped at a hotel to get some ice cream and encountered the reception of a French-Luxo-Italian wedding. After meeting many of those involved we were invited to come back in the evening for the "party". We returned later for dinner, singing with the guitar and dancing. We ended up staying up the whole night. The next day's picnic was followed by a 4-5 hour "nap".

Antal was also a Roman Catholic and we attended church the next day before heading for Belgium. In a precursor to what would in time result from the European Union there was no border guard between Luxembourg and Belgium. The language was Flemish or French and, for once, I was able to help Antal in the language department. We stopped at a beautiful hostel at Namur and took in the sites of the city lights at night. The following day we visited the site of the 1958 World's Fair at Brussels. We had a photo taken in front of the Atomium (symbol of the fair). When we later checked into the hostel at Ostende we found a great number of Americans due to this being a major port for the many ships which brought low budget travelers to Europe.

About this time I realized that the scooter was losing power as it had at times in the past and I took the day to take it to a local beach and remove the exhaust system with Antal's help. We cleaned it completely and the power returned to the point that it ran the best it had since I bought it. This was good in another way as Antal was driving a Zundap with a much bigger engine than mine and I could now keep up to him much easier. We noticed the wind being ever-present due to the flatness of the terrain. Of course it was A-OK when it was behind you.

Crossing into Holland I found it as I had always pictured it from books. It was neat and flat with many windmills and canals. I could easily picture Hans Brinker and the silver skates gliding along these very canals. Some local people still customarily wore wooden shoes. The language was Dutch but German was also spoken and understood. Money was in guildings one of which was equal to 27 cents US. We went on to Amsterdam and I took a small ferry to the Youth Hostel at Schoorl where I was re-met by Antal later. This location was near an old German radar site, which we checked out before continuing on. I took some photos in Grypskerk including Antal and a neat windmill.

Our last challenge in the cold and windy weather was to cross the Afsluitdijk which is 30 kilometers long (about 20 miles) and holds the North Sea from inundating a large part of the land of Holland. It creates the Zyder Zee. When we stopped in a rest area near the middle we ascended the lookout tower from which you can view the dike with the sea noticeably higher on the outside than inside. It is still obvious in the photo I took of Antal there.

Antal and the Afsluitdijk

# CHAPTER TWELVE

## Checkpoint Charlie

We crossed back into Germany and spent a couple of days with Antal's friend, Klaus Winter, and his family. They were extremely hospitable and insisted that we stay with them. During this visit Antal and I went to Bremen where we toured the Nordmende electronics plant and saw how the TV's and other items were manufactured. In Antal's job he works exclusively with Nordmende products. We later moved on to Hamburg where I called Barbara Volkenhauer whom I met when I passed there before with Peter. We checked into the Youth Hostel and went out for the night being the last we would be together. For a kick we decided to check out the St. Pauli area and Hebert Strasse., the infamous "red-light" district. Of course we were accosted by "pitch-men" in front of every club we passed. They would approach us in many common languages and we decided to play a game with them. We would answer them in the most remote languages we could remember including Hungarian, Swedish and Portuguese. This resulted in more than a little frustration on their part.

The following day I said a heartfelt farewell to Antal who had to head back to Denmark on his way home to Sweden. We had really hit it off as travel partners and it was a bit strange to be alone again although there are obvious benefits of this status. I went to visit Barbara Vokenhaur whose sister was engaged to be married the following day. The whole family seemed surprised that I had learned a fair amount of German since the last visit. By coincidence I was treated to a truly German event. That evening was the *Polter Abend* for Barbara's sister. It is a party on the night before the wedding where the couple is visited by their friends and family. The guests announce their arrival by breaking dishes and pottery outside the door, which has been placed there for that purpose. Then the bride and groom-to-be must clean up the mess and invite the guests in for food and beverages. On this night the bride's sister presents here with the bridal veil. As might be expected the mood was high and the entire night was filled with fun and good will. I was able to contribute to the festivities by having a session with the guitar and it always made me feel that I wasn't a drag on any gathering.

The alternate Youth Hostel that we had checked into was a sports stadium at which I had to make a "booking" to get a warm shower. I had to leave my sleeping area and take all my required items to another part of the stadium after having paid the required fee. I thought this to be a bit complicated to get a shower until much later when I was to find out how the rest of the world lived. I took this occasion to find a laundry-mat and give my few belongings a good wash.

I was pleasantly surprised when I inquired at the US Consul and found out that I could drive my scooter through East Germany to Berlin and even visit East Berlin. At Helmstedt I approached the border to E. Germany on the autobahn and had to pay a 4 DM toll fee ($1 US) and 3 DM for insurance. As I continued through the countryside of Communist Germany I noted that the highway itself was in bad condition. There were a great number of farms at which I saw many middle-aged and older females doing manual labor. There were few cars and fewer signs along the highway.

West Berlin was like an island of democracy in the middle of E. Germany. I passed into it with no problem and went to the Tegel Youth Hostel. I was surprised when I had to stop on the road when the barrier went across in order to let an airplane land at Tempelhof Airport. The runway cut right across several roads given the lack of open space in W. Berlin.

The following day I approached the Brandenburg Gate and Check-point Charlie and took several photos of each. The process of crossing into E. Berlin was not very burdensome but it included having to change 5 DM from the West to E. German marks. We were not allowed to take any photos in the area of the checkpoint but after that there were no apparent restrictions. I recognized that the majority of the old city center was located in E. Berlin. Buildings were drab, cars scarce and streetcars far outdated. On one beautiful old building (which was not being well maintained) I saw a sign which read the equivalent of, "Thank the Soviet Union for Twenty Years of Brotherly Help". I visited a Russian War Memorial where interred were 5-7 thousand Russian soldiers who had died in WW II. At the end of a long walkway was a shrine building in which the names of those buried here were listed. I was told that many Russian families came to pay respects to their fallen family members when it was allowed and financially possible. I reflected that this would be a natural tendency in any society. Upon returning to the check-point I had another humanistic experience while an East German border guard was checking my papers when a gust of wind blew a couple of them away. Straddling my scooter I could not jump off and chase them. However, the guard realized this and chased them himself. He had been surprised that I spoke enough German to have a conversation. The image of E. German soldiers as being communist robots to fear was easily being contradicted by some person-to-person experiences. Generally a traveler in this area would "walk on thin ice" in dealing with the communist authorities keeping in mind that they could mess up your travel plans in huge ways if they took a disliking to you.

Another example took place at the border to re-enter East Germany. I had completed the required paperwork in the office and received the appropriate stamps. Then each party had to get in line with their vehicles for the final check by a guard before crossing the borderline. When I arrived at the young guard I spoke to him in German and he wanted to know where I came from and where I was going. When I replied that I was coming from near Boston and was heading around the world he was in disbelief that my government would give me permission to do so. As he inquired more about my experiences thus far I noticed the line behind me getting longer by the minute. However, I also noticed that not one of the drivers was indicating any impatience with the process. In the USA that guard would have been inundated with honking and complaints. Maybe there was something to be said for other types of government. It worked for me in this situation.

I had decided to head south and re-entered West Germany at Hof. During that drive I stopped to have a picnic with items I had picked up at a store in W. Berlin. Coincidently a group of two boys and three girls from E. Germany had stopped nearby for lunch as well. My approach to them resulted in an invitation to join them for our picnic. The youngest of the girls was about 12 years old and had seen very little of her family. When she was very young she had been sent to a commune to be raised according to the State. I took photos of them and shared my cookies and apflesaft, which they thought were of good quality. They were reluctant to speak much about their daily lives. However, they did make it clear that the E. Germans did not believe all the propaganda about the "Paradise" in the east (Russia).

East German realistic youngsters

I continued to Lauf near Nurnberg and headed for the local Youth Hostel. It was totally full and so I ended up sharing a tent with three Australians. Of course this was the summer vacation season and I eventually got to the point of thinking as a mother of students, "Vacation, please end soon so I can get my life back to normal". I had driven 425 miles on this day, the longest of my travels so far. The following day I visited Nurnberg which is a true Bavarian city. As expected the marketplace was the center of early morning activity and was a charming setting for the sales of almost everything. The *Glockenspiel* was very beautiful but a little smaller than the one on the front of the *Ratthause* in Munich. After a few photos I headed south to Munich and out to Ebersberg for a cheerful reunion with the Ehrl family. I found a set of my slides waiting for me and I was able to show them a piece of my journey since I left them. It was July and the surroundings were just gorgeous.

During the following week Gusti headed for France for a working holiday and Zita left to work as a live-in housekeeper/baby sitter for an American family living south of here. The reduction of the family size for this period was balanced by the news that Frau Ehrl was expecting the 9th Ehrl soon. Of course, my sweet little nurse, Hiddi, was there to help me with my German and practice her English with me. I celebrated my 29th birthday with the Ehrl's and Hiddi made a great cake for the event. It was coincidental that I had observed my 28th birthday with Marie Needham in Ireland through whom I had been introduced to the Ehrl family

Thanks to the fine weather the family and I shared some memorable outdoor activities like the day we rode the scooter and bicycles to the forest to pick berries. We brought along a lunch and enjoyed the day in each other's company. We also took advantage of the near-by lake to have a refreshing swim. When I finally packed to leave on July 28th I was confronted by the tears of my nurse, Hiddi. She was a real sweetheart and as my scooter took me out of Ebersberg I found I could not hold back my tears either. Again I had been the recipient of great fortune and had the privilege of becoming a member of a local family where I was destined to get a valid look into the culture of this scenic land and its people.

I headed for Rottach-Egern where I fulfilled my promise to say hello to Zita. It was obvious that the woman of this American household was not too thrilled to have me stop by. From what I could determine her employers were typical "ugly Americans" relying on the power of the almighty dollar and looking down on those who didn't have enough. Despite living there for some period they did not speak German. I spent a little time with smiling Zita and reminded her in German that all American were not alike. Due to her maturity she had already understood this.

That day I had taken my noon lunch near the Tegern See. I had been given some ham chops from the Aunt's shop, which was new to me. They were in the form of pork chops but the meat looked and tasted like ham. They certainly were delicious as I consumed them with locally purchased bread and milk in full view of the distant Alps.

At one point in the drive I realized that I should be taking a right turn when I had almost passed the street. Trying to accommodate the turn I ended up hitting the curb and bending the fork of the scooter to a noticeable degree. I did some instant repairs but it was not to be totally repaired until many thousands of miles later.

I continued on to Berchtesgarden, a very popular vacation spot for locals as well as foreigners. It has a spectacular view of the Konig See, which had been visible to Adolf Hitler whose "Eagle's Nest" was just above in the hills. The house, which had been there had been long before torn down but I toured the underground bunker which was his safe haven. Of course, all furnishings had been removed and I found it quite damp and smelly. It was like paying an admission fee for the privilege of getting a head cold.

Next I drove to Salzburg where I joined other visitors in a tour of the Salzburgwerk, a salt mine which has been in continuous operation since 1570. There were still 100 men working on lower levels. The visitor must put on the uniform of the worker which consists of baggy pantaloons and jacket with a cap and a leather pad cinched around the waist and trailing down behind. Once suited up, we mounted a small narrow railway car with a straddle bench in the middle and ducked our heads as we made the two mile trip into the middle of the mountain. As we started our walking tour it was fascinating to see all of the walls, floors and ceilings to be of solid salt. We became aware of the need for the back-side pads when we had to go to a lower level. The guide would line us up behind each other like a bobsled team at the top of a long, twisting wooden slide. The highly polished wooden surface quickly took us to the next level below once the guide had given us a push start. At one point we had to board a small boat which took us across an underground lake. The elevator finally took us back to the surface to catch our small train, which took us back to the exit. It had been truly an intriguing trip.

# CHAPTER THIRTEEN

## Led by the Danube

From here I generally followed the Danube over the next two days stopping in Youth Hostels as I made my way slowly towards Vienna. On the outskirts of this elegant city I stopped in a local park to have my usual picnic lunch. I found a bench to be more applicable for this as it had been raining before and the ground was still wet. Not long after I set up my lunch and drink, a young man approached with a rather large, mean-looking boxer dog. Shortly the dog showed a greater interest in my lunch than he did in exercising in the park. His owner came over and restrained him and we ended up in conversation. He was Bruno Schneiderbauer and his dog was Terro. His English was quite good and he asked many questions about my trip to date and my future intentions. We seemed to hit it off quite well and he invited me to visit with him in his Vienna apartment where he was temporarily alone because his parents were on vacation. He gave me his address and I later looked him up. I was wondering at the wisdom of doing so when my knock was greeted by the low growl of Terro on the other side of the door. However, we became quick friends and my heart rate went back to normal.

Bruno worked at a local Youth Hostel and was studying economics at the university. We enjoyed each other's company so much that I ended up staying a whole week there. Bruno liked music and was learning the guitar so we had many sessions both at home and various bars/restaurants where we would meet his friends. Bruno had loaned me a set of keys to the apartment. I started to feel like one of the neighbors after a while. When Bruno went to work each day I would take Terro for a walk to the park where he could run around and exercise. According to local regulations, I had to put a muzzle and leash on him anywhere outside of the park. It was a bit strange for me as

I had to call him and give commands in German. On a couple of occasions I had prepared dinner for Bruno when he got home from work. Of course, we had Rooney-style spaghetti and, later in the week, Spanish *tortillas*. He just loved this new adventure in eating. One of my favorite snacks was hot *leberkäse* which was bought at a small kiosk along the main street. It was a delicious kind of meatloaf which was carved off a whole loaf depending how much you wished to pay for. It was sandwiched between slices of your favorite bread (pumpernickel for me) and flavored with your choice of mustards. I could easily make a meal of this with a drink.

Bruno & Terro—Vienna

As I toured this beautiful capital I visited The Prater, a huge park with a gigantic ferris wheel. It was not unusual to find some very accomplished amateur musicians entertaining others in the park with beautiful classical music. It was an appropriate setting given that the Vienna Opera House was not far away. Another notable visit was to Schloss Schonbrunn which has been used as the setting for many movie scenes. I shot several photos of this well-known castle with its extensive gardens. I would see many views of this location in my future.

Finally, with Terro looking particularly sad I wrote out some of Bruno's favorite songs and bade farewell to another personal cultural adventure. Our friendship was to last many years into the future. Following Bruno's directions I headed into the Austrian Alps to Zell um Zee with incredible scenery all around me. I found many perfect spots for my picnic and I would get a kick out of going to the local dairy store where you could buy fresh milk in any quantity poured into any container you brought with you. It was so fresh and tasty as well as cheap! To me the surroundings were somewhat like Yosemite National Park I had visited during my training for the Air Force in several locations.

At Innsbruck I visited the site of the Winter Olympics and checked at American Express for mail. I was pleased to see that I had nine letters, four of which were from sweet Hiddi. I guess it was not coincidental that she had been my nurse as she later went on to become a doctor. I continued on to Liechtenstein, which is within Switzerland. This principality is only 15 x 7 miles in area. From a vantage point near the Prince's castle at Vaduz I took a photo in which you can see the entire country.

I headed for Zug, Switzerland and again visited with the Brandenburgs for whom I made some tapes with the guitar. I took some photos and continued to Lucern where I received some more mail. The next day was one of challenge as I prepared to drive over the Gotthard Pass in the Alps. Although the scenery was gorgeous I couldn't appreciate much of it given the narrow roads and dense traffic. I would have to stop at the roadside to enjoy the surroundings. I decided not to use the rail tunnel which was expensive and for which there was a wait. So I urged my noble "steed" over the 6,916 feet of the pass taking a few photos along the way.

Although I was still in Switzerland, Italian was spoken in this area. So I bought Italian language book from the same author (Hugo) who had written the one I used for Spanish. Then, as I lounged on the poncho after my noon picnic, I would study Italian noting the similarities to Spanish. I was to realize that there are four languages spoken in Switzerland. It is no wonder that so many people in this part of the world are multi-lingual. Travel to other countries for Europeans might mean just a week-end trip.

The whole of Liechtenstein

# CHAPTER FOURTEEN

## "Ciao, Gerry"

Entering Italy was a bit frustrating given that I was forced to buy gas coupons without much explanation. It turned out later that they were to my advantage because by using them I could buy gas at a lower price. I was "given" a brochure only to find out later that I had paid 400 lira for it (exchange rate was 600 lira to 1 US dollar). It gave me an intial bad impression of Italy, but later I would find many wonderful new friends there who would restore my faith in my fellow man.

I noted that the traffic police were dressed in total white (I referred to them as "Mr. Clean") as I made my way to Bergamo where Pope John XXIII had studied in the seminary. I went to confession here in a combination of several languages but it seemed to work OK with the priest. I continued to Sotto il Monte where this "poor man's pope" had been born in November of 1881. He had been christened Angelo Guiseppe Roncalli and I toured his home where he shared one room with 14 other members of his family. Indeed, he knew the life of the common person as indicated by his enormous popularity wherever he went.

I returned to the area of Lake Como and spent lunch time at Lake Lecco where I was able to take a refreshing swim. I noted that there were many Germans on vacation in this area. It was Ferragosta (August vacation time) and many Italians were also enjoying the sun and beaches. For this festival the entire city would go on vacation at the same time with businesses closing, etc.

When I arrived at Milano I was truly impressed by the cathedral (*Il Duomo*), the largest in Italy. I stopped to change a $20 travelers check and received around 13,000 lira at the going rate. This amount would take me through many days and miles at my low-budget rate of spending. Later I visited a castle and took a stroll in the gardens beside it. The weather was great and many people were enjoying the outdoors. As I walked along I met a man who was doing the same and he struck up a conversation. He didn't speak English and I had not learned enough Italian so we ended up speaking German. He said he was a truck driver who made many deliveries to Germany and had learned the language along the way. He had some free time because he was waiting for his truck to be loaded at a nearby firm.

In one area we noticed a crowd of people around one man seated at a small folding table and they were playing some kind of game. My new acquaintance explained that it was a kind of card game where the player would bet an amount of money (minimum was 10,000 lira) and the dealer would shuffle three face-down cards in plain view. The player had to guess where the subject card would show up. To me it seemed too simple to be true. So, with the encouragement of my German-speaking friend I put down a 10,000-lira note and was stunned when the subject card showed up at the wrong place. I was in shock! How could the card come up in the wrong place when I watched it so closely? My friend tried to give me words of consolation but I couldn't even grasp that I had lost the largest part of all the money I had changed that day. In my haste to get even I wanted to play for the 2000 lira I still had but they would not take any bets less than 10,000 lira. Soon thereafter, the table was folded and the dealer was gone. When I finally realized what had happened I was livid with myself for falling into such a scheme. Only after I had walked much further alone did it hit me that my "friend" was a recruiter for the dealer. As a result I went into a depression that lasted several days. I noted the whole event in my diary as "My first real lesson in Italian". Of course there are opportunists in every country but the Italians had a knack for it.

On my way to Venice I took a cooling-off swim in Lake Garda and arrived in the water city to find that I could not drive to the Youth Hostel. I had too much baggage to walk there and I did not dare to leave my scooter overnight in an unattended area. After leaving it with an attendant at a parking lot (for a fee) I walked around this unique city of romance, art and history. I learned that everything is done on the water. There were water taxis, busses and even the Coca-Cola barge to make deliveries to the merchants. Piazza San Marco was a busy place with beautiful architectural surroundings. I re-met some young people from the USA whom I had met at other hostels and we visited Venice together ending with a huge songfest at an outdoors cafe. I later returned to my scooter and camped out at a camping site.

The following day I headed for Bologna and stopped along the road to help a man whose car was broken down. It turned out that Raoul Patergnani was a business man who ran a manufacturing firm in Adria and he had already called for one of his employees to bring another vehicle and take the inoperative one back, He knew very little English so we spoke French and seemed to understand each other quite well. He was surprised that I had stopped and invited me to lunch as we waited for the other car. He was amazed at my journey and invited me to visit him in Adria where he made farm machinery.

I continued to Sottomarina where a huge crowd of Italian vacationers was taking advantage of the last day of their holiday. The most logical place to sleep was camping out near the shore, which I did but didn't get much sleep due to the late night revelers. In the morning I prepared to leave but met an out-going fellow named Mario who was there with his extended family. At his invitation I joined them for lunch, a swim and a boisterous sing-along with the guitar. Even though I was in the early stages of learning Italian I found, as usual, that music is the most universal language and it allowed me to get close to many common people who gave me the true lessons of my sojourn.

Singing with Ferragosta revelers

Later that day as I entered Adria I located Raoul and was welcomed at his house which was almost empty given that his wife and children were at their summer camp for some days. In the evening he invited his cousin, Giorgio, his wife, Linda, and some other friends for dinner and a songfest. Raoul insisted on tape recording almost everything I sang. He would play it for the rest of the family when they returned. The following day I had the privilege of washing my clothes and repairing the scooter with his whole mechanics shop at my disposal. That night we had dinner at Linda's house and another song session. Italians sure do love music. I found the Italian dialect of this region to be somewhat like Portuguese and Mallorquin Spanish. Most Italians can understand Spanish and vice-versa. I also found out that Hawaii is a dream place for most Italians. They asked me to send souvenirs when I got there.

The next day was August 22 and I said farewell to Raoul who, like most Italians, is very sentimental. I stopped on my way to visit Ferrara and continued to Bologna where I met a young man from Argentina at the youth hostel. George (Jorge) Maceratesi had just won a trip to Europe through a college competition in architectural design. He had flight transportation between many large cities and he would fill in the gaps by hitch-hiking (sometimes referred to in Europe as "auto stop"). We went out to eat together that evening at a common local *ristorante* and he was able to use his good Italian to make sure we were not taken advantage of. As can be suspected by his name, his ancestors came from Italy some years ago. He was able to point out to me that most towers in Italy are not truly vertical (like Pisa). We were to swap a lot of information over many weeks as this was the first of four unplanned meetings along our separate paths through Italy. The second place was Florence the next day where we were again in the same youth hostel. It was a huge villa that was reportedly used by Mussolini.

The National Academy Gallery houses Michelangelo's *David* and it is a magnificent piece of work. The guide notes included the fact that the stone was originally given to another sculptor and that the left leg is slightly longer than the right. Not being a student of art I could only appreciate the craftsmanship of the work. This was many of the places to which admission was free with my Youth Hostel membership card. These types of tips are passed to others freely in youth hostels and allowed many to stretch their limited funds much further. The other sites of Florence (*Firenze*) are as attractive as the many depictions we see so often, such as the straw market on the bridge. I stopped in a small coffee shop and heard a beautiful song on the radio while there. I asked the waitress, Clarissa Vigni, what it was and she wrote the Italian words of "*Amore*

*Scusami"* for me. This would be the first song I would learn in Italian. Little did I know that Robert Goulet had a hit recording of it in the USA as "My Love Forgive Me". To this day I still have not learned the English words; the Italian sounds so much more authentic and romantic.

At Pisa I checked out the Tower and had my photo taken trying to prop it up. As always it was a very popular destination for visitors from near and far. I continued up the coast to find Marina di Massa of which I had heard so much. It is a villa with a beach just outside the courtyard. There are beautiful gardens, fountains and statues all around. We ate on the patio where a juke box was available for dancing at night. There were two unusual features of this place; it stayed open during the day and you could stay for as many nights as you wished. The wardens, "Mama and Papa", were great people and acted like parents to all visitors. This was my third meeting with George.

While at church I met Maruja from northern Italy and another traveler. She suggested that we could have lunch together. She would do the cooking if we bought the ingredients. We were all staying at the hostel where cooking facilities were available. We went to the local street markets and she bought the things she needed for her special spaghetti dish which I can still remember many years later. The sauce was not the traditional marinara type but much lighter with whole tomatoes, olive oil, lemon juice and several spices. I'm guessing it was her regional sauce and I have never tasted it again since that day. Given my love for food my memory easily makes note of such unique gastronomic experiences.

The next couple of days were marked by bad weather as I tried to get to Rome. However, a thunder and lightning storm slowed me down and I stopped in Livorno at the youth hostel. The next day was worse. Trying to get to Rome I came across a flood on the main road. At places there was four feet of water on the highway. I ended up with about 150-200 other travelers at the train station at Ladispoli about 35 kilometers north of Rome. During this period I had occasion to open the canned survival pack I had brought with me from the Air Force. It was quite a letdown although still edible. I noticed it had been originally packed in 1956.

The reports from the highway said that nobody was able to travel because the trains were out and the roads flooded. So, all of us tried to get comfortable in any way and spent the night at the train station. The conditions became obvious the following day when we continued to Rome on local roads. At times we had to push through a foot of soupy mud. That was about the most my scooter could take but it did not stop. It hit me that, apparently, "All roads didn't lead to Rome" at this time. When I finally arrived there (Sept. 2)

I found that many parts of the city did not have running water. Locals were lined up at fountains filling containers of many different sizes and shapes. I found the Vatican and toured St. Peter's where I paid a small fee to climb the copula so I could take a photo of St. Peter's Square below. I went to the Youth Hostel and found George but no admissions because of the water problem. We looked around and found a pension room for 1250 lira each. I was glad to check in as a cut that I got at the beach several days before started to really bother me. As a student of architecture George wanted to spend a significant amount of time in Rome visiting all the historic sites and I wanted to stay long enough to work and replenish my travel funds. George played piano in a college orchestra and knew many of the internationally known songs. I hoped to get work singing with my guitar. So, we headed out to visit many clubs to see if either of us could get work. We did not present ourselves as a musical duo. Generally there was not work but some people suggested other clubs to check. One of those was "Jerry's Luau" on Via Sardegna. When we got to talk to club owner, Jerry Chierchio, we found some luck because his piano player was in Venice making a film. We would have been happy if he had hired either of us but he said he knew how hard it was to make a few dollars and, so, hired both of us at 6,000 lira per night each to include dinner. We had hit the jackpot.

The club was a bar/restaurant with the L-shaped bar located on the main floor with one large table in the corner with plush seats around it. It was at one side of the steps which led to the lower dining area. On the other side was the piano with a boom mike facing the center of the room. Whatever music was played was piped throughout the club. When we realized that we were expected to start that night we had a real time crunch. We had decided to move into the rented room of an older couple who had been host to George's friend for quite a time. We could hardly have been more at home with "Mama" and "Papa" Repetto who virtually adopted us. We each paid 650 lira per night including breakfast. We had to transfer our things from the old room to Repetto's and get ready for starting that night at the club. To make things interesting George had lined us up for a double date also. Somehow it all worked and we settled into our new routine.

At the club I would usually start by doing a set of numbers mixed among old standards, popular folk songs and ballads. I would get many requests from the bar patrons as many of them were assigned to Rome in embassies or foreign company offices. As well, I was told that many entertainment dignitaries came to the club because it was more private than many of the other places. I would sit on the piano stool and sing into the boom mike. After

45 minutes or so George would take over and play a selection of standards and show tunes.

During one of my sets on the first night I noticed the star of TV's *Highway Patrol*, Broderick Crawford, come in with his wife and some Italian friends and sit in the settee across the stairs from the piano. During this set I noticed Mrs. Crawford go to the bar and speak with Jerry, the owner. When I finished one song she came over and asked if I might come to their table and do some songs for them. She indicated that she had checked with the boss and it was OK with him. I grabbed my neck cord and approached the table saying, "Good evening, Mr. Crawford. What can I sing for you?". In his typical gruff manner he answered, "To hell with this Mr. Crawford stuff. My name's Rod". That totally relaxed me and I did quite a few songs up to the point where Rod said, "You don't have to play that thing all night. Sit down and have a drink." With that he made everyone else push over to make room for me next to him and had me order a drink.

He explained to me that he was in Spain making a movie and they came to Rome for a break. While we chatted he related one of his more embarrassing moments in Spain. One evening after shooting all day they went out to dine and drink to relax. They often went to little-known places so they would not be recognized and they could be at ease. He indicated that it's challenging to keep your cool when your night is interrupted by fans seeking autographs and/or photos. On this particular night they were somewhat in the countryside and had been in the small club for some time when a well-dressed older man shuffled over to his table and excused himself but asked for an autograph. With a look of strained patience he prepared to give the man an autograph and asked for his name to personalize it. The gentleman answered, "Andre". Rod asked for his last name. The answer was, "Segovia". Rod almost fell out of his chair and spent the next several minutes apologizing to this genius of the classic guitar for his lack of enthusiasm. He queried as to why this famous individual would want his autograph. Mr. Segovia answered that he had enjoyed Rod's movies and TV shows greatly and considered himself lucky that they had met there.

Immediately Rod invited him to his table and they ended up having a great time together. After closing time Mr. Segovia went to his car and brought in two guitars for a brief concert. Rod told me that he was taught to play three notes on one guitar while Segovia played a symphony around those notes on the other. When they parted Segovia gave Rod his guitar, which became one of Rod's most cherished souvenirs from anywhere. Later someone tried to buy it from him and his answer contained a couple of expletives. Soon he told me that they had to move on to another place and left me a 6,400- lira tip, which was more than my regular pay for the night. So, I had gotten off to a great start in Rome.

The next day George and I had to go to the local police station to register because we intended to stay in Rome for more than two days. As well, we had to register with the local equivalent of ASCAP and pick up the forms on which we had to report every song we performed each night. In that manner the composers got royalties forever. If a song is performed but, not on the list, it costs the performer 3,500 lira.

Our daily routine was to wake up at around noon. Mama Repetto would have coffee, bread and butter ready for us. We would spend the days visiting friends, seeing the sites or other chores like repairing my scooter. I would check at American Express for my mail almost every day. This was one means of giving friends a forwarding address in my travels. Between 6:30 and 7:30 PM we would have dinner at the club with the rest of the staff. Then we would return to our room to get ready for work at the Luau. If we had prepared before dinner we would spend the next couple of hours strolling Via Veneto and/or sitting at an outdoor cafe on the same street sipping *capucino* while watching those who are strolling. One night I was surprised to meet Barbara from Bremen whose family I had visited there.

We would start entertaining at the club at 10:30 PM and I would always take the first shift. As the patrons got used to us they would want to hear my songs and sometimes sing along. Lucky George didn't know too many of these standards, so he got off easy with me doing 1:20 sets and him doing his usual 45-minute sets. It always amazed me how some people would be so upset if I happened not to know their favorite song. I would only do a song if I were confident that I knew all of the words and verses. Some thought I should know every song from every generation and most countries. Others heard songs they had not heard for a long time and came in to hear those songs over and over again. I got to know many new friends. Aside from the regular patrons we would have celebrities like Robert Mitchum Jr., Dale Roberts and Don Ameche who invited me to his table as he ate dinner by himself. He was intrigued by my trip and showed genuine interest in it. He was a true gentleman and very personable. We would finish at the club around 3:30 AM, do our homework (sheets) and head for the room on my scooter. We even got to know some of the faithful prostitutes who hung out on the same corners on our way home. We'd wave at them and greet them as we passed. We'd usually got to bed between 4:30 and 5:30 AM.

The area in which we lived was not far from the Vatican and I would often go to church there. I went to St. Peter's Square one day to view, and listen to, Pope Paul VI in his last appearance before making an historic trip to the United Nations in New York to plead for world peace. He spoke in Italian and later led the audience in prayers in Latin. This was the time of the Vatican Council and I was really surprised one evening as I drove through a crowded city street. I had to stop for some slow traffic in front and as I looked across the street I recognized Bishop Fulton Sheen whom I had seen on his TV programs many times. As he looked over I waved and said hello to him. He was true to his reputation as he left his party and crossed the street to chat with me. He was interested in where I was from, where I was going and what I was doing in Rome. After a few minutes chat he excused himself as others were waiting for him. He blessed me and wished me luck and safety in the rest of my journey. He made a lasting impression on this traveler.

During my 5 weeks in Rome I got to know some great people and see some of the most famous sites of our modern world. Of course these included the catacombs, the Coliseum, the Spanish Steps with the Trevi Fountain, the Sistine Chapel and the location of the earlier Summer Olympic Games. I found Rome (like most large international cities) to be full of several usual categories of people. There were the older rich men who spend a lot of lire for the privilege of having beautiful young women on their arms, beautiful young woman who are willing to pass the time with older men provided they have lots of money to spread around, middle-aged women who are desperately trying to preserve their youth and dashing young men who are interested in beautiful young women with the goal of seeing how long it would take to get them into their apartments. As well, there are many adventurous tourists who are out to have a great time including observing all of the above categories. It seems that I would find in my travels the same heterogeneous mixture of characters in every city or village I would visit. Sometimes it took a while to figure out who played which role but they were all there.

Often I would go to Mass at any near-by church on Sunday and pick up 200 lira of flowers on the way back to the room for Mama Repetto. She would just beam with this small gesture of affection. Very often the Repettos would invite us for Sunday dinner, which would be the traditional "soup to nuts" feast for which the Italians are known. Mario (Papa) was a former producer of films and was intrigued and frustrated by the potential of what I was doing. He would have seen it made into a film as a person-to-person cultural exchange at the grassroots level. However, he ultimately realized that he was beyond his productive days in the world of films.

George left Rome about a week before me and I did a solo at the club for a few days. They had lined up another piano player from the USA who was a great musician. We overlapped on a couple of days and enjoyed working together. On my last night I bought some fancy pastries for the staff and recorded some tapes for one of the Indonesian waitresses. She just loved *"When I Fall in Love"* and I had learned it for her while in Rome. The following morning I had to say good-by to all the neighbors and finally to the Repettos who had grown on me like another set of grandparents. As I headed away from the apartment building I could see Mama Repetto waving on the balcony with tears streaming down her full cheeks. I had truly been touched by the basic humanity of another beautiful person. It was October 11 and I headed south.

I drove to Naples and met George at the Youth Hostel. The following day I left my large bags at the hostel and we went to visit Pompeii, which was destroyed by hot cinders not fire or lava. There was much to see and we took several photos of the areas that were nearly intact. I noted here that what would appear to be a public toilet often turned out to be a local business with entrance fees of 25-50 lira. Certainly as you head further south you enter areas of Italy with few jobs and low wages. We took a pension room in Sorrento for 600 lira each and stayed overnight to catch the boat to Capri the next morning. I was allowed to leave my scooter at the pension. The trip to this famed island was beautiful and included a visit to the Blue Grotto. If you wanted to enter the grotto there was an additional fee. We transferred to one of many small rowboats which were waiting and headed for the opening to the grotto. It was small and varied in height as the swells of the ocean came and went. With well-practiced timing the oarsman grasped an overhead rail and at the right moment he pulled hard to thrust the boat through the opening as he laid down flat in the boat as we were. We popped up inside a huge cave, which had little light except for the outside light reflected under the water. It gave the entire cave an eerie blue shade, which was beautiful in itself.

Upon reaching Capri we found a great pension at Villa Marina with a fantastic balcony view for 700 lira (about $1.20) each. I found the island to be much like Ibiza; small and quite mountainous. There are no ocean beaches to speak of. The coast had a grainy gray surface. There were several swimming pools where visitors could pay a small fee to swim and take in the sun. We found many German and other European tourists here. There was an abundance of flowers everywhere you went. The Italians are dedicated gardeners. George and I got a super view of the island and its surroundings by taking a cable car tour to the top of the highest peak. We had the good luck of being there during a sparse tourist time.

When the boat returned us to Sorrento the next day we checked back into the same pension where I had left the scooter. Again we were serenaded in the evening by the accordion music from a nearby party. The atmosphere was classic. We went on to Salerno where I left George to hitchhike to Sicily. I then returned to Naples and re-claimed the rest of my baggage at the hostel. That evening I had a good test of my Italian as I helped the warden translate the English instructions for a new movie camera he bought. He was quite friendly and it was often the case where I would meet someone who had visited or worked in the USA and we would talk at length about their experiences. I well remember meeting one older man who had worked in the USA for many years and had returned to Italy after he retired and had a steady Social Security check. He could live very nicely there given the difference in the cost of living between Italy and the USA.

On my way to Santa Lucido I stopped at Paestum where I visited and photographed the Greek Temple of Neptune from 600 BC. It was almost totally intact. I was to find out that some of the best-preserved Greek temples were located outside of Greece. I completed the 390 kilometers to Santa Lucido and, upon inquiring locally, I was introduced to an older lady who not only rented me a room for 400 lira, but insisted that I also take my scooter into the room. I presume she felt somewhat responsible for its safe-keeping. The result was that I did not have to unpack everything that evening.

At Villa San Giovanni I bought a boat ticket for myself (100 lira) and my scooter (1000 lira) for the trip to Messina in Sicily. During the trip it rained strongly and all of my things got wet. A small compensation was that I was introduced to arranccini that is a ball of rice with meat and vegetables in the middle and is lightly deepfried. It is a very popular snack, which I thoroughly enjoyed on the boat. Once in Messina I headed for Taormina, a beautiful walled town perched on the side of the mountains overlooking the sea on the east coast of Sicily. The rain had continued and would be with me for more than four days. When I found George again I learned that hitchhiking in the south was very bad and he had to take a train to arrive here. He was staying with a friend so I found a reasonable pension and went about the task of trying to dry off my belongings. After two more days of rain we toured the local sites and found them very inviting. There was a Greek theater further up the hills and its view included Mt. Etna and the gorgeous coastline. The following day the weather was great so we headed south on my scooter to visit Catania and Sircusa where we visited another well-kept Greek theater dated at 480 BC. Both the architecture and the technology were exquisite. It is said that a silver dollar dropped on center stage could be heard at any location in the theater.

Fantastic view from Taormina

Mt. Etna with east coast Sicilian vista

Scooter at cold summit of Mt. Etna

I noted through chatting that schooling in the south only went to the 7th or 8th grades. However, educational TV was helping to make a difference for those who were still at home.

We passed through Catania on our way to see the top of Mt. Etna. The road was quite steep and I was not sure the scooter would carry both of us all the way. As we approached the top we drove through the clouds and, even though the sun came out, we found it quite chilly, as George had no sweater with him. At the highest point of the road we were at 1910 meters (about 6,200 feet) and the temperature was 2 degrees centigrade (just above freezing). With these conditions we did not stay long on the summit. We got some coffee, took some photos and returned to Taormina. The following day I was to say good-by to George for the last time. He was to head back to the north and I was to follow the "instep" of the "boot" to Brindisi at the "heel" where I would take the boat to Greece.

After an emotional "Ciao" to George I headed for Messina where the ticket salesman tried to charge me a significant amount more than I had paid a week before when I had arrived from the mainland. Thanks to having acquired enough ease in Italian, I was able to set him straight and I got the same tickets for my return. I then followed the coast through Calabria to a town of Crotone where I got a room for 700 lira and met the man who ran the local scooter repair shop. He was intrigued with my journey and insisted that I keep the Irish Rover safe at his shop overnight. The following day he would not accept a tip or fee which surprised me to the point of making a note of it in my diary. He was another special friend I would meet for only a fleeting moment in time.

As I stopped to have *colazzione* (breakfast) that morning at a small road-side restaurant I noted that there was an old man sitting on the curb at the road end of the walkway leading to the building. When I finished and was leaving I struck up a conversation with him to see what his daily living was like. As I suspected the biggest problem was that the economy was down and there were not many jobs in the area. In this rural setting I thought he might be a farmer. However, I had not learned the word for farmer in Italian and I was stumped—until I remembered the Latin word of "agricola". I used it and was easily understood by the gentleman.

There is some assurance in learning a "dead" language. I was seemingly blessed with an ear for languages and I found my high school Latin would come in handy when visiting any of the five countries where the Romance languages were spoken. However, to this day I find it much easier to express myself in a language than to understand that same tongue. As I moved from one language to another I identified the first useful words I wanted to learn and progressively moved into other useful words. I developed a number of techniques such as learning an adjective but not its antonym (opposite). I could instantly double my vocabulary by using the one adjective for both indications by using the negative of the verb. So, if I wanted to say in Spanish that something was expensive, could say that it was not cheap (*barato*). By using similar techniques I was quickly able to express myself to native speakers although I might have to use a complete sentence because I did not know a particular word. Thus, if I used proper grammar (a must, I believe) and had decent pronunciation, the native speaker could understand my meaning. However, when a native speaker talked to me he/she would use many words that I had not yet learned. This is the opposite of a bi-lingual person who learned the language from their parents or grandparents. They can usually understand the language better than they can speak it. One challenge is to convey to a stranger your actual level of ability in their language. Of course, if you come off quite fluently (even in a limited vocabulary), it is often assumed that you are completely fluent and the conversation will immediately proceed at that level of proficiency leaving the learner in a fog.

# CHAPTER FIFTEEN

## Leaving the "heel"

When I arrived in Brindisi (heel of the "boot" of Italy) I found the hostel and was pleased that it was very nice and had few guests. I made note that I had arrived at the end of the Appian Way from Rome even though by a circuitous route. It was from this port that the Roman armies departed for far off parts of the Roman Empire. It would also be the first part of the road journey that would return them to the ancient capital. It was October 30th when I bought my tickets for the boat trip and they cost 9,500 lira (about $15) for me and the scooter. I always worried a bit about going through customs with my scooter but in this case it was not a problem, as I had to serenade the custom officials when they saw my guitar. We became quick friends and I think I could have taken a pink elephant aboard with no problem. It didn't stop immediately as the crew of the ship must have been clued in and requested a session for them as soon as I got on the boat. As I often pondered, "music soothes the savage beast" and many potentially hard-nosed officials. I had no customs problems when I arrived in Kerkyra, Corfu. I checked into the local hostel and later went to church.

As usual I wanted to spend some time in a small village or town where I could become a temporary part of the local lifestyle. I looked at the map and picked Kassiopi which was located after about 36 kilometers of bad road on a beautiful small bay. The total population of this town was 650 people from 120 families. After a short search I found a room in a "hotel" which was a private home on the east side of the bay. It advertised that it had an indoor toilet, which was a bit rare in this extremely poor area. I rented the room for 15 drachmas (about .53 US). The owner, Basilios, was a great talker but not very ambitious. He was quite proud of the size and strength of his wife whom I saw carrying 65 pound bags of sand up to his house. He did the supervising.

Peaceful bay of Kassiopi

Innkeeper & prime laborer

He had two nieces, Fredericki and Agatha, who lived close by. Agatha had gone to Crete to learn how to use a rather primitive loom located in an old barn. She had learned to speak some English and immediately became my Greek teacher. Later as I roamed around the town I came to this barn where all of the women were engaged in chatting while they carried on almost every task in the making of wool fabrics. I took a photo of them with the sheep in the background. Once the sheep had been shorn, the balls of wool were spun into yarn by hand by the ladies standing around. They would pull off the fibers and use their fingers to spin the yarn, which was rolled into a ball with the other hand. They had a stand from which the wool was then transferred to the bobbins for the shuttle. Then Agatha took over for the process of weaving of some blanket or covering. Almost the entire process can be seen taking place in this photo. For some items the intermediate step of wool dying would take place. (Note: A beautiful red and black bureau scarf later sent to me by Agatha is what I refer to as a real souvenir of my trip. It adorns my bureau to this day.)

I noticed that the stand was broken so I repaired it and then gave the women a song fest with the guitar. They quickly "adopted" me including trying to match me with some of the local girls so I would settle down there. One of the true characters was Lene who performed a mock ceremony with Fredericki (Kiki) and me and pronounced us "married" to great laughs and

Total fabric production in one view

cheers from the group. I later rowed a boat across the bay for them where they would do the initial washing of a new blanket. The flat rocks at that location had been identified as being ideal for the purpose. They were near the water's edge and were just right for the amount of paddling that took place during the washing. The universal product I found to be used in this area for washing clothes was OMO, as popular as Tide back home. When washing small items they often used olive soap because of the salty seawater. Speaking of water, the only drinking version was found at the well in the town center. A frequent chore was to carry the clay jugs to the well and return with a supply for the family. I took part in this on several occasions.

I was fortunate to be in town when the van from the city came and set up the movie theater in the local restaurant. That evening a great crowd showed up for the Greek-made film which was quite poor in quality. It mattered not to the audience and I enjoyed their enjoyment of it. The entrance fee was only 4 DR (.14 US) about which nobody would complain. The restaurant was the only one in town and I had many of my meals there. I got to know the owners well and each time I entered I would go directly into the kitchen to see what was cooking. I would point to what I wanted and ask how to say it in Greek. When I had decided they would then serve me at the table. This was my standard approach in most Greek restaurants.

There was a juke box which had almost all Greek songs on it. Once in a while I'd play one or two just to get the atmosphere. One day I lucked out when a group of students from Kerkyra on an outing came to eat while I was there. As expected they played many songs and when the theme from "Zorba the Greek" came on they lined up and did a great version of the dance from the movie. It was as if I had a private floorshow. I could truly believe I was in the land of Zorba. This was also true at night when I would stroll around the bay area with the moon shining through ancient olive trees and bouncing off the water over which I could see the lights of Albania.

One evening I became aware of another pastime of the locals. Basilios mentioned that he was going fishing and invited me to come along. I thought this would be an interesting experience, as I never thought of going fishing at night. Once we had gathered the gear we headed around the bay to his favorite fishing spot. It was then that I found out that his fishing amounted to throwing a couple of lines in the bay, fastening them to a tree and heading for the bar to drink wine and chat. I reflected on how many other nationalities had a similar way to pass the boring nights. I noted that the common Greek wine is much thicker than the Italian or Spanish equivalent. I also noted that the most popular hot drink was Turkish coffee although the two nationalities seemed to have no great love for each other. A bit of caution came with the first cup of coffee consumed by a new visitor. The cup was small and the liquid quite thick. The taste was very good until you got within a half inch of the bottom. That is where the "sludge" was located and the uninitiated might end up with a mouthful of it. In a home setting the leavings were drained and the cup turned upside down to dry. Thereafter an "elder" would "read" the patterns much as was done by my relatives with loose tea.

One of the common local trades was fishing and many of the men were involved in it. While I was there they had a great catch of sardines, so much so that they could not sell all of them and the price plummeted to .06 US per pound. Their elation at the catch led to desperation at the selling price. To compound the local economic problem the olive crop was failing due to a lack of water. Making a living in this area was extremely difficult, but these citizens could not accumulate enough funds to consider moving. And even if they moved, they could not be sure that their new surroundings would be any better than where they were. It was hard to accept the idea that the future was so limited for these new friends who had the same basic needs and desires as all of us.

During the daily hours when I was not busy I disassembled the exhaust system of the scooter and found it to be quite dirty from the many hundreds of miles it had traveled since the last cleaning. Opening all of the ports and passageways in the system restored the power as it had done before. After a delay of one day for rain (which delighted my local friends) I headed out for the 20 kilometers of bad road leading back to the capital. The route kept up to its reputation as a particularly rocky area resulted in the housing of the flywheel being dented causing much noise and wear. It took about 40 minutes to repair it and continue on to Kerkyra. I continued to the south a bit and found another room in Benitse for 6 DR. The lady of this house was a widow and greatly lamented the fact that her daughter who was married with children lived in the city and only came to visit when she wanted to load up on the abundant citrus fruit from the trees ringing the house. Of course, the grandmother wished to be part of the upbringing of the kids.

In this area I found the local bread to be very good. I would buy the small round loaf when it was still warm and eat it for a meal with butter and jam. My landlord invited me to eat with her one evening and the most memorable item from the meal was some cabbage, which she had cooked and served with the citrus fruits from her garden. It was a unique taste for me that I never forgot. On one day when I was in town I bought a pound of hamburger and some tomato paste so I could make her and the other two older male guests a real Italian spaghetti dinner. However, when I was out taking a walk she decided to do the cooking and we all ate a typical Greek spaghetti dinner in which the sauce is more like beef gravy in color and taste. Oh well, I tried. I noted that the older men in Greece often fingered "worry beads" in relaxed company. This would carry into the entire mid-east as I would later learn.

As I walked around Benitse one day I came across a young man named Nicolas. He spoke good English due to the time he had spent working in a restaurant in Flushing, New York. He and his brother-in-law had jumped ship there and were working to save money when another Greek turned them in to the Immigration Service. He was particularly upset that another Greek would turn them in. They were sent back to Greece and their passports were retained in Athens for two years. Now he was helping his brother-in-law to build a new house that entailed much physical labor. I joined in the work and helped him for several days, which brought expressions of disbelief from many neighbors. We, from the USA, are not known for doing much manual labor. We were in the process of applying the external stucco to the outside of the walls. It took a bit of getting used to in order to do it properly. Ultimately I could keep up with Nicolas and others. I well remember the feast that took place during the noon break when all of the women would bring platters of all types of food for the workers.

Before leaving on November 13 I took advantage of my idle time and got a decent haircut for .33 US. On that day I drove to the pier in Kerkyra with a beautiful day all around me. However, during the long wait the dark rain clouds came across the area and we had to duck to keep dry. Before we left the rain had passed and we headed for the 1.75 hour crossing to Igoumenitsa on the mainland. Unfortunately we were traveling faster than the weather and we caught up to all the rain and had to go through it again. The trip cost just 1.00 US for the scooter me and. As we unloaded in Igoumenitsa the rain let up and I started the 104-kilometer trip to Ioanina. At about the 6-kilometer mark I got a flat tire, which I had to change at the side of the road. As I continued on I came across a long stretch of road where there was no pavement. Instead I was slowly progressing through 2 inches of soupy mud, which is very dangerous for the scooter. A local hot-rod approached from the front and hardly slowed down as he sprayed me, my scooter and all my baggage with soupy mud. I turned and "thanked" him in several languages.

Soon I was climbing into the mountains, which were quite rough going with country roads. As well, it was getting quite cold. Rain returned to be my company and I kept looking for Ioanina ahead of me. I had a small handicap in that the only map I had found of Greece was in French. It was a bit strange to see the names of the places on the map in French and then try to find them on road signs in Greek. After the sun went down I had to stop several times under trees to avoid the strong rain and what turned out to be a thunder and lightning storm. On a number of occasions I would see the lights of the city in front of me only to see the road turn away from that settlement as I approached. Much later I stopped at a restaurant where I ate liver and onions and drank tea to warm up. I found out that I was just 7 kilometers (4.5 miles) from Ioanina and I pressed on to the Youth Hostel there. I found only one other guest there, an American. I was able to take advantage of the lack of people in my dorm room and I spread all of my wet things around to dry. I finally put my weary body into bed after one of the most trying days of my journey thus far.

The following day was still rainy so I decided to stay over and take care of some other items beyond drying my clothes. I found a local gas station and got a young boy to repair my flat tire, which I then put back on for use. Being Sunday I also inquired if there was a Catholic church in the area. I was sent to several houses of worship none of which was Catholic. The last one I was sent to with assurance was an Evangelical church and I decided to stay there for the service. Not being able to understand the Greek of the sermon

I satisfied myself by reading the Mass in my own missalette. About the time the congregation got up to sing, I finished my Mass and left. They didn't bother me nor did I apparently bother them. This would be one of the few times I missed Mass in all my travels. By the time I returned to my scooter I found the "repaired" tire flat again. So I went to the station, bought some patches and glue and fixed it myself with the unbelieving boy looking on. While in this area I noted that the Greeks apparently don't mind eating their food cold. Sometimes a meal would be served and those partaking would continue to chat and drink and maybe 40-50 minutes later would consume the meal. I don't mind eating cold food if it's meant to be that way, but I prefer my hot food—hot.

On this Sunday evening I witnessed another event, which took place in many of the countries I visited but in individual styles. It was the weekly social event I refer to as the "stroll". The downtown streets would be blocked off and families and groups of young people would parade along the streets greeting their friends and commenting on items of local interest. Usually there was some music to be heard and tasty foods available from street-side vendors. One that I tried was *kokirets* which is spitted lamb with flavorings roasted on an open fire. I bought a 3-4 inch section and it was then chopped into cubes, salted and put into a paper container from which it was eaten as you stroll down the street. I always found the aroma of the meat being cooked outdoors as very enticing. I truly enjoyed this type of sampling.

On a bright day I headed south through Arta for Patras. Of course the last part of that journey involved getting the ferryboat for the 1.5 mile trip across the Straits of Corinth. It only cost me 8.5 DR (.30 US) but it was a very rough ride causing my scooter to fall over. However, within a short time I was in the Youth Hostel at Patras and had the first of many meetings with Daisy and Odile, two young girls from Paris. It was hard to believe that they had not told their families that they were going traveling but hid their luggage before "leaving for work" one morning. They then met and headed out of Paris in Odile's old car that broke down after only a few miles. They were not deterred and decided to hitchhike for the rest of their sojourn. I was concerned for their safety but I thought that this might be more acceptable among Europeans. Their goal was Istanbul and I would meet them several times along the way.

One of my prized vistas was that of Olympia, the home of the original Olympic Games. It is from this site that the Olympic Torch starts its journey to the games wherever they are to take place. I visited the location of the original stadium and the many temples of the location. It was a beautiful day with warm sun and a gentle breeze as I wandered through the groves of that setting. I used my Zeiss Ikon to record these scenes for the future. I continued on toward Tripolis through mountains that reminded me of Norway and Scotland. Due to bad weather I stopped in Vutina and got a first-class room in a hotel for .65 US. It was quite cold as I strolled around the town in the dense fog. The elevation there was 1053 meters (almost 3,500 feet) above sea level. The following day I passed Argos and went to Naplion where I found just two other guests at the new Youth Hostel. It was very nice and we had a jam session with the guitar in the evening.

Epidavros was a must-see according to all who had been in the area. It was only about 20 miles from the Youth Hostel and it was there that I saw the most beautifully preserved Greek theater anywhere. I spent a good part of the day here taking in the several views of the 14,000-seat theater and its surroundings. In the festival season you can attend original Greek plays in this place, a matter of enormous pride to the Greeks. On my return to Argos I passed on to Corinth and stopped to take some photos of another engineering marvel, the Isthmus of Corinth where the Corinth Canal was cut through at the time of Nero. By cutting this deep canal ships would be able to avoid the longer journey around the Peloponese when sailing for Athens from the west.

# CHAPTER SIXTEEN

## Ancient Athens

My day ended in the famed capital, Athens. I stopped in downtown and made some inquiries while I had some refreshments. I finally made some connections and got a room on Avenida Apollonos for 30 DR. This location was on the fringe of the traditional, old Plaka District. Looking over this from the back window of my room I had a direct view of the Parthenon. In the evening I visited the Plaka and could easily imagine life in past centuries as I wandered my way through the narrow streets with the smells and sounds of old Greece flowing around me. I re-met Odile and Daisy and learned that they had a room across the street from mine.

Daylight brought many other scenes to relish such as the Parthenon and a small temple of Hefaisto, which is one of the best preserved in Greece although it's often overlooked due to its proximity to the Parthenon. Even the roof of the building was intact which is quite rare. I visited the US Embassy and got tips on my future travels as well as information regarding the availability of vaccinations from the US Public Health Service at no cost to US citizens. I received shots for cholera and small pox, which were recommended for the areas of my intended sojourn. I went on to the embassies of Syria and Lebanon where I obtained my visas and learned that I would have no problem entering with my scooter. I noted that this was the first time in my journey that I was required to get a visa prior to entering the country. When speaking about possible travel to Israel, I was cautioned that I would not be allowed to enter any Arab country if I had an Israeli entree in my passport. Some people would visit all their intended Arab countries first and then visit Israel. Others would take a boat from Greece to Israel and leave the same way. In this case the Israeli officials would use a paper visa and entry document that could later be easily removed for further travel in the Mid-east.

I ended this day by driving my NSU up Lisabetto Hill where there was a small church and an out-door cafe. Sipping a drink and mixing with the locals made the time pass quickly and soon we were all presented with a gorgeous sunset over Athens looking all the way to Pireus, the port city to the west. It was in this type of setting that I became aware of *sulvaki,* soon to become one of my favorite foreign foods. It is meat roasted on a vertical spit from which the outside edges are trimmed and mixed with tomatoes, onions and dressings as it is rolled inside a huge pita bread. I was to find this delicious sandwich in most parts of the Mid-east although known by other local names.

It was in Greece that I first noticed a body-language sign from men when they wished to answer "no" to an inquiry. It it a distinct upward nod of the head. Later in the Arab countries I would find the same but usually accompanied by an oral click formed by releasing the tongue from the roof of the mouth. With practice I was able to use this response in appropriate discussions with locals.

On November 28 I left Athens and headed for another of the country's famed locations, Delphi. The ride was through very remote areas and I frequently wondered how the people in the tiny villages at the bottom of vast, deep valleys could keep in touch with the rest of the population. Of course, the answer was that they were quite self-sufficient, an ability from which many of us have been too isolated for most of our lives. When we think deeply enough about it, we can realize how little it takes to exist and how spoiled we have become from having too many benefits of life handed to us with little effort. I'm convinced that we humans only value and respect what we have in proportion to the personal effort expended on our part to obtain it. As well, it often amazes me to hear the amount of life's pleasures that are somehow "owed" to those in developed countries. We often demand our "rights" and turn totally away from any obligations. The people in these villages accept that their success in life depends mostly on their own ambition.

I re-met Odile and Daisy in Delphi and together we toured the ancient city, famous for the Oracle. The sports stadium and temple were outstanding. We viewed the ruins of an entire ancient city perched beautifully on the side of the mountain overlooking the Straits of Corinth. One could picture the ancient inhabitants treasuring the spectacular view of the surroundings. When I checked into the local hostel I found a similar view out my back window. Of course, I recorded the scene with my camera.

The next day I drove north through Lamias and Larissa to stop at the hostel near Mt. Olympus which towered at 2917 meters above sea level. The hostel was very nice and I was the only visitor, giving me an edge with the nearby citizens. When I went to the *taverna* for food I ended up having a great time with the owner who spoke German. I have often been impatient with school vacations during my travels as I find that available hostel, pension and hotel rooms are more difficult to find.

My northern route took me through Thessalonika after which I stopped to photograph a substantial roadside shrine. I was told that they are erected in the memory of those who have died in accidents. They were quite elaborate and reminded me of those I had seen in Ireland and other countries. I was surprised that there were not more of them when I considered the "king of the road" attitude of the average Greek driver. My route took me through Kavala and Komotini and I stopped for gas just 10 kilometers before Alexandroupolis in a small town of Markri. I happened to inquire of the mayor who insisted on treating me to the gas and offering me a place to sleep in the town hall. Although the accommodations were sparse I appreciated deeply the sentiment and kindness of this local politician who considered it his job to be the "welcoming committee" of the village.

On December 2nd I headed for the Turkish border but had to delay several times because of rain. When I approached any international border I was always apprehensive about what demands might be made on me regarding the papers for the scooter. When I arrived at the customs office I went through immigration easily and then went to join the short line waiting at customs. The group in front of me consisted of three young English girls who had given two young American guys a ride in their van. The father of the driver had obtained the full international insurance to cover the van in any country they might visit. In fact she had two documents, which confused the agent at the desk who spoke only broken English. He finally had to call the manager who spoke no English but did speak French. With things at a standstill I volunteered to help out in French. In reviewing the insurance papers I realized that one was just a calendar extension of the other. As well, the color had been indicated as something non-descript like mauve. When I explained this in French to the manager he was able to instruct the agent and he proceeded to complete the necessary documents. A short while thereafter the manager noticed me standing separate from the group and asked if I was with them. When I answered that I was not he became embarrassed that I who had willingly helped their situation was not being served. He quickly processed my scooter and baggage without review and I was on my way down the road with my questionable documents long before the girls and their totally genuine papers.

I could not change my 500-drachma note except in Istanbul. Luckily I still had two U.S dollars, which I could change and got enough gas for the rest of the trip to this famous city. It was a wild and windy stretch of road for another 300 plus kilometers of travel at night. I well remember that about 88 kilometers before Istanbul a gust of wind took my cap off my head and it was impossible to retrieve. Thus, I lost my world-traveled hat at this point.

When I finally made it into the center of Istanbul I had to pull over to the curb to search my Youth Hostel book to see if there were hostels in the city. This capital was a thriving city with throngs of pedestrians passing on the sidewalks. On several occasions people would stop and try to assist me and somehow the majority of them assumed I was German. They would greet me in German and I would answer them in German, but let them know I was from the USA. After a while a young, off-duty policeman came to be my savior and took it upon himself to find me a good, but reasonable, room for the night. He would run ahead of me to several hotels/inns and inquire as to the availability and price of lodging. There were no Youth Hostels in the area that we could become aware of. He finally found a room for 8 Turkish lira and I remember meeting a young girl from Alabama who was traveling through this whole area by herself. Although I was quite self-confident I was surprised at her daring. I certainly would not have recommended that situation for any lone, young female that I knew.

The next day I was shocked to find that even the local banks would not exchange any Greek money. I had a 500 DR note which was worth about $18 US. In my travels this was significant and would take me a long way. While I was inquiring about this at the US Consul office a man who was about to travel to Greece offered to exchange my drachmas for US dollars. He was like a lifesaver. Later I found the American Hostel across from the St. Sophia Mosque. The day rate was only 6 lira with hot showers and no curfews. It also had a place to wash your clothes. I noted that it was for men only. The hostel for girls and families was only open in the summer.

While looking around the city I ran out of gas and tried to get some help from a traffic cop who did not speak English or any other language that I might try. As I struggled a pedestrian came along who spoke German and he offered to show me where I could buy some gas. Ali had lived and worked in Germany and spoke it quite well. He invited me to his place, which turned out to be a single unfurnished room with a mattress on the floor and a box for a table. He prepared lunch for both of us and it was fish, tea, bread, margarine and maple butter. He was very anxious to talk about life outside of Turkey. He lived a very poor existence here as did most of the locals. He said that he was more frustrated than most people he knew here because he had lived in a developed country with a steady income and was very aware of the difference. Most of his neighbors and friends were not aware of any different standard of living and, thus, did not miss it. Soon, after checking his watch, he had to leave to make some change. I accompanied him to the local school yard during recess where he charged a few cents for students to shoot his air gun at some targets that he brought with him.

Later I met Daisy and Odile for the 5th time and we toured around the city. The Ian Sophia Mosque was built in 347 AD by Constantine and by this time was a revered museum. We also visited the Blue Mosque that is the only one in the world that has 6 minarets. Observing the customs we removed our shoes at the door and washed our feet. The interior was covered with carpets and was an architectural marvel. There were more than 500 Mosques in Istanbul. We went on to the Galata Bridge climbing the tower to view the Asian part of the city across the Straits of Bosphorus. It was a visual confirmation of the uniqueness of this city, which is the only one in the world located on two continents. As we walked through the sights it started to rain and we three ended up under my ever-faithful poncho. Although we attracted some stares I was quite content to share my shield with these two lovely young ladies.

After we parted company for the day I went on to the Galata bridge and found a new friend who worked there. On both sides of the main bridge was a lower level walking path on which were located many stores and kiosks. I met this bridge worker who spoke German and he invited me into the office where we could have some hot tea and *oralet*, a hot drink with a taste of oranges in it. It was good and I was able to warm myself as well as dry off some of my garments. Soon my host was making lunch for us and we enjoyed each other's company for several hours. This hard-working man was no celebrity but another human being who shared his meager means with me, a stranger from afar, whom he would never meet again.

Later in the day Daisy had the "great" idea of having coffee at the Hotel Hilton, which turned out to be 5 lira (.55 US) per cup. We laughed about it later; it was almost the price of our room. We did get a break when using the rare underground metro, which was free to tourists. Finally we had to

Daisy & Odile far from home

say the traditional fare well as I was to leave for the east the following day. We exchanged addresses and promised to keep in touch. These young ladies had been on their own in several foreign countries for almost five weeks. The next day was December 7th and I paid a grand total of 18 cents US for the ferryboat ride across the Bosphorus. In later years a modern bridge would span this waterway. On the far side I had arrived at another continent but was still in the same city. The prior day I had changed a $10 US bill and was able to get 11.5 lira/dollar in the bazaar compared to 9 lira at the bank. It was amazing to find young teen-aged boys doing recruiting for moneychangers in several languages. As always it paid to shop around.

As I headed east I started to get into more hilly terrain and colder weather. On this day I drove 445 kilometers (280 miles) to Ankara, capital of this diverse nation. I was getting used to the idea that people wanted to buy almost everything I had each time I stopped. That would include the scooter, my guitar and various pieces of clothing. I had heard that some travelers from the USA had paid for their entire trips by bringing extra pairs of Levi's with them and selling them along the way. Somehow there would always be someone who could come up with whatever money was asked for when it came to selling western items. I traveled very light and so I never had anything I could, or was willing to, sell.

When I entered Ankara I found my way to the local university where I befriended some of the students who let me stay in their dorm room for the night. Of course, this was on the floor in my sleeping bag. I noted that food was cheaper in Turkey than in Greece. Although the Greeks drank much Turkish coffee, the Turks seemed to prefer tea. Having been raised on tea from my Scottish immigrant parents I was quite content with tea although here it was never drunk with milk. At the price of 2.5 cents US per glass I was not going to quibble. It was usually made with a significant amount of sugar.

I left the capital the next day and turned south climbing into the mountains which formed the large plateau in the middle of the country. It got progressively colder and I ended up driving through thick fog high in the mountains. I stopped for some gas and was surprised to find that gas was 9 cents US per liter (.35 US/gal.). I continued until I came through the clouds and faced some strong winds. In Konya I found a good room and got away from the cold for a while. The following day I drove further south and stopped at Karaman where I had my first taste of *hummus*, which was served hot in a small casserole dish and had some tasty oil on the top. This was a puree of chickpeas and flavorings, which I would find throughout the mid-east. It was eaten with some leavened bread here in Turkey and it was so delicious I would look for it in many future locations. I found it often in my future travels but it was never served hot again. In other areas it was usually eaten with pieces of pita bread. This particular meal cost me only .31 US. By being willing to partake of local, common foods I saved many dollars but also learned of the food basics of the average citizen of the area.

Common market in southern Turkey

I was descending through the mountains in the south when I ran out of gas at night just 15 kilometers before Silifke. I was pushing the scooter for a while when a truck came by and stopped to assist me. The driver and his co-worker were very helpful and insisted on lifting the scooter up to the top of the full load and driving me to the next station where they also insisted on buying me dinner. Once the scooter was filled up I continued to Silifke and got a room. I was now on the south shore of this land and things started to change rather quickly. For one, the outlook and culture of the people of this area was much more like the Arabs than like the Turks. Women wore shawls and baggy pantaloons that were tight at the ankles. Men were almost always mustached and wore a type of pants, which hung down to the knees. I was told that these were designed for men who rode horseback. These residents apparently liked JFK but had no good words for LBJ. The climate was much warmer and I noted that towns and cities along this stretch were known for their citrus fruit especially Mersin. When I passed through small villages I would realize that they were not big enough for a mosque. So, they would have a minaret attached to the cleric's house.

My guides to ancient city of Neopolis

Along this coastline I stopped at an ancient city of Neopolis and found two young children who offered to be my guides. They didn't speak any foreign language but they knew all of the site's important features. The boy was about seven years old and his sister was younger. I followed them as they chatted their "spiel" and I gave them a tip after I was allowed to take their photo. As I left them I came across my first camels roaming at large. They were walking along the deserted beach area in the same direction as myself. I could find no keepers and I decided they must be wild. I next met a group of uniformed students walking to school, which must have been at a significant distance, as I had seen no buildings for quite some time.

Uniformed Turkish students walking to school

Along this road I saw a sign with a familiar name on it, Incerlik Air Force Base. I had had occasion to locate this base on maps when I was in the Strategic Air command. I visited the facility and found that it had now been turned over to the Turkish Air Force. My memory served me well as I confirmed with the gate guard that Gary Powers and others had flown their U-2 spy planes out of this base over Russia. The last Turkish city I passed through was Antakya (know in older times as Antioch). This road was quite mountainous and it finally led me to the Syrian border.

# CHAPTER SEVENTEEN

## The Arab bloc

Here the "guardian of the Arab bloc" delayed me for quite some time indicating his displeasure with my future travel plans. I had to describe what I had in my pannier bags down to the pairs of under-shorts although he did not insist on seeing them. At one point he asked me if I intended to enter Israel. I was so frustrated by then I told him that if I thought I would, I certainly would not tell him. Finally he charged me a modest entry fee and I was officially within the Arab block of nations. There was a note of disappointment here because I had been told that I would have to carry an affidavit from my local priest to prove that I was not Jewish as I entered the first Arab country. This official apparently had no interest in the note from Father Leahy which I had carried for more than a year as a guarantee that I would not have to prove my non-Jewish status in a much more physical manner.

I proceeded to the town of Banias where I stopped at a gas station to fill up. I found that there were 4 Syrian pounds to the US dollar. The young attendant was very friendly and invited me in for tea. I took the occasion to become familiar with a different style of toilet facility. In this case there was a hole in the floor with a fixture in it that was straddled for any and all operations. Flushing was a matter of using a convenient hose to wash down the inside of the bowl with water. While chatting with my host a motor scooter pulled up outside with two young men. They were greatly interested in my scooter with all of the baggage on it. This was the first time I would meet an Arab local who would become a good friend for many years to come. Harris Sulman was a student at the University of Lebanon in Beirut and his friend was Broheim about the same age. After a number of inquiries about my travels-to-date and my intentions Harris invited me to visit his home, which was not far away in the village of Herisoon.

I followed Harris to his home and met most of his family that consisted of nine brothers and two sisters. With him lived five brothers and one sister whose main job seemed to be cooking and cleaning after her brothers. She had a very good disposition but was out of sight unless fulfilling one of her functions. I was to find out that none of the women would be in any of the photos I took in the Arab countries. The house had several sparse rooms and I had difficulty in identifying the members of the family because friends were always dropping by and they were always quite welcome. When it came time to sleep those for whom there were no beds slept on the mats on the floor. Of course, Harris and some of his brothers and neighbors spoke English quite well allowing for me to start my study of Arabic. One aspect of the language that was intriguing was that verbs in the language are conjugated by changing the beginning of the verb rather than the ending as in most other languages. It is written from right to left and vowels are left out in the written form. I started writing down the basic vocabulary and grammar structure.

Harris and brothers in front of their home

I also learned that Banias, the closest town, was a port at which crude oil from Iraq was loaded onto tankers for shipment. Banias was the end of a 1000 kilometers (620 plus miles) long pipeline from Iraq which crossed the barren desert on its journey west. When I later visited Banias to go to church I found that I was in a Maronite church, which was part of the church under Rome but they did not use Latin in their liturgy. As it turns out they were a great jump ahead of the other Roman churches where the local language would be used later for the Mass.

One neighbor was Mersim who was quite well educated and we had a long talk about the political situation in the Mid-east at that time. The Arabs were quite unhappy with England and other countries of the west, which allowed Israel to take Arab land to build their country. They had revered JFK but were not too impressed with LBJ. Many Arabs believed that the Jews had Kennedy killed and that they had a plan to take over the world. The surrounding Arab countries had made an attempt at coordinating their agendas through the United Arab Republic but it ended in 1961.

One evening Harris and I visited the nearby home of his elder brother who had several children. Everyone was thrilled to have a visitor from the USA in their house and they showed great hospitality. We chatted, sang and ate some snacks among which were peanuts. However, these peanuts were still on the bush, which had been pulled up whole and suspended from the ceiling. Everyone helped themselves from the bushes and it was a new taste to try them without being roasted. For the next couple of days we had bad weather and I used the time to work on the scooter and visit with the other family members. When the sun finally came out I took a photo of Harris and his brothers outside their house. The house had neither running water nor electricity, which surprised me when I noticed a wire entering the house near the eaves. Upon inquiry I was informed that they had a telephone that could call around the world but no electricity. It made no difference whatsoever in the feeling of friendship that was ever-present. On the 16th of December I left with the promise to contact Harris in Beirut where he attended college.

When I arrived at the border of Lebanon the agent, whom I dubbed "the little god", decided that I might have stolen the scooter because the original owner's name was still on the registration paper. Despite showing him the bill-of sale and the original insurance papers (both in my name) I was forced to leave my scooter at the border after driving it 28,000 kilometers through 23 countries without a problem. I then had to find a way of getting to Beirut with all of my gear/luggage. Luckily after I waited a while I met a Danish man who worked for the UN in Beirut. I found a pension near where I was left off and got a room for 5 Lebanese pounds ($1.65) A trip to the post office produced 13 letters waiting for me. The clerk couldn't believe the pile.

After I had a chance to clean up and make myself presentable I went out in the evening and tried to look up some of Jerry Chierchio's friends. Marco was back in Italy but I met Aldo at the Excelsior Bar. He also knew Jerry. My last call of the night was at the Kit Kat Club owned by Rajah Marcodie. I met Rajah and conveyed the best wishes of Jerry and indicated that I had worked for him in Rome and inquired as to the possibility of finding some work here. He invited me in to the club and we sat down and had a drink as we talked about my trip and its intent. Next came the floor show after which the 4-piece band played music for dancing. He asked me to arrange with the musicians a couple of songs I might sing as an audition. When I approached the leader, Alberto Rey, he responded in a thick Italian accent by apologizing for his poor English. Thus, I had a chance to practice my Italian and it turned out that he and the group knew the Italian song I had learned along the way (*Amore scusami*). We were able to use the same arrangement as the one from which I learned and it came out quite well. One of my favorite songs that seemed to be known throughout the world was Tony Bennett's "I left my I Heart in San Francisco". Luckily I had also learned it in French, which was like a second language to most Lebanese. On the basis of these two I was signed up to perform at the club each night. As a costume I had Uncle Hughie's suit cleaned and pressed and I was good to go with a bow tie on which Rajah insisted. The deal also included dinner at the Colony Hotel also owned by Rajah.

Although I was busy each night at the club I had the days free and was able to visit many areas of Lebanon even though I didn't have my own transportation there. I had a joyous reunion with Harris and Broheim when they had a break from their classes. We hung out together and I ended the evening by taking them to their first cabaret show. They thought they were dreaming. I mentioned to Harris that I had to go shopping for some shoes in the bazaar. He pleaded with me not to go alone as I would be taken advantage of. So, we made a date and he gave me instructions to pretend that I was dumb (speechless). He arranged several hand signals we could use to communicate and we headed into the shopping area. I tried on several pairs of shoes that turned out to be not suitable. Finally I found some that were acceptable and he asked if they were OK. I gave him the signal that it depended on the price. He bargained for me and I bought them for about 60% of the original asking price. We then stopped for a drink and had some great laughs about the whole incident. (Note: I later referred to these shoes as my penance as they turned out to be too tight and I had to endure some pain every time I wore them. That'll teach me to pull a fast one on some poor shopkeeper in Beirut.)

Rajah was a shrewd businessman and he had a solid financial backing for whatever he wanted to pursue. On the first night I was at the club he invited me to accompany him to the Casino of Lebanon. It was the second largest casino in the world and I was overwhelmed by the plush surroundings and the big name stars who performed there. Many Lebanese viewed themselves as more European in their lifestyle and outlooks. Rajah liked to gamble at various tables. I just stood well behind him and marveled as he bet amounts, which would have lasted me 2-3 months in my low-budget travels. He also liked to bet on people. That is, he had identified several young entertainers who had some talent and promoted them through publicity, musical arrangements, costuming . . . etc. At the time I arrived he was doing the same for a young female singer from Dallas by the name of Vicky Lewis. She had been traveling with her guitar-playing boyfriend who, lucky for him, was included in her deal for support. She was part of the floorshow each night and Alberto Ray had made many arrangements for her songs. At one point Rajah asked me if I were interested in making singing a career. Although flattered, I let him know that I first intended to finish my world travels. He accepted that and was very helpful to me for the rest of my stay in Beirut.

My arrival in this "Paris of the East" coincided with the arrival of the USS Forrestal, aircraft carrier. There were 6500 US sailors around town and the Kit Kat put on an early show at 8:00 PM for the enlisted men who had to be back to the ship early. They made me the MC for this show and I sang a couple of numbers in it. I met a lot of homesick sailors who came to the club. I got a kick out of one of them who had fallen madly in love with our very curvaceous stripper. I didn't have the heart to tell him the *she* was really a *he*. During the daytime I met many sailors walking around town and spending lots of money on anything they could find. Of course, many spent sizeable sums on booze. Often this resulted in behavior that was not very impressive to the local population. I remember witnessing an incident in which a drunken sailor had been taken into custody by two S.P.'s. He was standing in front of the officer in charge and decided to "sucker punch" him in the stomach. He was quickly loaded into the back of a pick-up truck and taken away with four S.P.'s sitting on him for restraint. I thought that it was quite a shame that a young man might have totally messed up a good military record thanks to not being able to control the amount of alcohol he consumed. I was sure that he spent a few days in the brig.

One day when I was visiting around the town I re-met Joe and John, the young Americans who had been given a ride by the three English girls I helped at the Turkish border. They brought me up-to-date on the travel adventures of the girls. When they arrived at the Syrian border, the girls were tricked into showing the paper visas they had for Israel. Immediately they were denied entrance to Syria and any Arab country. Thus, they had to return to Turkey and take a boat to get to Israel without visiting any of the other mid-Eastern countries. I was told that, if a visitor came into Jordan and wanted to visit Israel, they could go through the Mandelbaum Gate only in the direction of Israel and not the reverse. Thus, they had to leave Israel by boat.

One of the acts at the Kit Kat Club was *Henri and Camelia*, two Egyptians who did a roller-skating act on the stage. Camelia was a young Moslem girl having a great time in the show business circuit. Henri was a Christian who felt the force of Gamel Abdul Naser, the dictatorial President of Egypt. Since he took over he kept telling the populace that Christians were black-hearted and greatly restricted any travel out of the country. Henri was able to leave only because he was a professional entertainer and had to return immediately after each engagement. He was trying anything to change his nationality. He had me check with the American embassy to see about the citizenship of a foreigner who married a citizen of the USA. He would pay a female citizen of the USA to marry him until he got a legal status. However, I was never aware that he was able to accomplish this.

We three socialized on several occasions and I got a real kick out of taking them to the Bristol Hotel, which had an ice rink in the lower level. I was amused to see these two struggle in their first attempts at ice skating when I watched their very professional roller skating act nightly at the Kit Kat Club. I was quite frustrated because the rink was small and round with too many people. Having been brought up near a lake in Wilmington I had acquired a facility on skates at an early age. As might be expected, both Henri and Camelia advanced quickly to decent levels of security on the blades.

After one of the shows at the Kit Kat I met a group of young Somalian students from the American University at Beirut. I was amused to find that I could practice my Italian with them because Somalia had been an Italian colony until 1960. They were intrigued by my travels and invited me to visit them in their dorm room at the university. We had long discussions about many international topics and they prepared a typical Somalian dish for lunch. It was a rice dish with a tomato-based sauce served in a large common dish put in the center of the table. Although they offered me a spoon, I insisted on following their eating custom of using their (well-washed) hands. The rice was gathered into the hand and formed into a small egg-shaped ball. Then it was swooped into the mouth with a deft movement of the thumb. It tasted great no matter how it was eaten.

As the conversation broached the subject of mankind and man's inability to get along with others, one of the students told a story about a teacher who had kept one of his students after school and wanted to keep him busy. He took a map of the world and tore it into several dozen pieces. He told the student he could go home when he had reconstructed the map. Thinking that it would take several hours, the teacher was amazed when the student finished the task in 20 minutes. He asked how it was possible to do so and the student took the map and turned it over to reveal a picture of a man. He replied that it was easier to deal with the problems of one man at a time. If each man could be made whole, then the world has to be right. I had certainly experienced this in my travels-to-date and I often regretted that we, as homo sapiens, had made such incredible technological advancements in the 20th century, but had not learned much about getting along together on the beautiful planet we occupy. It is within us to do so; we simply must make it a priority.

As the holidays approached the Century Club (upstairs) was also opened. The headliner there was a young returning native by the name of Maya Casabianca. She had made her name as a songstress in Europe and was welcomed home by huge, enthusiastic crowds. She sang in English, French and Arabic. Because Rajah owned both clubs I often sang in both on any given evening. On New Year's Eve (welcome 1966) both clubs were really jammed. One popular act, which joined us, was Pam and Billy McMahon from Queensland, Australia. They were a dancing duo with Billy doing solo tap numbers and a solo drum segment. He was quite short and energetic and reminded me of Mickey Rooney to whom I had often been compared. We got to be friendly and exchanged addresses for future encounters.

At Christmas I called my mother and it was $15.50 US for 3 minutes. Of course, I still had to book the call and wait for some time before the connection was made. As I chatted with her it hit me that I had called her last Christmas from Palma Mallorca, which is a flight of 3-4 hours from Beirut. I had taken a whole year to cover the distance. Thus, did my *eight-month* trip continually extend. Around this time I was getting my feet wet on occasion because when I left my rubbers at the door of the Colony Hotel during dinner, a doorman thought they were abandoned and threw them out to the street. I looked for them to no avail. Of course, some lucky local was now keeping his/her feet quite dry thanks to the loss of my world-traveled rubbers.

On January 23rd I ended my stay in Beirut and went to the club to say my final good-bys to all there. I noted that it was, somehow, easier to do so than in earlier times. However, there was one, which really got to me. Each night when we closed the club, three members of Alberto Rey's band would walk with me towards our separate lodgings. We would always stop at a small sandwich kiosk where we would have a bite to eat and share a bottle of wine. I noted that the old shopkeeper could be heard speaking 4-5 languages in a short period as he served his late-night entertainment customers from around the world. When finished we would continue to the corner and go our separate ways. On this last night Robi, the sentimental old man of the group, broke down in tears as he gave me a real *paisano embrazzo*. We had gotten to know each other quite well and I was particularly sad to leave him.

I had arranged for a ride to the Syrian border for $3.30 US and was relieved to find that my scooter was in good shape except that I had to push-start it because the batteries were low. I had resolved that I would not leave the scooter in such a situation again. Having not driven the scooter for 5 weeks I felt a bit awkward on it at first. I had taken the precaution to insure that my paperwork was acceptable to any border guard in the future.

My reunion with Harris' family was a joyous one with excited inquiries to find out what had happened to me since I left their home. I had brought some small souvenirs and some special candy to the delight of the many children of the clan. I found that there was the frequent rain that easily resulted in the rust-red mud, which got tracked everywhere. One day while heading for a friend's house we stopped at a small convenience store on the side of a dirt road. I bought some cigarettes (L and M) and Harris ordered something for us, which was contained in a large jar which looked much like a white lava lamp. This product was ladled out into small glass cups and was sipped until empty. As usual I was willing to partake of whatever was offered and soon realized that we were sipping a real basic version of yogurt. It was quite good.

On this same day I met Habibe, one of Harris' friends, who spoke English very well. When Harris had to return to the university in Beirut, Habibe invited me to visit his village of Srapion up in the nearby hills. On our way to the pick-up point we passed a scene which was quite intriguing to me. A number of the local women were gathered around a wood-fired oven, which looked like a small mud igloo with an opening on the side of the top. It was about 3.5 feet high and made of bricks and plaster of some kind. The women had formed a small production line to make authentic countryside bread. The balls of light-brown dough had been prepared ahead of time and one would start to flatten it. The next in line would continue the process until it was a large flat disc of about 12-15 inches. It was a single layer and was unleavened. The lady at the end of the line tended the oven and determined when the heat was right. She would then take a swish and dip it in water and spread it around the inside surface of the oven. She would then use her large hand to palm the disc of bread and slap it onto the inside surface of the oven. She timed it by experience for just a couple of minutes and then pealed the bread off and stacked it like so many oversized poker chips. This was the common bread that we all ate in that area with every meal. They would usually give me 3-4 discs to eat at a sitting. Most solid food was eaten with pieces of the bread torn off by hand and formed into a "U" shape in order to enclose the food from a common dish. Liquids were drunk from cups and things such as stew would be eaten with bread that had been formed into little cups. Sharing was always at the center of the local lifestyle.

Habibe and I soon met the 4-wheel drive landrover that was the only vehicle that could climb the rocky road to Srapion. This vehicle brought goods as well as passengers to the top of this local mountain. It was, indeed, a bumpy ride but worth the trip. We stayed at Habibe's uncle's house where I met another friend, Mohammed, who was the village comic. He was an ex-Army captain who had many stories to tell and kept everyone amused as we ate dinner sitting on floor mats.

I must note here that I was often asked about the many souvenirs I must have obtained while I was traveling. I had no use for the conventional items carried home by many tourists. I could not get excited about a camel saddle, which had been made in China or some other place far removed. However, there were certain personal items I was given which had true meaning to me because they represented a humanistic bond. As an example, when Habibe and I went out to visit the village the following morning we met many of his local friends all of whom invited us to visit them and allow them to show hospitality. Of course, we could not take all of them up on their offers. As we approached the village center Mohammed and some of his friends came from the intersecting pathway and we had a boisterous reunion. As we spoke I took out my L and M's and offered one to Mohammed who took it with a big smile. We both lit up and I threw the empty package on the side of the path, as the locals would do. Mohammed asked for a pardon as he admitted that he could not remember my name from the previous night. With that I picked up the L and M package, opened it and wrote my name in Arabic, which was the only word I had learned to write. As I passed it to him, he smiled again as he pronounced "Gerry" several times. He then carefully folded the pack and tucked it into his waistband for safekeeping. Not to be outdone, he then took the empty package of a local brand that he had and wrote "Mohammed" in Arabic for me. He passed it to me, I received it with respect and carefully tucked it into my pocket. *That is a souvenir* and I still have it to the day of this writing.

The following day we returned to Herisoon and went to the wake of a young boy who had been killed in an accident and buried several days before. The wake was in his father's house where only men were allowed into the main room. The women were separated into another room. As I was introduced by Habibe, we ended up in a long discussion mostly in French because the professional person there had learned French at some time in the past. They asked about Vietnam, Israel, prices and work in the USA and social security. I found them to be truly interested in life in other parts of the world.

I should note here that I had a great desire to retain a working knowledge of the languages I had used in my travels to date. I devised a daily routine that I would use almost every day that I was on the road. As I drove my NSU through the countryside of any land I would make myself recall all of the events of the prior day. Then I would recall them aloud in Spanish, French, Italian, German and (later) Japanese. My Greek and Arabic never got fluent enough to do this without a great amount of body language. I found that this linguistic exercise forced me to retain enough of each language so that I would feel somewhat comfortable when I had a need for it in the future.

On January 28th I headed for Damascus and was treated to tea by the guards at the military check-point. In Damascus I stayed at the youth hostel where I was able to exchange some travel info with those who had been where I was heading. This was certainly one of the great bonuses of staying at hostels. For example, I was tipped off to a restaurant called the Laterna where you could get a full course meal for 315 piasters (.83 US). I took advantage of this each day in Damascus. On one day I brought Henry and Camilia whom I had re-met at the club where they were performing. I also visited the Omayad Mosque where I viewed the tombs of Saladin and John the Baptist. This ancient city is filled with history.

During my 5 days here I re-met Habibe who was attending the university. I was a guest in his English class, which was taught by an American professor. Later that day he took a long time to relate to me a tragic tale which has to be considered in the context of their local customs. He had a girlfriend and he was first accused of flunking school because of her. He was forbidden to meet her. Later his father, uncle and other men of the village held a council against him accusing him of seducing this girl and other charges. His uncle wanted him to be executed. The girl's father arranged a marriage for her to another boy, in which she had no say or choice. Later, before the marriage, Habibe visited her village to find that she had committed suicide rather than go through with the undesired wedding. There were no local courts or law-enforcement agents involved in this matter. The village elders apparently had the power to decide such crucial life decisions. This was a bit of a "wake-up call" for me coming from a country where the law is primary and everyone is forbidden to take it into their own hands. Habibe also told me that there were many government detectives here and he was afraid to be seen with me for fear that he would get into trouble with those in power.

After leaving Habibe I headed for Jordan and found the land not as flat as I remembered Syria. I passed through Jerash and Jerasa where I stopped long enough to take some photos of the well-preserved 2nd century BC ruins. I continued on to the capital, Amman, which is small and nestled among several surrounding hills. I had decided to provide myself with an ouqual headscarf used commonly by local men. This would protect my fair skin from the brilliant sun of the roads ahead. Of course, making the purchase was a matter of bartering and I got it at a very reasonable price. Shortly thereafter I met a 21-year old Jordanian soldier named Samir. He had learned to speak English and was anxious to practice it with me. As we became acquainted, he insisted that I come to meet his family who were living in the poor section of the surrounding hills. He lived with his aunt, uncle and grandmother who was a true character. She always had a smile on her toothless face and had a heart of gold. She not only smoked but, cut tobacco and rolled her own cigarettes. I was also introduced to the neighbors including Ead with whom I had a big songfest with my guitar. Soon I had half of them singing "Lemon Tree". Samir's grandmother made a hit with all by doing "the twist" to one of my Elvis Presley's songs. These folks, including some Palestinian refugees, were truly hospitable in the most basic sense. Often in this type of situation my mind would race to evaluate the surroundings and the answer always was that I had met a group of people who had the same hopes, aspirations and dreams as most. When they met a stranger, they were not reluctant to express these same characteristics, which re-confirmed my trust in my fellow man.

When night came Samir and his family made a comfortable spot on mats for me on the kitchen floor. I had the novel experience of being kept awake for a while by the snoring of the chickens that shared the room with me. The following day, after breakfast with the family, we said our good-bys and I found the road leading to Jerusalem. I stopped to visit the Dead Sea, which is 1200 feet below sea level and noted the high salt concentration which allows almost anything to float in the water. From here I followed the Jordan River north to the spot where Christ was baptized by John the Baptist. At this spot I re-met a German boy who had driven a Mercedes car to the area. His

Jordanian friend, Maruk, was a businessman and invited me to use a vacated building in Jerusalem when I arrived there. I continued to Jericho, which is the oldest continually inhabited city in the world. It is quite tropical with dates, lemons and oranges growing in all directions. About 6 kilometers on the road to Jerusalem I got a flat tire that was a rare occurrence for me. After I mounted the spare I continued to Bethany where I ran out of gas—not a totally unusual day in the life of a traveler.

Ead, family and friends in Amman

I looked up Maruk at his Ritz Souvenir Shop and he gave me the keys to the building where I could stay. I thought this to be extraordinary trust to give the keys of his building to a total stranger—another lesson in trust. The building was used somewhat as a storage shed but had mats for my sleeping bag, a stove, a shower, a toilet and a radio. This was far beyond my daily expectations in this part of the world. I had just finished one of my films and I sent it for processing to Italy and used the Cairo American Express as the return address. In this manner I would be able to see the results of my camera's efforts periodically.

For the next six days I roamed the area where so much biblical history had taken place. I quickly realized that this was the holy city of the three major religions of the world: Judaism, Christianity and Islam. It was difficult to realize that I was actually present in many of the places referred to in our Bibles. One day I decided to follow the way of the cross (Via Dolorosa). Not

Jerusalem countryside much as Jesus saw it

all of the "stations" that we acknowledged in our churches were apparent. At one point I had to take a detour to go around an area, which had been totally renovated in the past 2000 years. The walls of the old city had been moved north putting the location of Calvary and the tomb within the current bounds of the city. The distance from the beginning to the end of the Way of the Cross seemed much shorter than is usually depicted. I was surprised to see that the Holy Sepulcher church contained both the split rock of Calvary and the reported tomb of Jesus. I was not totally convinced of the authenticity of these claims but it did not matter, as I knew I was wandering around the city where Jesus has passed some significant events in his life and was later crucified. The church was administered by five Christian sects and the many changes in this stewardship over the years had resulted in some strange architectural alterations.

Given that Jerusalem was at this time mostly located in Jordan, several of its gates facing west and south were fully sealed against transit to/from Israel. Slightly north of the city was the Mendalbaum Gate (located in Noman's Land), which was the only point at which anyone could cross to or from Israel. I was told that a person could only cross in one direction but not return. Thus, had I ventured into Israel, I would not have been allowed to visit any other Arab country. At this point I made a decision to by-pass Israel and continue within the Arab block.

In order to visit Bethlehem, which was in Jordan, I had to take a detour route to the southeast to skirt around the borders of Israel. Just before I arrived at Christ's birthplace I stopped to view and photograph a beautiful small church, the Church of the Shepherds, which had been erected by the Canadians in 1954. It was reportedly on the site of the caves where shepherds were tending their sheep when the angel appeared to them on that Holy Night. At first I found it locked and found out from a local shepherd that it would open in an hour. I asked if there was a coffee shop in the area to get some lunch and he ended up inviting me to eat with him. I was surprised to find out that he was an Arab Christian and that there were many in this area. I continued into Bethlehem and visited the church of the Nativity and the grotto within, the reported birth place of Jesus I observed that this church itself was unique in that apparently the only door through which one could enter was about four feet tall requiring everyone to lower themselves as they went through. I accepted this as a gesture of humility but it was never confirmed. The grotto was located beneath the main altar and only a limited number of visitors could enter it at a time given the small area involved.

On a beautiful February 10th I headed out of Jerusalem and stopped at Bethany to view the tomb of Lazarus. At the Dead Sea I tested the buoyancy of the water, which was 21 percent salt. It is 392 meters (more than 1,000 feet) below sea level and very hot. I waded in a bit and could feel the effect when I put my arm under the water. Luckily there was a fresh water shower available for use by any visitor. I met a Swedish couple there and we had a picnic on the beach together. I photographed the mountains to the south on the west bank of the sea where the Dead Sea Scrolls had been discovered in 1947. From the barrenness of the land it was easy to understand why that discovery had taken so long.

I continued on to Amman and re-met some friends who were excited that I had returned. I visited with Ead again and later stayed with his family overnight. I also saw Samir's family just before I broke a cable on the scooter. I asked my hosts if there was any kind of cycle shop around, as I was sure I could find some cable that I could modify to fit my scooter. One young man volunteered to show me where there was a cycle shop and he directed me there from the back seat. When we arrived at this "cycle" shop I was surprised and ecstatic to read the sign, which read "NSU Motor Scooter Distributorship". It was as if I had found gold in the desert. I not only bought the specific cable but an additional ignition key as a safeguard for the future. I noted that a new NSU scooter cost 160 dinars (about $460). With the help of Ead's brother, Mofat, I was able to repair the scooter and head for the desert.

(Note: When a Moslem man wishes to marry he must present 300-400 dinars ($800-1100) to the father of the bride as a dowry. In poor villages it is possible without payment but for the affluent it could be as high as $3,000. A Moslem man could have four wives but he would keep them in separate houses.)

# CHAPTER EIGHTEEN

## "Ahalem wa sahalem"

Heading south from Amman for the 210 mile trip to Aqaba, it became immediately apparent that there is not much to look forward to in regard to en route scenery. The land is flat and arid with very sparse vegetation. One consolation comes from the presence of the New Desert Highway, which is a well-paved, two-lane, hot-topped road. This was particularly significant in my case as I was riding a motor scooter, the small wheels of which do not readily lend themselves to ease of travel on anything but a hard surface. By this time I had put my cycle over most conceivable types of pavement and I was well acquainted with the performance limitations of this small combination of metal and rubber which had so faithfully carried me through many thousands of miles since I had left Ireland with it some 19 months prior. I grimaced when I thought of the work that would have been involved had I continued on the bicycle that the scooter had replaced after 1200 miles of peddling. At Na'ur, 15 kilometers (9 miles) from Amman, I turned onto the desert highway and headed directly south. It required only a few minutes of travel to make me aware that I had made a very wise investment in an Arabic headdress (ouqual) in the market place of Amman. So, I pulled to the side of the road and arranged the large cloth and double black cord, which is common attire for those who live in these surroundings. Several times thereafter, I had to stop again to make adjustments until I settled on a stable arrangement that would withstand the force of the wind as I traveled. Now, looking like a low-budget, modern day "Lawrence of Arabia", I started my assault on the open road leading to Aqaba.

Shortly after noon I stopped at one of the small villages, which all too infrequently dotted the path to the south. I was down to one liter of gas and decided that I'd better acquire some before chancing any more long vacant stretches of the highway. However, contrary to what I had read in a tourist pamphlet, gasoline was not readily available along my route, and specifically in this village. While explaining my plight to the owner of the small restaurant, I was informed that I would find no fuel until I came to El Hasa, another 50 kilometers down the road. Backtracking would be useless as I found out that there was no fuel for 124 kilometers (almost 80 miles) along that particular stretch. Eventually the shopkeeper agreed to sell me one liter of gas and the small amount of required oil from his own supply. As I had something to eat I pondered the possibility of reaching El Hasa with the two liters of fuel. I was getting 21 kilometers/liter for mileage and I couldn't think of any way to increase it. I remember a well-intended local teen-ager who tried to convince me that I surely had enough gas now with the other liter I had bought. When I had reviewed the mathematics of the situation with him, he still insisted that I could coast down hills, thus, decreasing my fuel consumption. Having already driven 117 kilometers on this road, I had great reservations regarding the number of hills I might be able to coast down. However, with no other alternatives presenting themselves, I decided to head out and hope that I might, somehow, have more fuel than the temperamental gauge indicated. I drove as economically as I could and, as suspected, found very few opportunities to save gas by coasting. The type of apprehension and suspense, which accompanied this part of the trip had been a factor with which I had learned to live in my world journey. Even now I can vividly recall passing over a railroad line and seeing a sign that indicated I had only 9 kilometers to go in order to squeak out of that predicament. Being a devout optimist, my spirits really took a plunge when the scooter coughed and came to a halt within 50 feet of the sign.

During the ensuing hours, as I pushed the scooter the 6.5 miles to El Hasa, I re-evaluated my opinion of these hills that were so small to coast down but so gigantic to push up. At least I did get a break on the downhill side. Somewhere along that part of the road I thought of the small amount of gas, which always remains in the float chamber of the carburetor. By using the primer knob I was able to get a ride for about a quarter of a mile. Having so much baggage added to the difficulty of pushing because I had to push from the side. Several vehicles passed by but, even if they had stopped, they probably couldn't have helped due to my need for a little oil to mix with any gas I might acquire. The sun beat down and I plodded on quite resigned to the fact that, if I were to continue my globetrotting, it would only be after I had expended the energy to get my "steed" to the next "water hole".

The attendant stood in wide-eyed disbelief as he filled the small tank. Somehow, he couldn't comprehend that I had covered the past 9 kilometers in the described manner. After having "tanked up" myself at the local restaurant, I headed on for the town of Ma'an where I intended to put up for the night. By this time it was dark and, at first, the cooler night air was a welcome change from the scorching heat of the day. However, as the miles passed it actually started to get too cold for comfort. When my speedometer told me that I was 34 kilometers short of my destination, I stopped to put on my bulky wool sweater, which, by this time, had earned a prominent place among my few treasured pieces of practical clothing. I had put down the kickstand and left the motor running as I went through the ritual of putting on the sweater and rearranging my headdress somewhere in the middle of the vast emptiness. When I had secured my saddlebags and turned to board the scooter, I found myself looking directly into the eyes of two Arab Bedouin tribesmen who faced me at a distance of about 10 feet. As could be expected, they were dressed completely in Arab desert garb with the addition of two curved knives and a pistol. I can remember theorizing about this kind of situation when we were telling scary stories as children. At this point in our daydreams, our first reaction would have been to jump on the scooter and "split". However, having traveled alone for over 19 months prior to this through many different kinds of personal trials, I was relatively shock proof. I simply looked up and said, *"Mudahuba, maza el hare. Shlounuk?"* (Hello, good evening. How are you?). They gave a similar friendly greeting and indicated that they thought I might have a problem. They had evidently heard the scooter motor running from their camp not far from the road, and they had investigated out of curiosity. When I told them that I had not stopped because of trouble but only to add some protection against the chilly air, they invited me to their living quarters to drink some hot tea and warm up. This offer was followed by a few minutes of small -talk as I mulled over in my mind the motives of these people who choose to lead such a different kind of existence. During those minutes, I decided that they quite obviously didn't have any evil designs on me or else they could have easily used their weapons and the element of surprise to subdue me long before this. So, I accepted their hospitality and pushed my scooter as we walked up the sand path to their little corner of the world. Often Bedouins live in tents but these people had two small wooden huts, indicating that they were probably from the upper middle class of the local society. We entered the smaller of the two structures and immediately one of the men started to make tea, as the other lit a gas vapor lamp.

The following two hours were spent drinking tea, smoking cigarettes., and discussing topics which ranged from the cost of guns and knives in the USA to the daily lives of the Bedouins. They had a few grazing animals which they had to move over a large area in order to find enough vegetation for them. They also had a few chickens. Bartering in Ma'an provided their other meager requirements. Living virtually alone in the desert, they had to police their own property and thus, the need for the show of weapons. They had to present the image of being able to take care of their belongings. Naturally the knives had very useful functions and I later noticed that the pistol didn't even have a clip in it. There probably wasn't a bullet within 100 miles of the place, but the firearm served its purpose well.

As time went on, one of the men decided to entertain and brought out a homemade musical instrument. The *robaba* is a small single-stringed instrument resembling a cello and is played with a bow. After this man had proudly displayed his talent, he allowed the other man to try it. Finally it was passed to me and I made a comical effort to handle the thing. Being one who can never pass up a jam session, I went out and got my guitar from its perch and brought it in to join the concert. Realizing that they would not understand any of the foreign languages in which I sing, I played songs with a variety of rhythms. I had not learned any Arabic songs, although I had managed to become somewhat conversant in the language during my prior three months in Arab countries. Soon I passed the guitar to my new friends and they didn't have a clue as to what to do with the other five strings. However, they were quite content to bang away and get this "wild different sound". Had I not trusted them, I might have suspected that their scrutiny of my instrument was in preparation to making six *robabas* out of it.

With time pressing in I excused myself, thanked them for their hospitality and prepared to leave. They asked me where I was heading and why, to which I replied that I was going into Ma'an where I would find a place to stay for the night. They wanted to know why I would go there when I was quite welcome to stay with them. They would not accept the idea that I would be a burden to them. With the realization that I might have some fears of staying there, they indicated that I would stay in that particular hut and they would sleep in the other one. They went into great detail to show me how the door could be bolted and locked on the inside making it quite secure (there were no windows). Not wanting to offend their gracious offer, I agreed at last and we settled down to chatting again.

Both of the men had about a week's growth of beard and one of them must have become a little self-conscious about it. Shortly he had his shaving equipment out and was preparing to use it. It consisted of a long-outmoded multi-piece razor and a small tube of brushless shaving cream. With the intention of introducing him to a little progress, I told him to wait a minute and I retrieved my shaving kit from my saddlebag. I told him to moisten his face as he normally would while I shook up my can of aerosol lather. This in itself prompted rather concerned glances from both men, but when I sprayed a large ball of the foam into the open hand, their eyes bulged in awe, as if having witnessed some type of magic. The smile and comments of the user confirmed the quality of the product. This encouraged me to finish off the job in high style wherein I produced my Old Spice after-shave lotion. Once he had applied it and smelled the resultant aroma, he perked up as though he was the "Sheik of the Desert". He would pretend not wanting to associate with the other bearded fellow and the sum total of the incident really tickled me.

All too soon the hour was late and they decided that we should all get some sleep. After reminding me of how to bolt the door, they wished me a good night and a pleasant sleep and then departed for the other building. I had already brought in my baggage. So, I went outside to answer a "call of nature" (that tea travels like a stampede). The room was furnished with a small table, two chairs and a cot with two blankets and a pillow, all of which had been used during our chat. I tucked in and shortly realized that my bunk-mate was the cat who snuggled in around my ankles. It didn't take long to fall asleep but during that interval I can remember reflecting how too often, and unjustly, we extrapolate the differences in culture and standard of living to include the humanistic out-looks of these whom we really don't understand. I was, at that time, a part or a direct contradiction to any such assumption. I distinctly remember being awed by the scenario of Gerry Rooney from Wilmington, Massachusetts, USA being the honored guest of newfound friends of a very different culture who were so willing to share their meager possessions with a total stranger. It made a profound impression on me.

Upon waking the following morning, I was surprised not to hear a sound from without and this became quite noticeable as I lay there for about ten minutes. I assumed that they must sleep late. When I finally arose and opened the door, I found my hosts sitting beside the door on the ground waiting very patiently, not wanting to disturb me. As soon as I presented myself, they jumped up with ear-to-ear grins and greeted me. It was then that I learned, for the first time, that one man had two children. They were playing near the other hut but there was no evidence of a mother. This could have been due to the presence of a foreigner. Immediately one man started preparing breakfast, as I got ready to shave. I was completely accustomed to shaving with cold water by this time, as I had been doing so for many months. However, they, somehow, knew that this was not customary in the West and they insisted on heating water for me, my pleas of this not being necessary notwithstanding. When I had finished, I allowed the other man to keep up with the Abduls by shaving with my gear also. When all was ready we sat down to an amazing breakfast of fried eggs, bread, tea and olives. This was a better meal than I had provided for myself on most mornings. Knowing their resources and their level of day-to-day living, I'm sure they sacrificed a large percent of their weekly food budget to provide this fine meal.

As I was packing my bags, I tried to think of what I might leave with them as a small token of my appreciation. I had noticed the night before that the string of the *robaba* was a piece of common wire, so I took out one of the extra strings which I carried in my guitar case and presented it to the musician. He was truly delighted and now probably has the "Stradivarius" of *robabas* in the area. As I loaded the scooter I overheard them talking and one of them was going into the town through which I would pass. Usually they try to hitch a ride on the top of a delivery truck going to Aqaba. I told him that he was quite welcome to ride the second seat of my scooter if he didn't mind holding onto my guitar, which normally occupied the bulk of that space. He declined saying that it would be too much of a bother for me, but I insisted on being allowed to do something to repay them. So, when I had the other baggage rearranged, I put him on the back seat holding my huge guitar case across his lap. With him in his Arab garb and me with my headdress, we started the 21-mile trip to Ma'an. For me the feature of this dual trip was the shocked expressions of the other Bedouins we passed along the highway. They seemingly couldn't tell whether we were two nutty foreigners or two locals who had flipped their lids. My travel mate was very quiet throughout the ride and only answered a nervous, "*Aiwa* (Yes)", to my inquiries regarding his well being. I suspect that he had never been on a two-wheeled motorized vehicle. In Ma'an he got off at a gas station where I tanked up. He thanked me profusely (I think he was more thankful to get off), wished me a good journey, invoked Allah's blessings upon me and disappeared down the narrow winding streets of the town.

As I continued my southern sojourn, my mind pulsated with an abundance of thoughts concerning my most recent experience. Up to that time I had repeatedly reaffirmed the universality of humanity and now I had just completed, what was probably, the most poignant example I would come across. What most people would have in their minds, at the point when I faced these two Bedouin tribesmen for the first time on the lonely desert highway, would have certainly been a gross misapprehension. All too often, when we try to picture people on this level of world society, we can not get beyond the image of a treacherous-looking Arab climbing into a hotel window with a knife in his teeth. From our ultra-sterilized sphere we tend to look down upon these "semi-primitive savages" without a willingness to try to understand them and their motives so that we can judge them in relation to their own standards. I believe that, all too often, we fail to realize that had we been brought up in the same surroundings with the same economic conditions dictating the common ways of doing things, we would conduct our lives in much the same manner as these whom we are too willing to degrade because they do not live up to our accepted norms of sanitation and cleanliness. Somehow, our sense of values equates education and progress with worthiness. These newfound friends had just proven their worth in a way that gave me the insight to look within their motivations. Through them, and many others I had met in that area of the world, I realized that a good part of their outlook towards others, especially strangers, comes from the Koran, the holy book of their Moslem religion. Their charity and consideration was real and much more impressive because it came from their need rather than abundance.

The double Arabic welcome, *Ahalem wa Sahalem*, could hardly relate to the Western mind the sincerity and intention behind it. From this point in my journey, I traveled with a renewed faith in people. I was to encounter others who would teach me much about humanity although they had never even had the start of a formal education. Sometimes the most significant lessons can come from the least suspected sources. All that is required of us in order to receive the wisdom of these unschooled humanitarians is to have enough tolerance to extend to them the courtesy and consideration they warrant by virtue of their existence as truly valued human beings.

# CHAPTER NINETEEN

## The "Pilot"

Another 25 miles of travel brought me to one of the great wonders of my entire journey. I had heard about Petra and was anxious to visit and view this city the buildings of which were carved out of the solid red sandstone of the mountains in the 4th century B.C. It had been occupied by the Edomites but fully developed by the Nabateens over a period of 500 years. It was a natural center of commerce in that it was surrounded by the mountains, had plenty of water and was the center of major trade routes of the time. Having invented the camel saddle the Nabateens were known as fierce fighters while mounted. Petra was quite isolated at the time I visited but the people were quite hospitable and friendly. Being late, for a small fee I stayed overnight in the police station of the village of Wadi Musa near the entrance to the valley.

The following day I visited the local convenience shop where I had some breakfast and talked at length with the two men who ran it. I was surprised that they were both from India. They indicated that India was so over-populated that their fellow countrymen often had to go far from home to make a decent living. Then, with my *ouqual* headress in place, I walked the 3.5 kilometers to arrive at the ancient city. This meant a stroll through the Siq, a narrow and steep cut in the rock, which led into the valley of the city. Most tourists ride into the city on horseback, but I opted to get the exercise and save the fee. As I walked I became aware of the carved water conduit on the side of the sheer wall several feet from the ground. In this manner the inhabitants obtained their steady supply of water from outside. The first view that you see as you emerge from the Siq is the beautiful Treasury building (*khazneh*). The architecture and craftsmanship were fantastic. I could not imagine an attempt at duplicating this beautiful edifice with our modern technology and tools. I could only speculate as to the resources on hand in the 4th century B.C. I spent the next several hours walking through the enormous development in which the carved structures varied from the exquisite Treasury building to rough-cut caves, which had been dwellings for the common people. I was told that some of the local poor people still live in those caves. I climbed to the top of one of the local peaks where the altar of sacrifice was located. From this point I photographed the valley below including the 3000- seat theater, which, likewise, had been carved out of the mountain.

Famous entrance (Siq) to Petra          Exquisite workmanship
                                        from 4th century B.C.

Significant buildings were widely separated and I took my time in arriving at the most beautiful one of all, *El Deir* (the monastery). As I approached I noticed that there were several men standing outside near the entrance and there was a small group of people apparently getting a tour inside the building. One of the men outside seemed quite casual with an open collar and rolled up sleeves. The others all seemed to be wearing military uniforms. As I got closer my suspicions were confirmed. The casual man noticed my camera, which I always had at the ready and asked if I wanted to take a photo. When

I answered in the affirmative he accommodated by posing about 15 feet away for my picture. Thus, did I record a prized photo of King Hussein of Jordan. I found out that the group he was waiting for included Prince Juan Carlos of Spain and his wife, Princess Sophia of Greece. He had flown them to Petra in his own helicopter. This confirmed my impressions of him as a very capable, modern leader. He also flew jet aircraft and drove racing cars.

Relaxed King Hussein and guests

I continued my tour of Petra and left to head for Aqaba about 75 miles further south. I arrived late and ended up sleeping on the beach like most of the low-budget travelers. The sand had been marked out with streets, lots . . . etc. Being that we were on the edge of the Red Sea the climate was great. From this point we could see four countries; Jordan, Israel, Egypt and Saudi Arabia. My plan had been to try to find a ship I could work on from here to Egypt but it turned out that there were very few going that way and without an Egyptian visa I would have trouble getting this break.

I did look up Haron El-Khatib whose friend, Hassan, in Petra had told me to meet him. Haron spoke very good English and ran Nasser Stores, a small variety store with practical merchandise. We had long talks due to his having worked for the film company that made "Lawrence of Arabia" in that locale some years before. He was in charge of signing up locals who would work as extras on the film. That night I stayed in Haron's room after having dinner with him and his father. The following day I checked on ships again with no luck. I did notice an extraordinary interest in my scooter in this area. I had, at least, ten offers to buy it. Of course it was out of the question. On this day I met Andy and Peg Creswell who were missionaries in this area and they invited me to lunch. Lunch included the use of their shower, which they rightly suspected I could well take advantage of. We had a long talk about this area and the situation of the world in general. As a parting gesture they gave me a small "New Testament" to keep me company on the rest of my journey.

On February 17th I checked for ships including at the office of the friendly Assistant Customs Chief who spoke German. He could not be optimistic for my chances so I left for Amman just after noon. Through some light rain I arrived in Amman at 11:30 PM and took a room for the night. The following day I left for Damascus and arrived there after 6 hours. My visa cost $2.00 plus $1.50 for the scooter with no problems. I checked into the same hostel as before and went to visit Henri and Camelia who had entertained at the Kit Kat Club in Beirut with me. They were surprised and happy to see me and we had a great re-union.

The following day I raced to Beirut to get to the Egyptian Embassy for my visa but it was closed. I dropped in on Roby and Cisco from the band and had dinner with them. I later checked into the same pension and visited other friends. I left my passport at the Egyptian Embassy and checked for ships going to Egypt. There was only one Russian ship going but I could not work for them. I re-visited the Colony Hotel and spent time with several friends from the Kit Kat Club. Finally on February 22, with 4 hours sleep, I started the frustrating process of booking the scooter and myself on the ship (the Syria) to Egypt. My ticket was $16.80 but the scooter had to be sent as cargo because I didn't have a Trip-tik. It cost $14.30 and was loaded onto the fore deck among about 35 horses, which would make the crossing. During the 27-hour journey I met the 3rd Officer, Amir, who let me sleep in his cabin. I also ate at the officers' mess.

# CHAPTER TWENTY

## Lure of the Nile

When the ship docked in Alexandria all the passengers left immediately. I had to wait for my scooter which would only be taken off after the 35 horses. It was a long process as one-at-a-time the horses were loaded into a small portable stall and then the crane would lift it and bring it down on the dock. Finally at 7:30 PM (after several hours) all of the horses were off and I anticipated the scooter would finally be next. I was dismayed when the workers started leaving the ship and turning out the lights. I rushed down to the agent screaming that they had to take off the scooter. Finally they did but indicated that the office for processing was now closed and I'd have to leave the scooter there. They would put it into a nearby shed and the worker insisted on driving it there (about 50 feet). I then had to gather up all my belongings and carry them to the customs area where I went through with no problem. It seemed like every other person (young and old) wanted to help me carry my things for *baksheesh* (a handout). Then I had to take a taxi to Amir's house where he and his family were waiting for me. We had dinner and his mother couldn't believe that I had been traveling as I did for so long. She got a real kick out of my primitive use of Arabic. She said she felt like I was one of her own sons. Of course I took close note of her very pretty daughters, Samia and Sauzan. Only later did I learn that Amir was one of 17 children. I checked into the local Youth Hostel and got a bit organized.

The following day I spent four hours walking around in a futile effort to retrieve my scooter. I was told that I would have to leave a deposit of 35 Egyptian pounds against selling it in the country. And I would have to wait until Saturday. In lieu of this I went to the American Consul and got an "Oath" signed by the consul that I would take the scooter out of the country when

I left. With this document after I spent 5 more hours at the dock paying 3 pounds for customs and 5 pounds for a "clearing agency" I was able to take the scooter. However, the key that they insisted on using could not be found. I was ripping mad and let everyone within earshot know how disgusted I was with the bureaucracy and cons. So, after I attached the two full-sized auto license plates to the scooter, I pushed it out of the gate mumbling all the way for effect knowing that luck had provided me with another key, which I had bought in Aman when I found the NSU dealership. Once outside the gate and out of view I found the key in my shoulder bag and started the scooter. I was quite relieved to have my own independent transportation again.

I noted that President Gamal Abdul Nasser was the first real Egyptian leader of his country in 800 years. He was very dedicated to progress but was trying to do things in too big a hurry. His was a very strict rule. Egyptians were not allowed to travel to any other country as tourists as this would take Egyptian money out of the country. Tax on imported items was as much as 260%. A roll of film that normally cost me $4.85 cost about $13 there. Quality items were scarce and expensive. The Christian population had decreased markedly due to Nassers assertion that any true Egyptian would be Moslem. Thus, I well understood my Christian friend, Henri, from the Kit Kat Club wanting to leave Egypt as soon as he could. Also locals were warned against mixing with foreigners which resulted in some of my new friends keeping their distance any time we were in public. I also noted that the daily dress for the common people was what looked like pajamas to me. They could be seen on most of the 12-15 young people hanging onto the outside of any bus that passed by. In several allies in any big city could be seen riot squads of police at the ready should anyone act out against the strict rule of Pres. Nasser. As I traveled the countryside I saw many warning signs at significant locations which prohibited photos including any bridges. Foreigners who stayed in the city for more than 2 days had to register with the police. I did not find this unusual for Egypt but it made me question again why I had to do the same in Sweden. One thing that I witnessed was that incoming mail was often opened by the postal employees and later forwarded with a note. This happened to me. I guess any foreigner was under suspicion.

I finally set off for Cairo through beautiful flat land of the Nile delta. It was obviously fertile and I noted that much of it was irrigated by ox-driven water wheels. When I arrived in the capital I looked up one of Henri's friends, Joseph Homesey, another Christian and later checked into the local Youth Hostel. From there it was only a 10-kilometer drive to view the grandeur of the Pyramids at Giza. I spent the earlier part of the day walking the area

Rich land along the Nile River

and taking photos. The two largest pyramids are those of Cheops (481 feet) and Cepheren (471 feet). Originally they had an alabaster coating but only a small amount that remained. The Sphinx was even larger than I had pictured it. I remained for the *"Son et lumiere"* (sound and light) show which cost 50 piasters. (Note: $1 = 42.5 piasters.) I found it hard to realize that I was sitting in an outdoor theater listening to the related stories of the Pyramids and the Pharaohs while looking at these same marvelous structures, which were progressively lighted as the story involved that particular area. It was portrayed that the laborers who provided the muscle to build the Pyramids did so from inspiration and commitment. It made me wonder why the normal depiction of the process involved so many whips. In all, the spectacle was unbelievable with the continuation of the beautiful weather.

The following day I (and others) had to move to another Youth Hostel that turned out to be a two-story boat tied up on the banks of the Nile. It was quite unique and was enjoyed by many of the international group, which usually is on hand. In the evening we could enjoy the night skyline of the tall buildings of Cairo from the upper deck. That night I went to church at a Greek Catholic Church and was surprised to have to enter by the back door. It was a nice church but the number of faithful had been decreasing steadily. I remet Joseph Homesey and his family with whom I had supper at their home. They spoke at length about how things had changed in Egypt especially for Christians. Many of their relatives (including father and mother) had already emigrated to Australia. They gave me their addresses and asked me to look them up if I ever got near them.

It quickly became apparent that it was not difficult to get a driver's license in Egypt. Most drivers didn't have a clue about basic rules of the road. As well, the pedestrians were not familiar with the idea that the roads were made for auto traffic and they should look before entering them. The result was a challenge to both with the drivers using their horns continually and the pedestrians not paying any attention to them. I noted this as I headed out of the city heading south for Luxor. Suburban driving was much more pleasant as I drove along the Nile Canal. The river was beyond the narrow strip of land on the other side of the canal. I had gone about 100 kilometers (66 miles) when the car in front of me without warning took a right turn and cut me off. I could not stop in time and contacted the rear bumper of the car that flipped the scooter over breaking the windshield and jamming my left hand under the handle bar. It turned out that the hand was OK but the windshield was broken diagonally in two large pieces. The driver looked into the rear view mirror and saw me standing straddling the scooter. I obviously was not dead so he continued on his way south. I then had to push the scooter into a nearby village and try to find some way to repair it. I was eventually led to the village blacksmith, a large man with a primitive shop. After looking it over he said he would put two steel plates across the tops and bottoms of the pieces and drill through to bolt them together. I questioned as to whether, or not, that would be strong enough. He assured me that it would be and proceeded to bring out the material. The "steel" plate was like a piece of tin from a can. I protested that it was not strong enough with him disagreeing. Finally I had to "pull rank" and let him know that I was a graduate engineer and I had a different method of doing it. I suggested that we overlap the two large pieces and drill directly through them to attach the screws, washers and nuts. Finally he agreed that it was a better idea. I paid him 75 piasters during which time I let the surrounding crowd know what I thought of their drivers.

Back on the road to Luxor it was now quite dark and there was no light given that the road was across the canal from all of the settlements. I was only about 6 kilometers before Manfalut when I came across four men standing behind their car trying to flag down another vehicle. None would stop but flew by quickly. When I got to that point I stopped to see if I could help. The leader of the men (driver) indicated that their only problem was that they had run out of gas. I had some gas in the gallon can I kept with me since I ran out in the desert. I told the man that he was welcome to the quart or so that was there but cautioned that it had a small amount of oil in it, which was necessary for my 2-stroke engine. At first he looked at the can in thought and then took a swig of it. I guess he determined that it was okay for him and, therefore, must be okay for his car. He put it in, got the car started and asked me to follow him into the village over the canal bridge. We arrived at the local gas station where he insisted on filling up the entire gallon with gas-oil mixture and sent a young boy for tea for all of us to drink. As we had our tea inside with others he loudly lectured those present regarding his plight. I could not understand all of the Arabic but what I could make out was his disgust with his fellow Egyptians who passed him by when this lone foreigner had stopped to help him out. I thought "One vote against the ugly American". They had determined that it was too late for me to continue on and so we ended up having a song session with the guitar in the middle of the town square. Later I was introduced to Mohamed and Hussein, two Red Cross attendants, with whom I stayed overnight in their station dormitory.

After breakfast the next day I left with a promise to visit again on my way back from Luxor. I took a photo of the lush green Nile valley and crossed to the eastern side at Nag Hamadi where 150 kilometers of dusty unpaved road started. This slowed me greatly as it was rather treacherous for the small wheels of the scooter. I was still driving through this when I had to stop at night in a village to get directions. I seemed to attract all the village children and it took me a while to find which road to take to leave. As I left the children decided that I would be a good target for their rock-throwing practice. Thus, I found out what it was like to be stoned out of a town. Luckily the stones were small enough not to hurt or damage very much. Finally I arrived in Luxor dirty and in a bad mood due to the abundant flies. I checked into the Youth Hostel and tried to clean up and get some sleep. A man I met wanted me to work in a movie for 2 Egyptian pounds (less than $5) the following day. When I found out that it was for the whole day I told him to forget it. I was at a loss as to how the locals put up with the abundant flies that seemed to be everywhere. I learned to pull up a hand full of long weeds and to use them like a swish around my face to keep the flies away. Local hawkers would sell small bundles of these stems tied with colored string to the tourists who frequented the area.

The next day was March 9th and I visited Karnak Temple which is the site of the ancient city of Thebes. The main temple is that of Amon with 134 columns. Outside lay an obelisk which had never been entirely finished. It was about 5 feet square and about 50-60 feet long. I marveled when I learned that the stone from which it was being made was not to be found in the area for many miles. I strained my engineering schooling to understand how this piece of rock could have been brought to this site given that it had to weigh hundreds of tons. The quest for that knowledge was matched only by that which would explain how these massive columns had been raised to their vertical positions. I recorded in my mind a congratulatory greeting to those who were able to accomplish such incredible feats in those days without our modern machines and technology.

I put the scooter on a small ferry and crossed to the west side of the Nile where lies the Valley of the Kings. After the considerable drive to these historic sites I learned that the tickets for entry had to be purchased at the dock. With that I decided that I didn't really have to see the inside. Upon my return to the dock I found that I was quite thirsty and parked my scooter to look for a source of some drink. The only place I could find was a local cafe located under a tent-like structure at the side of the road. It had rough benches that were about half full of working-class Egyptians. To their surprise I entered and sat down and ordered a juice drink, which came in a bottle. It did not satisfy my deep thirst so I asked if there was any water. The young waiter went to a large open vat and scooped some water into a well-used oilcan and brought it to me. I surmised that it was the "community can" and had long since been relieved of any oil traces. Certainly there was no taste of anything in particular as I drank the contents of the can. Being an obvious foreigner I often attracted attention when I joined any local group for whatever reason. I found that one way of making people feel at ease was to perform one of many humanistic gestures, which assured the others that you are a person much like them in basic ways. These would include burping, yawning, stretching, coughing, scratching and hiccupping. The reactions I got from any of these showed a lowering of nervousness if it had been present.

Back in Luxor I had lubricated the scooter and left by train for my journey to Aswan where I would view the progress in the building of the great dam that would create Lake Nasser. The train left 1.5 hours late but I had plenty of time. As usual I rode in 3rd class with the common people where I found rubble on the floor, abundant flies, dirty and sweaty people, nursing mothers and tea vendors. The seats were wooden benches and the windows, which had no glass were permanently open. It was a 4.5-hour trip and cost 85 piasters ($2.00).

Once in Aswan I inquired at the office of the dam project regarding an opportunity to see the dam work in progress. I was told that there would be tours conducted for tourists in the afternoon that would have meant my waiting several hours. When I pressed the point I was informed that I could go out on the workers' train if I didn't mind the conditions. I caught it just 30 minutes later and was amused by the workers who were taking a rest on the way to work. One way in which this was accomplished was to sleep in the overhead luggage racks. They were easy-going and quite friendly. Of course I was sitting there wearing my *ouqual* headdress, which is not commonly used in Egypt. The 10-kilometer trip took just 30 minutes.

When we arrived at the site of the dam I followed the crowd to the dusty location in which I found a huge number of laborers and vehicles. I saw the many Russian trucks that were being used and remembered that the USSR had out-maneuvered the USA in lending its expertise to the project. The irony was that I was told that the Russians did not provide spare parts. Thus, these Soviet machines were roving all over the worksite with General Motors parts in them.

I walked around as though I was an inspector from a foreign country with my shoulder bag containing my valuables. There were many police at this location but most had to do with directing the constant flow of traffic of the many huge construction vehicles. Any time I noticed one of them looking at me suspiciously, I would use an old adage, "The best defense is a good offense." So I would directly approach the officer and after greeting him I would ask if he knew where I might find some water. Immediately he became my buddy and anxiously directed me to the nearest source of drinking water. I thanked him in Arabic and asked Allah to be with him. Having satisfied his curiosity I then went about checking out the ongoing construction which included the power plant that was about 80% complete

I noted at this time that a Moslem man could have four wives and often did. This results in too many children to raise and the chances of any of them getting educated is slim. Thus, there was a consistent lack of development within the general population.

I later returned to the workers' train and road it back to Aswam. During that journey we had to pull to a sidetrack to allow another train to pass. We stopped adjacent to a sugar cane car and my fellow passengers pulled many stalks of sugar cane into our car to take advantage of the sweet liquid trapped therein. They would break off a section of cane and use their teeth to strip back the tough outer shell. When the inner pulp was exposed they would bite off a mouth full and chew it to wring out the juice. The remaining wad of pulp was then spit out on the floor. They offered me a section of the cane and watched to see what I would do with it. I just followed their lead and was soon munching and spitting with the best of them. Needless to say, the rail car was quite a mess by the time we returned to Aswan.

The following day I started to make my way back to the north. At the end of 150 kilometers of bad road I found that I had a flat tire. Once I repaired it, I continued to Manfalut where I remet my Red Cross friends, Mohammed and Hussein. They gave me an enthusiastic greeting and wanted to know all about my journey to the great dam. We passed the night drinking tea and talking about all manner of things. In the process I exchanged small photos with Hussein.

The next day I departed with some sorrow after having breakfast with my hosts. Then I continued back to Cairo along the Nile canal road. The trip was 674 kilometers and required 26 liters of gas. This amounted to almost 60 miles per gallon, which was not really great for the scooter. Then I remembered the many miles of "bull dust" roads where I had to cruise slowly in first gear. Here I noted that the local taxi was a model T Ford. It ran the north-south route along the same road and passengers would flag it down to hop aboard for the part of the trip that interested them. I returned to the boat hostel on the Nile and remet some of the other visitors. I remember speaking to one of them who was Japanese. I was asking about the Japanese language and he told me that the pronunciation was not difficult especially if a person spoke any of the Latin languages. This was due to the fact that the vowels were always pronounced in a consistent manner unlike the variations we use in English. Later I was to find that this was quite true.

Model T Ford taxi

During the next few days I did some repair/tune-up work on the scooter and gave it a well-needed cleaning after my trip to the south. I attended church again at the Greek church and was invited to dinner by Joseph and Rosa. Paula and "Zuzu" were also present. When I recounted the details of my trip to Aswam Joseph was aghast that I had stopped at all in Manfalut which is known for thieves and robbers. I stated that I had treated those residents with respect and kindness and they had done the same to me. They were still shaking their heads. They couldn't believe that I would travel without plans and a specific schedule.

It was now March 15th and I took the desert road to the east leading to Suez. There I found the Canal, which was like a strung-out swimming pool with clear blue water. I followed the Canal to Port Said on the northern end where I stopped for gas and met Mohammed who couldn't believe I was an American traveling as I did. My hope was that I would be able to find work on a ship which would be headed somewhere to the east along a path that I would find acceptable. I checked with the US Consul and various travel agencies to find out that I could not work on US ships due to the unions. Later I found this to be true of ships from Great Britain, Australia, Japan, Germany and others. The best bet was any ship from the Scandinavian countries.

Suez Canal—like a swimming pool

I found a bed at the local Youth Hostel and set about making plans to leave Egypt. Daily I would check for ships at the Canal Authority to find out their flag, destination and arrival date. As I visited around Port Said I found it quite modern and quiet. At the hostel I met Norio Tokumitsu and Shiro Kanda, two Japanese youngsters who were traveling and we exchanged addresses. As well, there were two groups of female students from Cairo. One was from a high school where they were primarily learning English and the other learning French. I was called upon at all times to help them practice their language skills. It was good practice for me as well, especially the French.

The most interesting person I met at the hostel was another Japanese boy, Hiroshi Nishida. He was a college student at Kei Hospital University in Tokyo and he had been working his summer break at a youth hostel in Germany. He was traveling with an Austrian friend who spoke only German. Thus, when we three went out on the town to eat in the evening we spoke mostly in German. This seemed to surprise many of those nearby. Hiroshi spoke English and German quite well and certainly better than my level. I could never guess at this point the life-long relationship that would develop between us in the years to come.

# CHAPTER TWENTY-ONE

## "Down under"

Finally after many days of checking I was accepted to work on the MS Tudor, a Norwegian ship from the Wilhelmsen line. This ship was to make a short stop in Aden (Yemen) and then go directly across the Indian Ocean to Freemantle, the port city of Perth, Australia. I had hoped to see parts of the Indian sub-continent but it did not look promising after a week of waiting. So, I decided that I would make this major leap in geography while I had the chance. I had spoken to the captain and explained my goals and reasons for my travel having finished my 5 years in the US Air Force. He later told me that, had I tried to pass myself off as a struggling student, he would not have taken me aboard. That line had been overused by too many in the past. I needed an Australian visa, which I had obtained in Cairo and I had to sign a release form to hold the company harmless for any accident or injury I might sustain. So, on March 26th we left port and headed through the Suez Canal. I had been assigned to a cabin, which was really a luxury for me. My scooter had been hoisted aboard using a special rope configuration that left it in an upright position. The bosun showed me how to do this and I was to use it many times in the future.

The meals were balanced and plentiful. We had self-service for snacks at any time. I appreciated the meals although many of the other crewmembers made a habit of complaining about them. Unfortunately for them they had to listen to a series of lectures from me regarding the food limitations on many of my newfound friends in the Arab world. I well remember in my own reflections having a feeling of "running out" on those I had gotten to know in these Arab countries where I had spent the prior four and a half months. Their daily lives were so markedly different from my own and I could truly appreciate what I had back home.

The mixed crew of the MS Tudor

The MS Tudor was a freighter with 14 first-class passengers aboard. Most of them were from countries in Europe and were immigrating to Australia. One family had immigrated years back from England and were returning from a visit back home. The crew consisted of 24 seamen and 5 officers. The crew included 3 from Spain, 1 from Portugal, 1 from Greece, 1 Australian and many Norwegians. The cook was Chinese and the bosun was Norwegian. I was referred to as a "work-away", not paid but working for my passage to include the scooter. (Note: The term seaman is a misnomer; the crew are laborers who work on a ship. Most of them would get lost in a bath tub with rubber dinghy.) The cargo was wire, paper and cars. The ship was 450' long and it displaced 10,000 tons. The engines ran on SAE 95 oil and could run for 23 days with a full load of 800 tons. Diesel fuel was used in the ports for better maneuverability. As always my guitar was my best introduction to anyone. When there were parties on the ship for officers and passengers or for the crew I was invited to all of them provided I brought the guitar.

Our daily schedule was: up at 6:00 AM, coffee at 6:30, work from 7-8, breakfast 8-8:30, work 8:30-12 noon, lunch 12-1, work 1-3, coffee 3-3:30, work 3:30-5, wash up 5-5:30, supper 5:30 PM and then free for the night. The next day was Sunday so we had a break from work.

One evening as we traversed the canal I went up on deck to view the shoreline. As expected, the water was very calm and the passage quite enjoyable. I happened to meet the canal pilot who boarded the ship in Port Said and would leave it at the southern end at Suez. I greeted him in Arabic and he immediately wanted to know where I was from; Jordan? Syria? Lebanon? For my answer in each case I responded in the mid-east manner of "no" by nodding my head upward and giving a slight clicking sound with my mouth while half closing the eyes. I finally told him I was from the USA, which he wouldn't believe. I showed him my passport as we switched to English that he spoke very well. He said I might have a USA passport but I was not American based in his many years of seeing foreigners come through the canal. After a bit of small talk he finally realized where I was from and why I was reluctant to tell him. I was Jewish from Israel. I thought of the astonishment my mother would have felt if her Scottish son with the name of Gerald Patrick Rooney had been mistaken for being Jewish. She was put out enough when people mistook me for being Irish.

Our daily routine had mostly to do with scraping and painting the ship. On our way to Australia we would paint the entire external surface of the ship. Once in the Red Sea the sea became quite choppy which didn't help the stomach upset I still had from Port Said. One night I was given permission to visit the Captain on the bridge. With my Air Force background I was naturally interested in the navigation across the ocean. I noted the presence of a radar unit, which the Captain said was not working very well. Of course it was usually used only near the shoreline. I asked if he had the maintenance manual for it, which he did. I told him that when I had some free time I would check it over in the same manner we had to do in-flight maintenance in the B-52, if it was okay with him. He immediately said I could work on it any time I wished regardless of the work schedule. The next day I borrowed some tools from the bosun and opened up the radar unit. I went through several procedures to tune up the unit including tuning the crystals. The result was not as I would have liked it for flying but it was markedly better and the Captain was overjoyed. Note: This was to bode well for the letter of recommendation he would give me as I left the ship.

On my mother's birthday, March 31, we arrived in Aden (Yemen), which was a British Protectorate at the time. The ship could not tie up at the small dock so small launches ferried people to the immigration dock and back. Of those on the ship the officers, the passengers and I were allowed to go ashore. The seamen would have to stay aboard. Aden was a duty-free port so most of those going ashore wanted to do some shopping. As we walked away from the dockside it was obvious that there was significant unrest here as British soldiers patrolled the streets as if on jungle watch. I stayed with a couple of the young male immigrants as we visited several shops. The only shopping I was interested in was to buy a hat to protect my head form the sun (my old one had blown overboard within the first few days at sea). We had been told that the motor launch would return to the ship at 6:30 PM and 9:00 PM. The English family was visiting military friends in the English quarter and they were the only ones with me who were to take the later launch. So, after dark I wandered down the main street, which was like in England but had high prices. I noted that a haircut was 6 shillings. I cut through the alleys and continued walking down the back streets looking for a place to get a haircut. I finally located what appeared to be a barber given the striped pole in front of his building. The barber was sitting on the front step sleeping. I had to wake him in order to bargain for a haircut. He said he would give me a good one for 3 shillings. I remember the barber chair was a padded lounge chair from someone's living room. However, I did get quite a decent cut and continued walking through the back streets including the "Crater Zone" which I later found out was considered extremely dangerous with many terrorists in the area. I strolled along and stopped for some native food at a street stall not thinking how much I must have looked like an off-duty British soldier. Finally I made my way back to the dock where I met the English family (the Beebe's) and we returned to the ship, which then left within the next two hours. The following day we were surprised when some of the crew heard over the radio that the cruise ship, Galileo, had arrived that day in Aden and when the launches took the passengers to the same immigration dock, some terrorists threw a number of bombs and five tourists were killed.

As we continued our journey through the Indian Ocean a few surprises were in store for this "land-lubber". On one of the first days when I got up, dressed and went on deck I was taken aback by the fact that when I looked out at the upper level of the ocean, it was about 10-12 feet higher than the deck I was standing on. Of course we were on the lower part of a swell. When I later went forward to the bow I was surprised to see a school of porpoises keeping ahead of the ship. They were joined by a number of flying fish at times.

On April 5 we actually crossed the equator but the traditional ceremony was not conducted until the following day. King Neptune took over the ship and initiated all those who were crossing this unseen divider for the first time. The initiates had been told they might get wet and they wisely donned their swimsuits. They were cleansed with a colored foam swabbing and then presented to the "King" for his blessing and the reception of their maritime name and certificate of initiation. It was a fun party and was followed by refreshments and quality chat time.

Four days later the Captain put on separate pre-Easter parties for the officers and passengers and the ordinary crew. I (with guitar) was invited to both. I enjoyed entertaining all those present as the amount of entertainment at sea was very limited. Most people had radios and once in a while a movie would be shown in the crew mess hall in the evening.

Once we had passed the equator I was able to take advantage of a geographic fact for the first time. Having done my Air Force navigation in the mid-northern latitudes, I was never able to see a number of the stars near the southern celestial pole. So in the evening I would borrow the star charts from the bridge and find a totally dark location atop the stern and seek all those celestial bodies I had known in theory only. It was a pleasant place to relax and think about all that had transpired in my trip and to speculate as to what would come in my future travels.

As we progressed towards Australia all became involved with, and concerned about, the strict regulations, which must be observed for any ship wishing to land there. By this time we had painted the entire ship above the deck. The bosun found a specialized job for me and I was anxious to have something a bit more challenging. Every hold on the ship had specifically assigned shackles, which could not be used anywhere else. I had to check each of the shackles with a master list and insure that they were in the right place. If one was lost or damaged, I would replace it with a new one on which I had to stamp the serial number assigned. As well, each of the booms for lifting had to be identified as to how many tons it could carry at particular angles (30 degrees or 45 degrees). These limits had to be painted clearly in large letters on each boom. This also became my job using stencils and a bit of free-hand technique.

On April 14 we arrived off the port of Freemantle at 9:30 PM. We could not dock at night so we anchored in the harbor and got ready to go ashore the next day. Australia was also very strict regarding any foreign plants, etc. being brought into the country. Inspectors came aboard while we were still at anchor and checked out every nook of the ship. The following day we tied up at the dock and I started to prepare my scooter for the next big road tour. The bosun was great in this effort as he found gasoline and mixed it with oil to give me an initial supply. He and a couple of other crewmembers helped me carry the scooter down the gangway. I then had to have the scooter steam cleaned as a precaution against bringing in any plant seeds or the like in the dirt that had accumulated from many countries. It cost a mere $2 AUS. I was sought out by a reporter from the Daily News for any interview about my travels. Later a photographer came by and snapped a couple of shots with my guitar. The Captain was kind enough to give me a letter of recommendation including the various roles I had played as part of the crew. When I had a chance to leave the dock area I found a telephone at the post office and called Nola Downey, one of the traveling Aussies I had met in Seville, Spain. Her mother answered the phone and let me know tha Nola was on the East Coast (of Australia) on her honeymoon. I mentioned to her mother how I had met her more than a year before and she said that she was sure that Nola's sister, Pam, and her husband, Jack, would enjoy meeting me. She gave me the address of the scuba diving shop that he ran and suggested I stop in there when I had the chance.

I returned to the dock to say a final farewell to the crew of the Tudor. I had become particularly fond of the bosun and I noticed his eyes getting misty as we said our good-bys. Then it was off to discover this huge continent, which was about the size of the USA with the population of the city of Tokyo. I started by taking a room for the night in Freemantle for just $2.50 A. The following day I called Pam Sue and then went to the scuba shop at 871 Hay St. in Perth. There I met Jack and his son, Barry, and started a treasured relationship based on the extraordinary background and outlook of Jack. They invited me to stay with them in the suburb of Kalamunda not far away. I was given the address and directions as to how to get there. Then I toured around Perth and Freemantle visiting Kings Park where I photographed a statue of Queen Victoria overlooking the mouth of the Swan River with Perth in the background. There was something very familiar about this great land 'Down Under" and its people. At first the accent I heard seemed quite like British English. However, it did not take long for me to realize the Aussies were uniquely different from most others. Ultimately I wrote my Aussie dictionary in order to keep track of the word use and accent. I did note that I had mixed emotions about re-entering our modern type of society after so many months in areas where many locals did not know if they would eat anything on a given day.

Later that day I drove to 22 James Road, Kalamunda and met all of the Sue's. Jack's wife was Pam and they had four children; Barry, Glenda, Graham and Anita. The whole crew included Irene, the house girl, and Tubby, the friendly black lab. They had a very comfortable home with a huge garage on a hill overlooking Perth the lights of which could be seen at night. Jack was a man of many parts whom I got to know as time went on. He ran W. A. Skindivers where he sold and serviced all manner of scuba tanks and equipment. In another building close by he had a small manufacturing plant where the master machinist, Peter Van Dyke, oversaw the production of spear guns and many other small pieces of equipment. Having been an underwater expert in the "Z" force during WW II, Jack instructed in scuba diving as well. He was mentioned in a book called "The Heroes" by Ron McKee, which related the ultimate fate of a group of Z force members who made two secret raids on Japanese shipping in the middle of Singapore Harbor while the Japanese occupied the whole area. Jack had had his own clandestine experience in Borneo of which he would write many years later.

Jack and family at Kalamunda

He was a freelance photographer for both the local newspaper and the local TV station. He had a weekly TV program called "Down Under" on which he used much of the film he had shot in his own ventures. And, as if he were not busy enough, he led his own dance band on the weekends. He was of Chinese parentage and was small and slight of build. I was to find out later the depth of this extraordinary man.

Immediately I was accepted by the Sue's as one of the family and I tried to do my part in keeping up with things around the house. In the time I spent with them I repaired the Hoover (vacuum cleaner), the radiogram, Pam's Morris Oxford car and an old motor scooter, which Barry and I had to completely overhaul. While I was doing this I had the opportunity to straighten the fork on my scooter and discover the steering lock located inside the front panel. Had I realized this from the start I would have avoided the theft of the scooter in Spain (although I got it back when it was abandoned when it would not start). I also managed to obtain a Bosch (recommended) spark plug for the first time since I had the scooter. I bought two new tires for it at $6.65 AUS each and it had a total new "lease on life".

The first week-end I was there I accompanied the family to the ANZAC (Australian-New Zealand Army Corps) day parade and reception. On that occasion Jack received a medal from the US government, which he should have received long before for his heroic duty in WW II. He had been a member of the special forces (Z Force) and was held in very high esteem by those who had participated in WW II in the south Pacific. It would be many years thereafter that I would become aware of the particular duties, which justifiably earned him that award.

The days passed like a shot with this family given the breadth of Jack's involvement in the community. The Sue's had a summerhouse in Yanshup, which we visited and upgraded with a new water tank. On that particular day, May 15, I celebrated my "2-year" mark in my journey. When I became aware that they could use some help in the manufacturing shop behind W.A. Skin Divers I ended up swapping theory for experience under the tutelage of Peter in the machine shop. I had not made much official use of my Chemical Engineering degree but I always preferred the practical application of the lessons I had learned in the classroom and lab. The equipment was somewhat dated which lent itself to more basic applications of the principles of engineering. We used an old style turret lathe to make ferules for spear guns. They were used to attach the thick rubber bands to the gun. When the production of ferules became boring Peter challenged me to make a new set of bushings for a compressor shaft in the shop. It actually came out quite well thanks to his expertise and guidance. It was a job that required a great deal of patience as well as skill. I was actually on the payroll although I objected given the hospitality being shown to me by the Sue's. As usual, I tried to give back to my hosts in all cases by doing things for them that I was able to do such as repair household items, automobiles, etc. as well as entertain them and their friends. I did note that General Motors had produced a line of cars that were sold in Australia but not in the USA. It was the General Motors Holden, which was extremely popular in Australia. Luckily for me most of the systems were similar to those of the Chevrolet and, therefore, familiar.

On one occasion I went with Barry and other family members to see an Australian Rules football game. It was quite different from rugby and American football, which they refer to as "gridiron". There were 20 players on a side and the field is oval in shape. There are four vertical goalposts at each end and the ball must pass between the middle two to score 6 points. If it passes between the outer poles it scores 1 point. The ball can be kicked, thrown, lateralled and carried on the run. The action is more like rugby than US football. The ball is shaped like our football but, a bit rounder and larger. Still I could get my hand far enough around it to throw it like a forward pass, which amazed the onlookers as it is not thrown that way in their game. When the full teams were on the field it seemed like a mass riot to me. However, everyone enjoyed the action and nobody got seriously hurt.

The greatest adventure we had together was when we visited Canarvon and stayed at the sole local hotel run by Carry, a great friend of the Sue's. On the way up we had traveled at night and one of the challenges was to keep from hitting the many kangaroos that jumped across the highway in front of us. Carry was a strong, but gentle, woman of many talents and she had become the sole manager of the business due to the death of her husband, Charlie, in an automobile accident just months before. A soon as the word went around that Jack Sue was in town all those in the surrounding community knew that there would be dance music in the hotel that evening. I was able to use the electric pick-up for my guitar for the first time and I joined Jack and Kerry's son, Neil, in helping to provide a night of rythms for those who packed the beer garden of the hotel.

One of the main goals of our northern sojourn was to take a trip to the deserted islands off the coast of Canarvon and spend some days exploring and spear-fishing. Dorre and Bernier Islands had been leper colonies for woman and men respectively until 1919. Between them they were 60 miles long and stood 30 miles off shore. We were supposed to leave at 9:00 AM but by the time all was ready it was 11:45 AM. There were Jack, Neil, Barry, Glenda and I in the 21' boat. We were to head for Disaster Cove on Dorre Island, a 4.5-hour trip. However, six or seven times along the way we had to stop and clean the carburetor and fuel bowl due to water in the petrol. In the process we drifted far to the south and arrived after dark in a rainstorm at Dorre Island 7 hours later. Thanks to the experience of Jack we were able to find the cove after a search along the coast. Ultimately Jack had to sit on the roof of the cab and use the powerful flashlight to find the haven. Once inside the cove the boat went hard aground and we were in fear that it would capsize. We had to jump out and ferry our supplies up to the beach. In the process most of our things got wet and our feet got cut on the sharp rocks below. Finally we re-floated the boat and tied it securely behind the oyster rock barrier of the cove. In the meanwhile Jack and Glenda had found a camping hollow and made a fire. Once we had put all of our gear high on the beach we relaxed with some food and settled down for the night amid some blowing sand.

Beautiful cove—now calm

The next morning we removed the rest of our supplies from the boat, set up the portable cooler, and organized our campsite. Then we went for a hike of 10-12 miles to discover the layout of this island. Jack had been here before and was searching for a particular jetty. On the way we saw a sea cow, a manatee, which is much like a human female in that it nurses its young. I was also told that it provides all types of meat cuts. We did not attempt to capture it. As we walked this lifeless island I realized that my feet were getting quite scratched from the briars and I needed more suntan lotion. Later in the day we went to the oyster rocks located on the northern coast of Dorre Island and had an appetizer of raw oysters directly from the shells. The process was to use a rock to knock the shells off the ledge, pry open the shell, remove the oyster, rinse it in seawater and pop it into your mouth. It was the first time for me and I thought that the taste of the oyster contained a hint of watermelon.

At night Neil, Barry and I went to the ocean side of the island to the shelf rocks to look for crayfish. When the tide would go out they would get caught in the small natural pools in the rocks. In our case we caught a mere 3 in 2.5 hours. The following day with the weather much calmer we all went spear fishing and caught about 160 pounds of fish in one hour, mostly due to Jack's efforts. He caught Norwest Cod and Bullchin groper. Neil and Barry had caught some smaller fish (baramunji) by rod in the cove earlier. With the cleaned catch in the cooler we settled down for a great feast of fish that evening. Of course I took the occasion to record many of these events with my Zeis Ikon camera.

Roughing it—nothing new for Jack

Before leaving for home we went back to the oyster rocks to fill a jar of oysters for Carry. We then stopped at a site off Bernier Island to try the fishing. We noted there were still some wild goats on this island. The fishing was not good so we headed for home in the afternoon. A short while at sea Neil discovered that the cooling system for the engine was apparently not working. We ended up rigging the hand bilge pump in a 5-gallon bucket with a 2-gallon bucket to fill it up. This pump had to be pumped by hand all the way home. Shortly after this event the carburetor started acting up again. About half way to home the engine quit. Neil tried over and over to get it going again but it would not catch. In the process he wore down the batteries. Thereafter the only way to try was to use the hand crank, which was not effective except to skin the knuckles of Neil's hand. Neil who was known to be short-tempered was howling by this time. We put down a pic, sea anchor, and I tried to SOS to the nearby fishing fleet with a Big Jim light. Although they acknowledged our lights nobody came to our help. After many more tries we decided that we would have to wait out the night. We all tried to make ourselves comfortable but it was of little use in the angrily tossing sea. The following morning we tried to fire off flares, which did not work because the wind was so strong. At the same time we fired the 303 rifle several times but it brought us no notice. We decided that we had to get the motor going again. Upon inspection I noticed that a grounding wire on the engine was broken. With that repaired we coaxed the engine into action with a combination of the electric starter and a pull-line around the shaft. We had drifted from 9:00 PM to 9:00 AM. With us manning the hand bilge pump the rest of the way we arrived at Canarvon at 12:30 PM. We were glad to unload, shower, have a meal and hit the sack.

The next day we had an opportunity to say "g'day" to another of Jack's good friends, Dominic. He was an Italian immigrant who had a small banana plantation. Jack's nickname for him was "Ba-goom". He was built like the stump of a tree and as strong as an ox. He was very jovial and showed us around his groves. Of course he insisted on giving Jack a stalk of bananas to take home. So he took his "pocketknife" (machete) and found a full stalk of bananas to his liking. He held the stalk with one hand and swung the machete deftly with the other to dislodge the near-ripe fruit. It was only when he passed it to me to take back to the car did I realize how heavy it was. I was really challenged to make it all the way without stopping. That stalk hung in Jack's garage for many weeks thereafter as we all sampled the delicious fruits of "Ba-goom's" labor.

Dominic with a stock of bananas

That evening we had a good session at the hotel beer garden and left at 1:30 AM after one of Carry's famous suppers. She would not take anything from me for my room and board but invited me to come back for race week in September and entertain in the beer garden. On the way back we had some problems with the car. At night while I was driving I hit a roo that went under the car and broke part of the exhaust manifold. We made some temporary repairs and continued on. Later in the morning a wheel bearing froze and Jack had to hitchhike for parts while I spent the time removing the ball bearing race from the hub of the front wheel. We were truly in the "outback" and I quickly became aware of the problem with flies in the countryside. Jack returned with the parts some hours later and we put all together and were on our way. We arrived at the house at 1:30 AM and tucked in to catch up on sleep.

The following days and weeks were filled with the many adventures of the Sue's and meeting interesting people as I continued on my quest to absorb the Aussie culture. One incident bothered me a bit. One of the Sue's good friends was an older woman by the name of Dot. I had been introduced to her and had chatted with her on several occasions when our paths crossed. One day she asked me a favor. She lived alone with her old dog and the poor animal was suffering from some disease, which could not be cured. She asked me if I could "put him down". I said I would out of friendship to her and not wanting to see the poor animal suffer. I took the dog to a wooded area not far away and tied him to a tree. I had already dug a sizeable hole when I cocked the 22 rifle and fired the one fatal shot. I quickly buried the dog and let Dot know that all had been taken care of. What bothered me when I later thought about it was how unemotional I was as I ended the dog's suffering. I started to wonder if my travels had hardened me to emotional issues. Later, to my relief, I found this concern to be inapplicable.

Over a period of weeks I was able to assemble all of the required components for Barry's scooter. At last we had it operational and he spent some time practicing after I had given him some initial instructions. The family decided to name the scooter "Jerry" (the way I was spelling my name at that time). He really took a shine to having his own motorized transportation.

As was the case so many times before, at last I had to part with this super family in order to continue my journey which I originally thought might take 8-10 months. They had given me the names and addresses of several friends who were along my intended route although they well knew that my path wandered as I saw fit on any given day. Thus, I left their home in Kalamunda on June 30, 1966 to head for Melbourne and the home of Diane Tipper. I had met her in Mallorca, Spain heading in the opposite direction around the world and she had stayed with my family just outside of Boston. This journey was about the same as leaving Los Angeles for Miami and I had a total of $22 A in my pocket at the time. Of course the Sue's had no idea of this or they would have been shocked and insisted on my taking a "loan" from them. However, I had learned to stretch funds long before this in my trip. So, I was not concerned about how I would get along. One of my last remembrances of Kalamunda was hearing the teary shouts of good-by from Barry as he ran far down the road until I disappeared. They pierced me with the warmth and frustration of real friendship.

# CHAPTER TWENTY-TWO

## The Nullabor Plain

My first stop was at the home of the Lemera's in Bunbury, south of Perth. Jim was an avid scuba diver friend of Jack and an accountant for the local Holden dealer. He, his wife (Midge) and their two kids (Terry and Rob) couldn't have been more welcoming. I stayed with these hospitable people for a couple of days during which they showed me around their area as we got briefly acquainted. He had intended to take me scuba diving but the rainy, blustery weather put a damper on that activity. Instead we toured the rugged west coast and viewed the crashing waves of the angry sea. Later one of my nieces would become a pen pal of Jim's daughter, Terry. While visiting with this family I found myself earning my keep by cutting a fair amount of jarra wood. While in the area I always used my guitar and songs to get to know people. After a session with the Lemera's Jim got me booked for a session at the Highway Hotel. I did two sets for $6A, which added greatly to my available resources to reach Melbourne.

I continued on through the southwestern corner of Australia by way of Donnybrook known for its apples. I also found some other new trees such as carrie in the timber country. As I passed through Manjimup I recalled that the suffix ". . . up" at the end of a name means watering place in the Aboriginal language. Shortly thereafter I ran out of gas about 7 miles before the town of Shannon, a timber mill town. I hid the scooter and caught a ride to Shannon where I bought the petrol and started walking back due to the lack of traffic. It was a bit weird walking alone through the pitch blackness on the narrow windy road while I could hear any number of roos jumping around me. I finally got a ride from two "roo-jackers" who were headed for Pemberton where they would do some betting at the TAB (Totalizer Agency Board) unknown to their wives. I was not able to locate the scooter so I took the ride with these two loggers and waited until their "sure thing" came in last. On their way back I found the scooter, gassed it up and drove into Shanon where I "camped" on the veranda of a vacant home. The following day I photographed some of the beautiful coast line as I approached Albany. Albany harbor had been the departure point for the massed ANZACs leaving to fight in WW I. There was a statue of soldiers there, which had originally been in Port Said, Egypt until it was defaced. It was then brought to Australia as a fitting tribute to those who had gone so far to fight for the cause of freedom.

I found a great B and B at the County Woman's Association Pyrmont Residence for $2.25. I found a very friendly group of teachers (male and female) staying there. After leaving the next morning I headed for Ravensthorpe and found the last 35 miles of that journey on an unpaved road. Due to the small wheels on a scooter it greatly slows progress when not on a solid pavement. I stayed over in Ravensthorpe camping in with a cobber I met in the only local bar. The next day the road led to Esperance. Along the way I photo'd some famous Aussie sheep. In Esperance I met Keith McLean, his wife (Joan) and daughter (Sue). He ran the food land and was very hospitable. He invited me to stay with him and we had a great session with the guitar that night. The following day I arranged a gig at the Traveler's Inn and then drove out to see the "pink lake". I had been told of this phenomenon but couldn't believe it until I saw it and took some photos. Apparently the color comes from red algae in the water and become more colorful as the wind increases. This is a quickly developing area. Art Linkletter reportedly had a huge spread of land just east of here. My session at the Inn went well and I received $5 for my efforts. I helped Keith in the store several times and took the challenge of chopping maley roots, which give off great heat but are tough to chop due to the twisted wood grain.

As usual the time to leave came too quickly and I was on the road to Norseman. With petrol stations very scarce I ran out of gas and acquired electrical problems just as I entered town. I got the gas and made my way to George Warry's Ampol station. It was located at the entrance to the Eyre Highway, which stretches across the southern Nullarbor Plain to Adelaide. I found that the contact points in the voltage regulator were shorted out. George let me stay in the unused district shack behind the station as I waited for a truck, which might take me and the scooter across the Nullabor. As I waited I tried to repair the scooter. I found petrol and oil in the ignition system and the commutators were fouled. During one of my short test runs someone stole my hunting knife, which I had been using as a tool. I had carried it half way around the world and it always made me depressed when I lost any of my journey mates.

Even if the scooter were in top condition I did not intend to try to drive it across the Eyre Highway. I took a photo of the sign to Adelaide, the next city east. It read, "Adelaide—1249 miles". I also came to learn that 580 of those miles were unpaved. Instead any driver would traverse deep ruts in grainy "bull-dust". Thus, after two days of waiting I was elated when Reg Clark came along heading east and agreed to take me along with my scooter. He owned his own truck and had 14 tons of jarra wood on it. Because of its weight it did not take too much space and there was plenty for the scooter. We left at 5:30 PM in his Dodge semi-trailer, which surprisingly had a regular Valiant car engine of about 85 HP in it. On his return trip to Perth he would bring 7 Valiant cars. I was shocked that the engine was not bigger but Reg said it was just fine with enough gears.

Start of the Eyre Highway

He would drive continuously with 1-2 hour stops for food and a nap. Along the highway we lost a wheel bearing and had to stop. We had to jack off the wheel and straighten everything and replace the old bearing hoping that it would last. At Madura we stopped and I found Jack Smith to whom I conveyed greetings from the Sue's. Here the table land drops to the flat along the sea on the way to Eucla where we entered South Australia. The land was dry and arid with little vegetation. It was not long hereafter that we entered the 580 miles of unpaved road. I was glad that I had not talked myself into trying to make it through this area with my scooter. I well remember the trouble I had with the short distance I had to drive in this type of sand when I was traveling down the Nile in Egypt. The first night in this environment just after Ceduna we came across a truck accident. The truck had overturned and the driver was lying in shock beside a fire. Others had already stopped to assist and a girl from the Wirrulla Hotel had come out to make him comfortable until an ambulance could arrive. Reg commented on the apparent sturdiness of this girl named Irene as she brought huge branches to the fire from some distance. When I got to talk to her I found out that she had escaped from Czechoslovakia by herself as a teenager and ended up in a relocation camp in Italy. At this point her Italian was better than her English so we used the former. She had had a truly treacherous escape from behind the "Iron Curtain". She gave me her address and asked me to drop a line if I could. With nothing more we could do we moved on towards Adelaide.

The rest of the journey was uneventful and we pulled into Adelaide at noon the next day. We unloaded the truck and I then called Les Smith, a friend of the Sue's. He invited me for tea and picked me up. He was quite hospitable and made me truly welcome. However, the open dissatisfaction of his wife at my presence drove me to thank an embarrassed Les and leave to sleep in Reg's truck. On searching for something to eat in a small convenience store I met a Latvian shopkeeper named John who was quite friendly. The little time I spent with him easily countered the coldness of Les's wife.

The following day I pushed the scooter to Harold Dewhurst's auto electric repair shop on South Road where I swapped some of my mechanical work for his electronic expertise. I had told him that I didn't have much money but I could do the mechanical work on the scooter if he could do the electric work to adjust the voltage regulator. Of course I would pay him for his part of the work. He said he would do so but I'd have to wait a bit because of the shop being so busy. He suggested that, if I could do the mechanical work, I could remove the generator from a waiting car and the other staff on the crew would show me how to use the equipment to test it and re-build it. I did so and replaced the generator and all was well. He later adjusted my scooter and said we would call it even. Seeing that he was so busy I asked if he might be able to use another helper for a few days. He said he could and I later checked into the local YMCA for $2.50A (bed and breakfast) and spent the next few days learning a lot about starters, generators, alternators . . . etc as well as adding to my depleting travel funds. I was able to link my theoretical engineering with the practicality of the physical items.

I was still having problems with the voltage regulator, which would not re-charge the battery. About this time I learned through trial and error that the scooter would probably run without the battery if I could get it running. I found I could "pop start" it by pushing it fast and popping first gear. I was to use this mechanism on many an occasion. Aside from Harold there were three other workers in the shop. Vic was a very bright apprentice and he invited me to have dinner with his family. There I met his parents, Ellen (adopted Aboriginal sister), Jeff and Lee (a real cutie). After dinner we road to Windy Point from which we could see the lights of Adelaide surrounded by hills and the sea. This family was very sincere and interesting. As I had seen in countless other locations they formed the basic building block of the local society and I was extremely happy to be able to spend time with them even on a limited basis.

The following day was July 22 and I worked my final day at the shop and said my good-by's to all the crew. I was paid $20A by Harold who appreciated my situation and that insured the funding for the rest of my journey to the east coast. I left the following morning on a fine day and did 320 miles which was a record for me in one day on the scooter. I stopped in Stawell, famous for "the gift" foot race but I wasn't in any shape for any race by that time. I slept at a campsite on a concrete floor. The next day I continued to Ararat where I went to church and had breakfast. Soon thereafter I was stopped by the police and told that I had to use a helmet in Victoria. He checked my driver's license, which would run out the next day (my birthday).

I continued and arrived at the Tipper's house at 5:00 PM to a royal welcome by Diane's whole family. There was father (Ben), mother (Yeta) and Mike (younger brother), I had not seen Diane since we parted in Palma, Majorca in January of 1965. Along her journey she had stayed with my family north of Boston before completing her travels around the world some months before. In short order I felt like I was a returning son. The Tipper's had even placed their caravan (small camping trailer) next to their house for my use so I could come and go as I pleased. After a shower and change of clothes I was ready to meet my "Australian Family" for a true get-acquainted session. At their home I had received a set of slides from the Agfa lab and I was able to show them to the Tippers as we got to know one another. These slides were mostly of the Mid-east and they found them fascinating. As I chatted with "Dad", a semi-retired auctioneer, "Mom" busied herself in preparing one of her incredible meals, which were due to spoil me for the road thereafter. I later learned that Diane had been shocked when her father offered me a glass of sherry and we sipped a few before dinner. When she had met me in Spain I had just arrived there and was a hopeless "tea-totaler ". She had thus sternly warned her family against offering me any alcoholic drink. What she did not count on was my gradual entree into the realm of wine. By the time I had visited families in Spain, Portugal, France, Germany and Italy, I had joined the ranks of those who truly enjoyed a glass or two with a good dinner.

The Tippers—Diane, Michael & parents

Mom, Dad & I in front of my "digs"

That night we easily talked through dinner and ended up with a great songfest with my guitar. When I recounted that I had been stopped by the police for not wearing a helmet, they insisted on providing one as a birthday present on the next day when I turned 30. As I searched for the right place to buy it the next day, I was whistled at by almost every cop I passed on the scooter. Rather than take the time to explain to each one my circumstances, I just kept going in the belief that they had more important things to do than to chase me.

I had also received several letters and cards from friends and family. It was noteworthy that it was July 25th and I had just received an international money order for $250 from my mother who had access to my bank account. Many friends have asked me how I could afford to travel for so long a period through so many countries. A combination of factors made it possible including my willingness to work at whatever small jobs I could find along the way and my desire to live simply and as close as possible to the living standards of the local citizens. However, the most universal contribution to the extension of my own funds was the incredible hospitality I found throughout all the lands I visited. So often a casual conversation in a language I was struggling with ended in an invitation to visit a local home which not only saved me a huge amount of funds, but gave me a true lesson in local family life with new-found friends.

In the following days I found my photo and article in the Herald newspaper and I sang and was interviewed on Channel 9 where I was paid a stipend of $55. At the encouragement of the family members I applied for some entertainment work at the Stage Coach Inn and was accepted to entertain table-to-table at this popular Italian restaurant. I sang with the guitar 3-4 nights per week for 3 hours and was paid $16 per night plus some very generous tips. Thus, I was easily able to buy two new batteries for the scooter at $23 for the pair. Although the Tippers would not let me pay for anything, I'd bring home some flowers for "Mom" when I had the chance and she would make a huge big deal of it.

In order to feel like I'd been accepted by the family I insisted on doing whatever odd jobs they had around the house. Soon I cleaned out the garage so I could work on Diane's Fiat and "Mom's" Ford Zephyr both of which needed some attention. Next I realized that the bathroom had no light in it. I installed one and put in a shelf where "Mom" could store the linens . . . etc. Later I repaired Mike's Morris 1100 and "Dad's" motorboat. Shortly after arriving I had been introduced to the Wright-Smith family across the street and took a liking to their three small children who reminded me of my 46 nephews and nieces back home. The oldest was Peter who had a great liking for airplanes and flying. One day I took him with the scooter to the local airport and we got permission to enter a Cessna 172 and let him take the controls. We visited the control tower where I learned that there were only four omni stations in the whole of the country. These are the omni-directional electronic transmitters that allow airlines and others to fly on designated "airways" between points on the map. We talked "flying" and had lunch there in what was a pleasant day for me and a true thrill for him. I found out later that his home also lacked sufficient electric outlets so I installed three more of them, which was a particular challenge as the walls had horizontal beams running through them at varying heights. Being typically me, I also repaired my shoes by attaching a new set of heels (comes naturally when you are the product of two Scottish immigrants). Now I was ready for many more hundreds of walking miles.

During my time with the Tippers, Jack Sue made a trip to Melbourne to photograph the administration buildings of the "Z" force of which he had been a part. The Tippers welcomed him and he stayed with me in the caravan during the two days we used to find the desired buildings. I became aware of a book by Ron McKie called "The Heroes" recounting the hair-raising events of an attack on Singapore Harbor in WW II by allied soldiers who had left Australia and made their way in a discarded Japanese fishing boat (the Krait) to this Japanese stronghold and blew up 38,000 tons of shipping there. They later sailed back to Australia without being caught nor suspected. In the first part of that book which recounts the training of these men in Cairns, Jack Sue is mentioned as a trainee for other missions. His own best-selling book would be published many years later.

Through the publicity I received in Melbourne I was contacted by Brian O'Riley of the Moe Rotary club to ask if I could be contracted to entertain for the annual Ladies' Night banquet. Brian and his wife were the perfect hosts and insisted on my staying at their beautiful home while I was in Moe. At a BBQ at their house I met many of their friends including John Ellis, a very likeable fellow. The banquet went well and the entertainment was well received. I took the liberty of interspersing my songs with some of Bob Newhart's monologues, which I properly attributed to him. He is one of my favorite comedians. Despite my typical "Yank" accent, all seemed to appreciate his humor. I was paid $30 for my performance and I added it to the travel fund. While in that area I looked up Jack Davidson, a friend of the Needham's, who ran a paper mill. He was surprised to meet me and he gave me the grand tour of the plant followed by lunch together.

A couple I found quite interesting was Ken and Claudia Boyd. Diane had introduced me to them as we had lunch one day. Ken had been one of the "Whiz Kids" on a TV program called "Pick a box". He was a Scot and most likely had a genius IQ. Yet I was quite surprised to hear him express his envy and wonder at my travels, language skills and mechanical ability. We met on several occasions thereafter and had long discussions about many subjects from opposite ends of the educational sphere. I really enjoyed our time together.

# CHAPTER TWENTY-THREE

## "Lambing . . . etc"

I was truly fortunate to experience a real "Aussie" adventure by visiting one of Diane's old school mates who had married a sheep ranger living in the outback. For Diane and I the first part of our journey took us to Mildura where we visited the parents of her friend, Agi. The Sandors ran a motel and treated us like family. The father spoke German and we had a great time together. After a monstrous meal we continued on to Bunerungee Station and met Bob, Agi, their daughter, Dood, and a niece and nephew (Jane and Mike). Their modern cream-colored brick home was almost out of place in the middle of their 32,000 acres with 6,000 Merino sheep. The Anna branch of the Darling River cut through their property and passed in front of the house. The closest neighbor lived 18 miles down the road. The nearest town was 42 miles and the city was 60 miles. Station owners had to be truly self-reliant people.

On the first morning when I awoke I went into the kitchen and turned on a light. At first nothing seemed to happen. Then I heard the slow acceleration of a chugging engine, as the gas-fired generator got up to speed. As it did the lights slowly increased in intensity until all looked normal. Of course, they also had their own well for water. Life was quite hard for these stalwart friends but they enjoyed the solitude and loved the surroundings and life-style.

The fleet at the station consisted of Bob's car, an International Scout ute (pick-up truck), a Vespa motor scooter and 3 horses. Diane decided to learn to ride while there although she was petrified of horses. She used her determination to get up to trotting but did not quite get into cantering. My limited experience with horses was called into play one day when it was time for the muster of sheep. I was one of the three on horseback and we started out and got to a point where Bob said, "Ok here we split up. Gerry, you follow this fence for several miles and round up any stray sheep. We'll meet you at the 5 mile pens." Between us we covered an area 5 miles by 16 miles in three and a half hours. You can bet my bottom was sore by then. Often these operations are layed out on a "mud map" drawn on the ground.

Bunerungee—Bob, Agi & kids with mud map

At the 5 mile pen we were marking and spraying the yearlings which included ear punching, ear tagging, castration and tail-cutting all of which requires about 60 seconds per lamb. On the second day I got to do several of these complete operations including the castration which is a dental extraction (nothing to do with the lamb's teeth). By this time I had learned that a ewe was a female, a ram a male, a wether is a former male, a hogarth is a young unshorn sheep and a stag is a male of half potential. Later I had the experience of shearing a sheep also. I thought that the equipment was bit awkward but managed to get the fleece off in one piece.

The hired hand named Bob was known for not taking very good care of the equipment. He often drove the ute and caused considerable damage through his reckless ways. For example, I had to spend a lot of time repairing and straightening the tie rods when he ran over a stump about 2.5 feet high while chasing sheep. He later had a "row" with the owner and was fired during our visit. Evenings were spent watching TV, talking about all kinds of things and having songfests with Bob's guitar and mine. Food was good and plentiful and usually included some form of lamb.

Quick processing by varied means

On Sunday we took the 60-mile drive to Mildura to go to church. The majority of that road was unpaved and became very dusty as we sped along. The Mass was said in Italian and we later had lunch with Diane's friends, Allen and Jenny Bond. He was the only doctor in the 230 bed hospital. Like teachers in Australia, doctors are financially assisted through school and then have to complete three years of assigned work wherever the government wishes. Diane had done the same as a teacher. When we finally left Bunerungee we re-traced this road to Mildura and visited the Sandors again where we were loaded up with oranges, grapefruits and all types of wonderful fruits to take back to Melbourne.

On September 26 I packed and said a truly sad farewell to the Tipper's and headed east towards Eden. There were enough tears to go around for everyone. Diane later told me her mother cried for two weeks thereafter. I had said good-by to the crew at the Stage Coach Inn and the others I had gotten to know like Toni the jeweler who insisted on giving me a gold pen as a gift. As I headed out it occurred to me that, as we get into adulthood, we should reject the admonition of most mothers. They would always tell us not to talk to strangers. That's very valid advice when young. However, if we remain communicating with only those around us we miss the opportunity to discover new ideas, outlooks and philosophies. In most local settings the inhabitants exchange mostly mundane thoughts and ideas. If they took every opportunity to speak with others from far away or who are quite different, they would increase their grasp of the humanity of man. That type of outlook had certainly served me extremely well in the two years plus during which I had traveled through 28 countries. As my family and friends know, I am a talker and never hesitate to strike up a conversation with another person who holds the potential to teach me something. And I believe that everyone I meet knows something that I don't and, thus, can be my instructor, Common people in many countries had taught me so much in my journey to date.

As I traveled east I came to Moe and stopped to say hello to Brian O'Riley again. There I coincidentally re-met John Ellis who gave me a note and directions in case I wanted to use his cabin near Eden. As I followed the coast to the East I noticed a strange sound coming from the scooter. I tried some quick checking and adjustments but it was to no avail. I had to limp into Eden, which was the old whaling capital of Australia. After a supper of fish and chips (first time for shark) I headed out towards John's cabin. I wasn't a mile and a half out of town when the scooter came to an abrupt halt and there seemed to be something catching in the drive train. I shut it off and tried to push it off the road. At times it would move a few feet and then get caught again. I turned it around and headed back towards the town making slow and noisy progress. As I passed one of the few houses in the area a man came out and asked if he could help. When I explained the situation he said I could leave the scooter in his shed until the next day and he would give me a ride out to John's cabin, which he knew. We drove to Gregs Flats where I woke Frank Burton to get the cabin key. He was also very helpful and understanding.

Great resting place during scooter repair

The cabin did not have the electricity on but I was happy to be somewhere I could place my things and relax. There was a single bed, a table, chairs and a sink. There was also a stove but it was not needed at this time of the year. I tucked in and slept well after considerable consideration of what challenge I would face in trying to get me scooter operational again. The following morning I made some basic breakfast and hitched a ride into town where I had left the scooter. A local fellow named Rene Davidson had heard of my problem and he was looking over the scooter when I arrived. He volunteered to use his pick-up truck to take the scooter to the local Golden Fleece petrol station where he knew the owner, Brian Henson. He correctly predicted that Brian would let me repair the scooter in the unused maintenance section of his building. Rene was a plant maintenance man and he lent me a number of tools so I could start taking apart the drive train of the NSU. It turned out that some very unique tools were called for and I spent most of the day making these with what I could find in the area. At the end of the first day of repair I tried to hitch a ride to the cabin but ended up walking 5 miles. The next morning I made it back to the station and was able to finally get the entire drive train broken down. As I suspected the two swirled bevel gears which operate at 90 degrees to each other had loosened enough to the point of minimum contact. The result was that both gears were almost totally stripped. At this point I had to make a crucial decision. If I couldn't find replacement parts I might have to abandon my "faithful steed" and search for another way to complete my travels. Given the amount of baggage I had with me it would take another similar cycle to continue with all my gear. I surely couldn't afford to buy a new scooter and finding an old one, which would fill the gap, would be nearly impossible in this rural location. My affection for the NSU and what we had been through together prompted me to decide that I would repair it no matter what it took. I called the NSU dealer in Sydney to fine that they did not have replacement parts. They recommended A. Honey Wrecking and I located an old scooter there from which I could get the gears. Brian was to visit Sydney the next day and I went with him for the 300-mile journey. This trip was along the beautiful coastline of the Tasman Sea and required a stop in Wollongong where I stayed in the YMCA for $3.00 (BandB). The next day was Saturday and I hitched the remaining 55 miles to Sydney. The cycle shop closed at noon which meant I had about two and a half hours to take apart the old scooter when it had taken me two days to take apart my own in Eden. Of course I was greatly helped by having recently done it and the assistance of Laurie, the chief mechanic with all of his appropriate tools. I paid $12 for the two parts and left to hitch back to Eden. I only got as far as Marooma but it was too late to get a room. So I hung out around the post office, which had a bench in front. I sat and/or slept on that bench through the night and almost scared the socks off a local who came to drop a letter in the outside box. In the morning I got back on the road and made it back to the cabin by 2:00 PM. I dropped off to sleep and slept through the night. Then next day, after breakfast with neighbor Ray Severs and his wife, I returned to the station and re-assembled the drive train of the scooter. Thinking that all was set I headed out to the cabin and had the start of the same noise on the road. I didn't dare to try to drive it back to town so I left it concealed in the bushes, hitched to town and brought the tools back to re-make all the adjustments on the side of the road.

The next day I went into town again and a similar thing happened. I took it all apart again and found that a spacing ring was out of place. Finally I had figured out the exact purpose and place for every part of the unit. With the scooter running fine I was talked into staying a few days longer to take care of the petrol station while Brian had to be out of town. His young brother, Henry, was a big help when I needed extra hands. Most of the days were spent pumping petrol and doing the normal things, which were considered full service at that time.

"Minding the store" at Golden Fleece

That would be washing the windshield, checking the oil level and inspecting the drive belts for the accessories. I was able to repair the windshield wipers of one old car for which I charged $5 to the delight of the older couple. I stayed at the station where I started reading Ken Boyd's "Sun, Sand and Stars". I called the Tipper's and had a delightful chat with all in the family. When Brian returned he paid me $20 for minding the station for three days and we were both quite satisfied with that.

As I contemplated my leaving of this quaint town I took the time to write my "Aussie dictionary" of words not used in the USA or used in different ways. Some of them are from British English. They are as follows:

| Australian | USA English | Australian | USA English |
|---|---|---|---|
| tucker | food | wether | castrated male sheep |
| bash up | beat up, fight | jumbuck | Merino wether |
| juice | petrol, gas | billibong | bend of a stream |
| herbs | power | billy | tin for boiling water |
| go for six | fall down | be in it | partake |
| buggered | impaired, confused | shoot through | pass by, leave |
| take on the knuckle | start a fight with | a do | party, celebration |
| get stuck into | become involved with | dill | simpleton |
| grog | booze | my word! | emphatic agreement |
| Abo | aboriginal | toot | toilet |
| "good on you" | well done | flog | sell, get rid of |
| roo | kangaroo | shout | treat |
| cup-a | cup of tea | give away | quit |
| chook | chicken | rough as bags | common |
| bickie | cookie | frock | dress |
| crook | angry, sick | prang | accident |
| beaut | fine, outstanding | plonk | booz, wine |
| bugger all | nothing | pram | baby carriage |
| ute | pick-up truck | lollies | candy |
| dinkum | true, correct | burn | short ride |
| sheila | girl | swaggie | tramp |

On October 12 I cleaned the cabin and said good-by to Mrs. Severs and Frank Burton. Now I was back on the road again having visited Eden since September 27. I drove through Bega and headed up Brown Mountain, which was a good test for the scooter at 4500'. Most of the road was unpaved and I noted seeing a bit of rare snow at the higher levels. I continued to the capital at Canberra, which is a new city half way between Sydney and Melbourne given that it could not be decided in which to locate it. It is within the Australian Capital Territory (ACT) much like the District of Columbia (DC) in the USA. It was designed over a lake, which was named after the American architect, Burley Griffin, who laid out the design. It gave me the impression of being a cross between Perth and a little Washington.

I contacted Dick Greenish, a Z force buddy of Jack Sue and he was an extremely busy guy. He ran a brokerage and was an ombudsman for anyone's problems. Eventually we met and he was excited and intrigued with my journey. He arranged interviews with the local press and TV stations. He was running as an independent for the Member of Parliament (MP) seat from ACT. As well he was associated with the ACT United Nations Committee. Given that the following week was United Nations Week he offered me a job to visit local high schools and speak to the students about matters of the world I had experienced in my trip. He and his wife, Roma, invited me to stay with them while I was in Canberra. She was the widow of Robert Page who was one of the "Heroes". Their crew had been captured on their second raid into Singapore in WW II and they were ultimately beheaded following the code of brave Japanese heroes.

Dick was involved in most events around the capital and when he brought me to a Rotary Club meeting it was assumed by many that I was one of the advanced party for President Lyndon B. Johnson's up-coming visit. When reviewing the itinerary set up for LBJ we were disgusted that they were going to throw a Texas-style BBQ for him instead of allowing him to try the great variety of Aussie food offerings. I wrote a satirical poem about the visit and Dick had 50 copies made right away so he could pass them to his colleagues. He was delighted when I put it to music at the piano. One feature of their house was somewhat unique. They had a swimming pool on top of the attached garage. I remember well using that nice, sunny location to catch up on my amplified diary of my trip. As usual I sent home 10-12 full 8.5 x 11 pages in a package hoping I would be able to locate them once I returned. As part of my desire to contribute something to my hosts I tuned up their lawn mower and cars.

During the following weeks I spoke at about 8 high schools around the area and met some truly wonderful new friends. We joined some of Dick's friends to welcome our President, LBJ, on October 21 when he toured the War Museum near Dick's house. On another occasion I visited their Parliament and was surprised to see the feisty, circus-like atmosphere that seems to exist there. Members expressed their disagreement by trying to shout down the person at the podium. Somehow I expected a bit of decorum at the forum, which represented the highest level of government in the country.

Having left the Greenish's I headed north and stopped in to meet and see the relatives of Joseph Homsey from Egypt. They were the Manouk's (Robert and Toni), the Gouda's (Peter and Mary) and their parents, the Naggar's. I had promised to read a message to them from their brother-in-law, Zuzu in Cairo. We spent the day exchanging information and news of their relatives while I had a sentimental journey as I once again ate some of the unique and delightful foods of their culture. It was interesting to learn of the culture of Australia through the eyes of new immigrants. On other occasions I had heard that, if Italians moved into a particular neighborhood, locals would start moving out. The next in line were the Greeks. There was an unofficial color bar at that time. I never really got to understand what it took to be a "fairdinkum Aussie". It might have to do with how long your family had lived "Down Under".

On the way to Sydney I got a BandB room at the Golden Fleece for $3.00 after traveling in the rain. The next day I decided to catch up on writing as it was still raining. While there I repaired the lock on my room door that had not seemed to bother the owner. On October 9 I continued to Sydney and located Bondi Junction where I would look up a relative from Scotland who had immigrated there some years back. Ruby Alan worked at the Grace Brothers store and I wanted to make an initial contact with her. I parked my scooter on Waverly Street at the corner of Oxford, a very busy intersection. My theory had always been that, if I tried to hide the scooter and someone found it, they would have a secluded situation in which to take whatever they wanted. The flow of traffic would ward off anyone with evil intentions.

So, I went into the store and met Ruby for the first time. We chatted and she gave me her address and phone number so I could contact her thereafter. I stopped at street level to get a quick sandwich and within a half hour returned to the scooter. My heart dropped when I realized the guitar was not longer on top of the load. Someone had cut the ropes and walked away with my world-traveled companion. I was crazed as I ran around to try to spot it. I ran to a cop directing traffic and, of course, he had not seen anything. I cruised the area on the scooter as a police car did the same. Despite my depression and rage, I could not retrieve this inexpensive instrument, which had been such an integral part of my life through 28 countries. I remember thinking that many people would have warned me against visiting certain of those countries based on the untrustworthy nature of the local residents. Yet, here in the most modern city on the continent it only took 30 minutes to have my guitar stolen. In fairness I had to admit the same could have occurred in New York City or Boston. In the following weeks I attempted a long series of TV, radio and newspaper interviews during which I made pleas for my guitar. I was even willing to buy it back but I didn't have any luck. Ted Knots of the Wayside Chapel in Kings Cross made a plea for my guitar to no avail. So much for my theory of parking in a busy spot.

Around the city I looked up a lot of friends whom I had met in my earlier travels. I ended up staying with Dom Hamilton and Bruce Simpson, friends of Diane Tipper. They had an apartment in Kirribilli just north of the Sydney Harbor Bridge. I noted that the toll for the bridge for a cycle was 2 cents, finally something I could easily afford. Her other friend, Peter Philips

Beautiful span for only 2 cent toll

had moved out shortly before. He was engaged to Dawn, a real sweetheart. Through them I met Andre and Margaret Benoit who operated Andre's Buffet Bar. They were a great couple with two daughters, Louise and Catherine. He was from Belgium where he had learned his culinary art. She was a local beauty who was very talented in art. Often we, apartment guys, would get food at Andre's. It was very tasty and quite reasonable. As I tried pawnshops to find my guitar I got several bookings on TV. Bob Sanders had lined me up for Ch. 2 and ABC rented a guitar for my performance. They sent a car for me and Peter and Dawn went along for the venture. All went well and I was paid $20 for my travel fund. I remet Jackie Hanna and her friends whom I had met in Innsbruck, Austria more than a year before.

I visited Ruby and Ian Alan and met many more of my distant relatives from Scotland. John Gelespie was my second cousin on my father's side although he referred to himself as "your 42nd cousin". They were all very hospitable to me and greatly regretted the loss of my instrument. Being in the midst of the brogue I was taken back to earlier days of my family and more recent times in Scotland. We enjoyed the afternoon and evening together.

With no hope of getting my guitar back I bought a new Japanese-made model for $32 at Elliot's and a used case for $3. It needed a bit of repair but I could easily take care of that. I looked around and bought some heavy plastic material from which to make the rain cover for the guitar. I was not as lucky looking for a 32" zipper to use on the cover. I spent most of the day around Sydney and finally was able to purchase one although it would take another 10 days to get the sewing done at an auto seat cover company. They did a fine job for $2.50.

As I had often done in other countries I had my mail sent to the General Delivery section of the main post office. Coincidentally at this time Mickey Rooney was in town performing at the Chevron Hotel. When I presented my passport to the postal clerk he kept looking at me as he searched for any mail. Finally his curiosity overcame him and he said, "You're not his son are you?" I could easily understand his assumption as I was from the USA, short of stature (not unlike Mickey) and had the last name of Rooney. It was only later that I learned that Rooney was not his real last name. He was born as Joe Yule, Jr. and had it changed as he started his show business career. Our resemblance would also be more believable when I found out that his father was an immigrant from Edinburgh, Scotland as was mine. The father relationship would be a stretch as he was only 16 years older than I.

As time went on I inquired about entertainment work at many different locations including the popular sports clubs, TV, nightclubs and restaurants.

I did get a spot on the Australian version of the "Tonight Show" hosted by an American, Don Lane. Through a newfound friend, Margo Reid from Kansas, I was able to do a TV spot on "Beauty and the Beast". I did many auditions but most turned out to be dead ends. I met Jess Williams, a Scot from Reg Grundy Enterprises, who connected me to his associate, Gwen Iliffe, in Brisbane. She wanted me to do the "I've Got a Secret" program when I get to Brisbane.

One of my general plans of travel was to try to visit New Zealand before I went north to the Orient. However, when I inquired at the New Zealand embassy I found that they were much more strict than most other countries. I would have to have my tickets for entering and leaving the country in hand before they would consider giving me a visa. They did not allow for low budget work-away's like me who would try to work his passage in both directions. Certainly I did not have the financial means to buy such tickets. I made several suggestions to the clerk as to how I might be able to visit by alternate means. All was to no avail and I had to abandon the idea of seeing another "Down Under" land.

The harbor of Sydney is very deep and beautiful to behold. Under a partially cloudy blue sky from the roof of our apartment building we watched the approach into the harbor of a small sailing craft. It was an historic day when Sir Francis Chichester of England made his only stop on his around-the-world solo journey. At 65 years of age he had covered the 13,000 miles from Plymouth in 107 days. He was greeted by an armada of private boats and water canons from the harbor patrol. He docked just below our building at the Sydney Yacht Club. His feat was immediately beamed around the world in the press and on TV. He rightfully became an instant celebrity throughout Australia.

I had been working on my Christmas card mailings, which I finally finished on November 27. When I totaled them I had sent 107 cards to 22 countries in 5 languages. This was one of the few "projects" I truly required myself to do in order to keep in touch with those I had met along the way. I was sure the numbers would increase significantly by the time I would reach home.

At some point I remembered that I had an insurance policy with the United Services Automobile Association that was available to US military officers. It was a mutual company and had great services throughout the world. I wrote to the headquarters in San Antonio, Texas to inquire as to whether, or not, my policy covered personal possessions. They sent me the standard form for making a claim and I made it out as much as I could. It asked for the original price and depreciation of each item. I could only insert the original prices and purchase dates not knowing anything about depreciation rates. With an accompanying note I explained this and left it to them to consider the depreciation if they would cover any of the items. I was later to be surprised in Brisbane to receive a check from USAA for $77, the total brand-new price of all stolen items. At the rate I was spending money that would take me many weeks and hundreds of miles. That's an A-1 insurance company!

Sundays were days of leisure and one of the fun things to do was to visit the Domain, which is a huge park. On Sundays many local "speakers", politicians and evangelists came there and used step ladders and boxes on which to elevate themselves from the crowd as they delivered their messages of self-proclaimed importance. Margo Reid and I frequently visited this area when bored. It very much reminded me of Hyde Park in London where I had started my journey three years before.

Having been brought up as a strict Catholic I usually found a local church to attend and went to confession as often as I could. As indicated before, I often had to use a mixture of languages is some countries. I was to become much more open-minded regarding other religions as a result of my travels. I found out that the Catholic Church differed greatly in different areas. In Australia they did not observe several of the feast days we had in the USA. Also in Australia all Catholic children had to attend Catholic schools. Any exceptions had to be requested from the Bishop.

As time went by I got to learn that Peter and Dawn were planning their wedding and had bought a modest old house in a rather crowded neighborhood of Sydney. There was a mountain of work to be done to it before they could consider having their wedding and reception there. I visited one day and helped Peter do some painting. The whole house needed a total makeover. It seemed obvious to me that Pete was struggling pretty much alone with this huge project. His mates would come over to visit once in a while and mainly spent the time drinking beer. One item that was truly lacking was any semblance of electrical capacity. I volunteered to do the electric work for Peter and we quickly took a list of supplies to the local store and I started the project. It consisted of a main power distribution box, additional main leads, twelve light fixtures with wall switches, four double plug outlets and an electric water heater. It took several days to run new lines and install all of the units. At one point Peter came out to the front of the house and looked up in dismay as he saw 18 wires hanging out of a main junction box. He just shook his head and went back to painting. As the day of the wedding approached a few of the gang came by to do some last minute cleaning.

On that special day I was still connecting circuits as guests arrived. Finally I finished the last unit, the hot water heater, and was able to test it with a good soothing shower. The ceremony was to be performed by Peter's friend, "Pappy", a lawyer and Justice of the Peace. Andre had delivered the food in the early afternoon and was shocked at the amount of work left to be done. However, everything was finally ready and "Pappy" mounted the stairway as a dais and announced that there would be no wedding that day. To his stunned audience he quickly clarified that the couple had actually been married in early December. With that the celebration truly began. During the required remarks by Peter I was made to feel much appreciated as he related to the crowd that my willingness to pitch in and spend so much time in helping a relative stranger had completely changed his opinion of "yanks" from the USA. The party went on to 4:00 AM at which time Peter pronounced it a success as he had provided more food and drink than the guests could consume, a unique, but common, measure of a gathering's rating.

I had sent a Christmas gift to my mother on December 13th and was surprised that she had already received it when I called on December 18th. I had to wait 30 minutes for the connection to be made but the quality and volume were great. It cost me $8.80 for three minutes and I did a little catching up on the family news. Being the only single one of seven children in a good Catholic family, you would correctly guess that I had a "bunch" of nephews and nieces in several places. The first to marry was the second oldest, Alice, and she set the pace by having 10 children. The others had added theirs to a total of 46 by this time. I was reminded of them as I spent Christmas morning with the Benoit's having delivered some small presents for the girls. I couldn't believe that it was 77 degrees outside, a typical December day "Down Under".

As I spent the days driving all around Sydney and its surrounding towns I noticed that the scooter was loosing power. I had the coil tested and it was fine. I then remembered the several times in my journey that I had the same problem and it turned out to be that the exhaust system was clogged. Thus, I planned an afternoon for the project and took my time to clean as much soot and grime from the tubes and parts as I could, given that I did not have a fire or torch to burn off the residue as I had done in the past. However, the effort paid off and the scooter jumped back to full life when I tried it out. This always renewed my challenged travel spirit as much as it did the power of my travel companion.

On New Year's Eve I went to a house party with some of my friends and spent the next day at Manly Beach being taught how to body-surf. Surfing is a huge sport in Australia and they often dominate the world competition. Their life-saving crew games are known far and wide. It was noteworthy that, by law, the entire coastline of the country is reserved for "public only" use. Nobody can own a piece of the seashore anywhere.

On January 2 Dom and I had a reunion as we picked up Diane Tipper at the airport. She had come to Sydney where she would leave on a ship for another adventure. She took Dom and Bruce up on their offer to stay at the apartment. During the day we borrowed a car and took her around Sydney including the South Heads where an immigrant ship had sunk within a hundred yards of shore after coming all the way from England. At night Di and I visited Kings Cross on the scooter and had a blast. We ended up testing our Italian as we ate at an Italian restaurant where one of the staff somehow decided I was Arabic. Two days later Dom and I put Di on the "Acadia" and almost sailed with her as we were the last two guests to leave the ship. I later called her family to insure them that her departure was quite uneventful and on time.

On January 7 Dom had a big party at the apartment for a lot of his friends. I had volunteered to cook spaghetti for the gang, which turned out to be 24 people. I met a lot of great new friends including some really beautiful girls with whom I would chat when I had time. As usual, most of the men were involved in drinking beer and swapping stories about jacking roos and football. I was told that the Aussie men prized beer, sports and women in that order. A lot of their outlook was showcased in a movie I had seen called, "They're a Weird Mob". I was really upset when I had to get busy cooking and several of the girls left because nobody paid any attention to them including the guys who brought them. I had to bite my tongue in order not to ruin the party for Dom and his mates. I would not have made a very good "Aussie" in those areas.

# CHAPTER TWENTY-FOUR

## So long Sydney

On January 9, after making my sad round of good-bys I finally left this dynamic city and headed north towards Queensland. I had only done 124 miles to Newcastle when a gear adjustment bolt loosened and I had to stop for repairs. As I pushed the scooter along the deserted countryside road a car stopped and four young brothers offered to help me. They knew of a petrol station further down the road and maybe I could get some help there. After they helped tow the scooter there we found a "friendly" owner who was quite unwilling to help at all. The boys suggested that I come to their house and repair the cycle there where I could use their tools. They towed me the 3 miles to their house, which is quite dangerous especially at night. However, they were quite hospitable and their father invited me to stay the night and do the repairs in the daylight. I was surprised at how much the accent of these country boys reminded me of the hillbillies of the W. Virginia area. Their dad had brought them up and they were poor but ambitious. They invited me to dinner after which we talked for quite a time. Finally I bedded down on the porch floor with my sleeping bag and everyone had to use some means of keeping the swarms of mosquitoes off. For me they burned several of the repellent coils that produce a mild smoke. I had to remind myself that I was heading north and in this hemisphere that means it's getting more tropical every mile. After breakfast the next morning I managed to use their tools and mine to repair the "Irish Rover" in temperatures of 90's at 8:00 AM. It took me two hours to get the job done, which seemed like four due to the flies and mosquitoes. Finally I went on my way with many handshakes and sincere good wishes. I only traveled 40 miles when the same problem occurred again. Despite the 104 degrees temperature it only took one and a half hours (getting better at it) to get back on the road.

As I passed through Port McQuarie, Kempsey and McLean I noticed that the gear change cables were wearing thin. I made a temporary repair and adjusted the gears again. I noted that the area north of Coffs Harbor was good for razing cattle, bananas, sugar cane and pineapple (inland). It was also known for low rivers and instant washouts during heavy rains. I learned that there are 15 rivers in the world that have a flow rate greater than all the Australian rivers combined. I would guess that this would depend on what time of the year the comparison was made. I continued to Coolangatta where I got a room with Vince Heffernan, a retired Brisbane policeman. He was as friendly as he was skilled. His hobby was making beautiful violins, which he carved on his knee with no workbench. He had learned the basics of playing so he could test the tone of his work. It would require 2-3 months to make one violin and then he took delight in naming them after his friends and family. The names were painted inside the support structure of the body. He preferred Swiss Pine wood for the main body but had difficulty in finding any in Australia. I wrote a letter to a company in Switzerland in an attempt to find some source he could buy from.

Vince Heffernan with one of his jewels

I was able to locate Irene again in this town and we had a great re-union. She was extremely hardworking and ambitious although she had some problems to deal with. She liked the songs I would sing especially "Green Fields". She was familiar with it and gave me the Czech words. She had become intrigued with Australia when she had been in a relocation camp in Italy and decided to move here. One of her favorite books was "Coonadoo", a story about an Aboriginal girl who was a servant on a sheep station and was taken advantage of by her white boss. Irene believed in delving into the real value of a person or friend. She was never impressed by external aspects of a person's personality such as make-up, styles and fancy hairdos. She had developed a means of prying into a person's core values and basing her impressions on realistic factors. She was quite brave and wanted to experience the world in all its facets.

I went on to Brisbane and looked up the LeRay family the daughter of which I had entertained with in Beirut. Pam and her husband, Billy, had done a song and dance routine at the Kit Kat club where I introduced them. The LeRay's "adopted" me for the next couple of weeks as I, once again, had the privilege of living with a local family and learning about the true life of the average citizens. They were Jack (father), Alice (hard-working mother), Pop (her 83 year old father from Scotland), Pam (still away), Sandra, Diane, Pierre, Ian and Lance. Jack was a superintendent at the colliery in Ipswich. He worked hard but had to be "pushed" by Alice to do chores around the house. I gave him a hand to do some alterations in the kitchen and he declared that he was now about two weeks ahead of schedule. As always I tried to show my appreciation for the kindness by repairing and building things around the house. I enjoyed the day-to-day life of this typical family as we toured the local area including the colliery where Jack worked.

While with them I got in touch with several agents and was booked to entertain in a number of local clubs. Some were real dives while others had a great crowd who enjoyed the offerings. I also did some TV shows. The most memorable of those was "I've Got a Secret", a take-off on the US version. It had been arranged by Jesse Williamson and Gwen Iliffe of the Reg Grundy Enterprises. As often happened the MC, Don Secoumb, interviewed me about my trip and I did a song for the audience. Then we played "I've Got a Secret" where I would try to stump a panel regarding some secret I had. They could ask questions for "yes" and "no" answers only ultimately trying to guess my secret. After introducing me he would say, "And now Gerry will whisper his secret to me as the home audience learns it". He had told me, "Don't say the real answer as the panel could be lip-reading". He obviously knew it already so he told me to say anything, it didn't matter. My secret was that I was now carrying my guitar around the world; what had I carried around the world before this? The answer was "nuclear bombs" on the SAC B-52 airplane. Finally when Don said, "And now Gerry will tell me what he carried around the world before as our TV audience learns it" I leaned over to him and with a deadpan face whispered "syphilis". Poor Don broke up so badly he couldn't continue for about a long 45 seconds. All the time I sat with a serious face. The panel did not guess the secret and Don's story made the rounds of the crew immediately. We all enjoyed the entire evening.

I was shocked one day when I read in the local paper that three of the original Mercury astronauts had died in their capsule during a practice. One was Gus Grissom whom we had seen with his six other crewmen at Stead Air Force Base when I was taking a pre-SAC survival course. The seven astronauts were there for special training having to do with a potential moon landing. It would take another eight years before Neil Armstrong would take that historic step. As well, about this time I heard the news of the 7-day war in the mid-East. Israel had been attacked and had taken the Sinai Peninsula, the West Bank and parts of Syria. This event would change the entire geography of the area that I had left just one year before.

I had no intention of traveling further north on the east coast and I started to make plans to leave this vast country. I got two cholera shots and found that my small pox vaccination was still valid. At this time there were many stringent rules about inoculations before entering specific countries. As a precaution I obtained a visa for the Philippines in case a ship would be going there. I had decided that I wanted to spend a significant amount of time in one Asian country and I picked Japan. I would be willing to pass through several others to get there but I would not spend much time in the others. With this in mind I started to study the small Japanese grammar book that I had bought in Sydney. I had obtained it because I had been told that the grammar of this language was quite different from English. Of course, the book instructed in basic vocabulary also.

I started to read the "Australian" newspaper, which listed the comings and goings of all the ships in the Brisbane harbor. I made many trips to the Brisbane dock area in pursuit of a ship to work on. On Feb. 3 I went to Hamilton Gate for this purpose and was turned down as often happened. However, the day was one of my favorites in Aussie as I met the dock gateman, Archie Kadell. Arch was a tall, easy-going man in his 50's and he was interested in just about everything. He loved to joke and have a good laugh even if it was on himself. His uniform was a T-shirt, Bermuda shorts, a jungle pith helmet and sneakers. During the seven weeks I stayed in Brisbane Arch and I spent a lot of time together. When I visited the port for any reason I'd drop by his gate and we'd have a coke together as we solved the majority of the problems of the world. He invited me to dinner at his house where his wife, Jo, prepared a wonderful meal. The bonus of the night was in meeting his aged mother who had a great spirit despite her years. Archie also introduced me to many of the unique Australian fruits. It was the first time I had tried mangos and papaws. He made me aware of *moustera deliciosa* which is a hybrid fruit containing several flavors from other fruits. It looks like a foot-long, elongated, slim green pepper and, as it is eaten from the end, the flavor changes about every two inches. Australia truly has a vast variety of fruits and flowers.

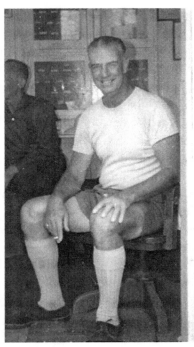

Archie Kadell—A true Aussie cobber

As the weeks went by I started to consider buying a ticket to Japan but it turned out that the cheapest one available was $250 on the Eastern Saga. It would have been only $160 on the Eastern Queen but it was fully booked. Many of the ships that came to the port had western officers. But they had Chinese crews and they were reluctant to take a Caucasian to work with them. I would have to find a ship without this restriction. Of course, I had long ago realized that the best bet for a "work-away" was with Scandinavian ships. While I was passing the time here I received two letters from a lonely widow who had two teen-aged daughters. She was asking if I would like to visit her home and get acquainted so she would have some companionship. If I could believe her background as presented, it was quite pathetic and truly sad. However, I was not going to get involved with anyone who would set my progress back any more than it had. My original idea was to possibly take 8 months to a year to travel around Europe and my lack of schedule and time constraints had resulted in my being two thirds of the way around the world after more than 2 and a half years. I was constantly balancing travel progress with the desire to truly learn of the cultures I was involved in.

One day while having dinner with the LeRay's I chipped a tooth and had to find a local dentist who could take care of the problem. I ended up at the office of Dr. Martini with whom I spoke almost exclusively in Italian. He was totally intrigued by my travels and insisted on his services being a donation to my travel fund. Again I had found a person who bolstered my faith in humanity. He did not know of me but became an instant advocate soon after I met him. These new friends made my world trip a true education and these lessons would serve me well into my distant future.

Based on the recommendations of many local friends I was convinced to visit Surfer's Paradise, a well-known holiday destination at the ocean shore. As a public relations move the local Chamber of Commerce employed several beautiful young ladies who were clad in gold bikinis as they went about their work. Their job was to observe the parking meters where out-of-state cars were left and to insure that these meters always had time on them saving the out-of-towners any parking tickets. Two of them walked their beats while a third, Veronica, made her rounds on a motorbike. I got to talk with Terry who was about to leave for Hollywood to make a film with Dean Martin. On the way back to Brisbane I looked up Vince Heffernan and had a cup of tea with him. I checked on Irene but was told by her landlady that she had left in a huff with no information.

During this period I noticed that one of the molded handgrips of the scooter was wearing out. I contacted the dealer in Sydney where I had bought the gears and they were going to send the part if it were still on the old one. However, after several weeks I had to admit that I would not receive it from there. So, I bought a local 2nd hand one that needed some work ($4.50) and had it welded for $1.40. With the new one installed my scooter was again ready for the road.

One day Jack took me to a rugby match where he was an official. This was Rugby League where there are 13 players on a side. In Rugby Union there are 15 per side. The ball is rounder than an American football and is only passed as a lateral. It can be handled by anyone and there is no blocking. The action is started with a scrum in which all players are interlocked to see if the one with the ball can break out. The field is 100 yards like a football field. A try (goal) is 3 points while a conversion is 2 points. The action is continuous like soccer.

# CHAPTER TWENTY-FIVE

## "West meets East"

I had read of the ship, Robert Maersk, coming to Brisbane and heading for Hong Kong with the possibility of going to Japan thereafter. I had found out that most foreigners including those from the USA could spend 14 days in Hong Kong without a visa, which made life a little easier. I went to visit and was told I'd have to wait until they contacted the home office. I was to come back in two days before they sailed. I learned that two of the crew were sick, one having had his appendix removed in a Brisbane hospital. My hopes were rising. I later was told that I could ship out with them if I took over the duties of the officers' mess boy. He was Chinese and going home to Hong Kong on the ship but he could not work due to his operation.

On March 8 I said good-by to the LeRay's who had become like my Australian family. I bought them a cutlery set and a ukulele for Vance to see if he might be interested in music. I got a kick out of playing it myself having started my involvement with strings with a ukulele and the Arthur Godfrey TV lessons in the 50's. I made the rounds at the harbor and said good-by to George Duffy and all of Archie's mates there. Finally I had to give a sincere farewell to this close cobber who had been a very special acquaintance during my time in Queensland. Both Archie and I had tears in our eyes as we wished each other all the best. I boarded the ship at about noon and the process of loading the 6,400 tons of wheat was continuing. The grain was being air-blown into the holds with a hose of about 12" diameter. It took a full two days to complete the loading. An ocean pilot had come aboard, as the ship would travel within the Great Barrier Reef as it skirted the NE coast. The loading finished at 7:00 PM and we were under way by 11:30 PM. I was assigned to a double cabin and was quite comfortable settling in although it turned out to be too hot being next to the engine room. The ship was so heavily laden that, on our cabin deck, we could not open the portholes, as they would be completely submerged when the ship rolled to any degree. I suspected I might look out and see Moby Dick at any time.

Because of the heat I had trouble sleeping at all when I got a surprise at 3:30 AM the first morning at which time I was told I had to prepare to serve breakfast to two officers coming off duty and tea and snacks to the officer coming on duty on the bridge. The cook was awake and had things ready. I served the two officers in the officers' mess and then had to load a tray with all manner of possible choices for the officer on the bridge. Loading was a big enough challenge but then I had to carry it up several flights of stairs as the ship rolled and pitched a bit. I don't know how I didn't spill half of what I was carrying. I later determined that the breakfast routine involved 202 steps. (Note: Later I documented that my total daily routine involved a total of 920 vertical steps for work purposes.) When I arrived there the officer took only a cup of tea and some toast although I had carried a virtual buffet of breakfast "goodies" all the way there. That night I got about one half hour sleep.

The following day I got a briefing on my work requirements and organized my time. I also pre-determined what would be desired on the bridge at 4:00 AM so I would carry only those few items. I must say that this part of my duty allowed me to study the stars on clear nights. I learned that marine navigators don't take celestial readings at night. They don't use a false horizon. So they shoot the sun using the ocean horizon during the day. Of course, their progress from day to day is so much slower than a jet airplane they don't have to check their position as often.

My mess duties included watch-change breakfast at 4:00 AM, regular breakfast for all officers at 8:00 AM, coffee time at 10:00 AM, lunch at 12:00 noon, coffee and cake at 3:00 PM (1500) with dinner at 5:30 PM (1730). I would set the tables, serve the platters of food and drinks, replenish as needed and later clean the tables, wash the dishes and get ready for the next meal. One thing that bothered me quite a bit resulting in a notation in my diary was the amount of food that was thrown over the side every day. I couldn't help but think of some of the friends I had met in poorer countries who could easily survive for weeks on what we throw away each day. Anything left in the serving pans would be dropped overboard after the meal. This gave me a renewed sense of the importance of not wasting any source of nourishment. I had always felt that way having come from a lower-middle class family of nine.

On the first day at sea I had asked the Purser if I could buy a bottle of soda. I asked if I should pay for it then or wait until the end of the trip. He said they would take it out of my pay. What? I was being paid? What a boost! I thought I was working for my passage but I was, in fact, receiving the wage of the mess boy. Later he asked me if I would take half the duties of the cabin boy who was missing. This would be considered overtime for pay purposes. From then on I cleaned 5 cabins a day in between my other duties. So, here I was getting free passage for the motor scooter and me from Australia to Hong Kong and earning some travel money along the way. This is the type of situation that helped me to stretch my funds to a great degree.

I had a unique experience one day when I went out on deck during break time to find many of the crew sunning themselves. I happened to meet the Chinese boy whose place I was taking and he was heading for home in Hong Kong. He was anxious to soak up some sun because he was afraid that when he arrived home his mother would think he was too sickly as he might be too *yellow*. It just hit me in a strange way. Normally those I knew would be accused of being too pale (white). He had a good spirit and we joked about it.

On the third day at sea they started the air conditioning and we all thought we were in paradise, especially me when I transferred to a single cabin that had its own bathroom . . . etc. However, we were brought back down to reality that evening when it stopped again. Many lost sleep because of a combination of heat and getting used to the movements of the ship (getting your sea legs). I was told that even experienced seamen take some time back at sea to get their "sea legs" if they've been ashore for a while.

I quickly wrote letters to my mother, the LeRay's, Archie and Dick Greenish so I could give them to the Ocean Pilot with money for stamps so he could mail them after he got off the ship at Thursday Island. As well, I repaired my watch and clock, which ran the best in years thereafter. I had started studying Japanese and was making fair progress. Among other times I would study in the pantry when all the officers were supplied with ample food. One thing that made my job a bit more challenging was that, due to miss loading, we had to start water rationing after 8 days. Water was only turned on from 0630-0730 and 1700-1800. I had to set water aside to insure that I could wash the dishes after meals.

I noted that we were taking a good portion of the route of the "Krait" which carried the "Z" force members all the way to Singapore Harbor in WW II. It was featured on the book "The Heroes". However, we did not go through the Lumbock Straits as it did. We did pass the equator and I was able to experiment with the coriolis affect. It implies that water going down a drain in the northern hemisphere would flow clockwise and the opposite in the southern hemisphere. I checked it over a couple of days and found it to be true. We continued past many of the 3000 thousands islands of the Philippines. In that area I noted several pods of porpoises (bottled nosed dolphins). I also realized that we could now see Polaris (the north star) again. Given that we were traveling northwest twice we had to set our clocks back an hour.

I was really getting attached to the crew and we spent many a night having jam sessions and songfests with the guitar. Of course, this involved me and others losing a lot of sleep. We figured we could always catch a nap in between times during the day. I found that the moisture of the ocean and heat resulted in the sciatic pain in my right knee being almost constant at times. That didn't help with all the stairs I had to climb. However, I took it as part of the meager price I was paying to have the sojourn of a lifetime.

After fourteen days on the ocean we arrived in Hong Kong in the evening of March 22nd in very rainy weather. Almost all commercial ships must anchor in the harbor with only a few military ships tied up at berths. The following morning I was awakened by the sound of many people climbing the gangway to get on deck. They were middle-aged and older women with a few middle-age men. They carried brooms and shovels and went straight to work to shovel the 6,400 tons of wheat off that ship. Once the holds had been opened a large tarp was spread over a section of the wheat and the women would shovel the grain into it. When it was full a foreman (man) would gather the corners, attach them to a cable from the derrick and the load would be dropped into a factory barge lashed to the side of the ship. I was amazed that this labor-intense crew could shovel off the entire load in three days when it had taken two days to load it by powered machinery in Brisbane. These workers continued day and night in shifts and only stopped to eat their meager meals, which one of them had prepared on the deck. I went to shore several times during these days and would come back at night to see the same old lady still shoveling several stories below me in the hold.

When we arrived in Hong Kong the Captain still didn't know where he would be going from there. It was possible that they would go to Japan or to Thailand and then Japan. Either option would have been great for me. Being Holy Week I tried to arrange my time so I could attend church at least once. I had missed all of the Easter holidays the prior year. My time ashore was cut up given that I still had all of my duties to attend to on the ship. I found out that I would have no problem with immigration if I paid off from the ship there. I confirmed this at the US. Consul.

One evening after dinner I was surprised to hear a clattering on the gangway and found four or five beautiful Chinese ladies boarding the ship. They were well dressed and seemed out of place to me. However, hardly anybody else on the ship was surprised. In fact a number of the veteran sailors knew some of them personally. I was later informed that they were referred to as the "Sunday School Girls" and were a traditional group of prostitutes who came on to serve the desires of the seamen who were not allowed to leave the ship. They all spoke English and some other languages as well. They were quite attractive and very outgoing. Everyone gathered in the lounge and got acquainted. At the request of some of the guys I got the guitar and we had quite a songfest as individual crewmen made their bargains and disappeared with a female for various periods of time. One young, new seaman was "treated" by one of his buddies to his first time encounter and much was made of it upon his return with toasts . . . etc. I had made it clear that I had no interest in any bargaining. After many songs and drinks I decided to turn in as I had my usual schedule for the following day. After I tucked into bed the girlfriend of one seaman who had just gone on duty came knocking at my cabin door offering a "freebee" for all the entertainment I had provided. Rather than get into any embarrassing discussion I made believe that I was asleep and she finally left.

On March 26th I got a shock when I found out that the ships orders had come in and it was going straight back to Australia and then to Japan. This would involve an additional 5-6 weeks, which I was not ready to experience. At this time a problem surfaced; the immigration authorities would let me off the ship only if the ship's company would guarantee that I would leave Hong Kong (they didn't want me to stay and end up on welfare.). Their young Chinese agent on the ship said they could not do that, as I was not an employee. I almost panicked. If I didn't find a way to get off I'd be sailing out of the harbor in a few hours in a direction I didn't want to go.

I knew that the Captain wanted me to leave at this point as he was getting new crewmembers. After my arguing my case and a number of phone calls to the local office by the agent with no positive results, I took a different approach. I handed the agent 5—$20 American Express Traveler's Checks and said his company could keep them while I was in Hong Kong and use them to buy me a ticket out of the Colony if I tried to stay there. With a last phone call he was told that would be acceptable. He apparently didn't realize that he could not have used the checks without my second signature. For me it got the required results. I was then paid off from the ship and received $70

US, which was fortunate since the $100 dollars I had given the agent was the bulk of all funds I had with me at the time.

Then I had to make hasty plans to get my gear, especially my scooter, off the ship. I went ashore on the motor launch and found a small sampan along the shore. The man and his family lived on the small craft and I asked if I could hire him to get my gear off the ship. I made a bargain with him for $15 HK ($2.50 US) and we headed to the ship where he tied up to the gangway as I raced up to find the crew to operate the derrick. I had been shown by my first bosun how to rig the thick rope on the scooter so it was lifted in an upright position and was quite secure. I had to make sure by having it lifted a couple of feet and then trying to dislodge it by pulling and putting my weight on it. I knew if we put it over the side and it slipped out it would be lost forever in the deep waters of the harbor. When ready I rushed down the gangway, got in the sampan and directed the owner to tie up along the starboard side of the ship. The crew lowered the "Irish Rover" until I could guide it into the narrow opening of the small boat. When it was securely inside I untied it and we went back to the gangway so I could get the rest of my gear and say my quick good-by's. After a short trip to the shore the man helped me to get the 270-pound scooter up a flight of about 10 steep steps. With his wife and children following with my gear I was finally on *terra firma*. By the time I did my business at the nearby immigration office and came outside, I watched as the Robert Maersk edged slowly out of the harbor on its return trip to Aussie-land without me. I had dodged another bullet in my travels.

I inquired for lodging at the seamen's mission but was refused, as I didn't have seamen's papers. I hurried to the Cathedral, went to confession and attended Easter Mass. I then took the car ferry to Kowloon (mainland) for a meager .10 US. I noted the transportation was very cheap there. I went to the Western YMCA and got a room for $3 US per night, which was actually overpriced for Hong Kong given the condition of the room. Meals were available, cheap and good. On several occasions I visited the Ocean Terminal Center that is like a huge mall with goods from every corner of the world. Prices were very reasonable. It was the largest such marketplace in the world. As I visited the city of Victoria (often referred to as Hong Kong) I realized that Hong Kong is the island of 29 square miles. I was stunned to see that some of the buildings, which had looked so majestic and beautiful from the ship were anything but on the inside. The population was 3.5 million of which 150,000 were listed as "marine inhabitants". They were born, and lived their entire lives, on a variety of boats that plied the busy harbor by day and tied up at night. Children under the age of 15 represented 40 percent of the population. The international airport, Kai Tak, was located close to the ocean in Kowloon. I noted that the northwest approach is quite difficult over the mountains. I also came to know that Macao (formerly Portuguese) is a famous gambling spot just four hours away by motor launch. It's like the Las Vegas of the area.

One day I was in a clothing store to buy a birthday gift for my mother and I had no problem chatting with the Chinese clerk who also spoke English. This was the norm given that Hong Kong was part of the British Empire at that time. However, I took note of a Japanese man who came to shop for a particular item. He did not speak Chinese nor English and was having a hard time explaining what he wanted to purchase. Finally he held up one hand and with the index finger of the other he traced a kanji character on his palm. Immediately the clerk understood what he desired. I was to later learn that the Japanese written language consists of the same Chinese characters (kanji) as well as two modern syllabaries known as kana. The kanji characters are word-pictures and mean the same thing in both languages. However, the pronunciation is totally different. So, the Japanese and Chinese cannot talk to each other but can write messages that are generally understood by the other.

I was immediately busy checking on ships on which I might get to Japan. Many came from various countries and I would find their locations and use the company motor launch to visit and try to talk the captain into taking me. While visiting the Isarstein I was turned down by the captain despite my attempts to impress him with my German. However, I was befriended by the 2nd engineer who invited me to drinks and dinner as his guest. He explained to me that it was virtually impossible to get a job as a "work-away" on a German ship due to bureaucratic procedures and rules. Thus, I added Germany to the list of "no-go" nations whose ships would not take me. This list now included the USA, Britain, Japan, Australia, France, Canada and others that I had not yet encountered. At least, knowing this avoided a lot of frustration in my future searches. The bottom line was that the Scandinavian ships were the best prospects. I narrowed my pursuits thereafter to ships of Norway, Denmark, Sweden and Finland.

I decided to move to the Chinese YMCA, which was brand new and cheaper at only $14 HK per day. Having situated myself in my new digs I decided to buy some rubber cement for my tire-patching kit in the business district of Kowloon. When I came back to the street I could not find my scooter. I searched frantically for it until a local merchant told me that the police had towed it away for over-parking. I called the police and found that it had been taken to the impoundment area at the airport. The fine was $50

HK and that was almost the remainder of my cash. I had no idea how long it would take me to find a ship for Japan at which time I'd be able to reclaim my $100 US from the agent. Later the Chief Inspector determined that it should not have been towed as it belonged to a foreigner. So, I was permitted to claim the scooter at no charge. A local young American motorcyclist offered to give me a ride to the airport and I well remember holding my breath on a couple of sharp turns through the streets, which he obviously knew quite well. I was truly relieved when I could take possession of my own independent means of travel.

When I wasn't checking on shipping I would spend the time visiting the local sites. I took the cable car up the "Peak" and was able to look at both sides of the Hong Kong Island. It was very mountainous and reminded me of Capri in Italy. I also went up to the peak on the Kowloon side from which one could see past the New Territories into Communist China. The terrain was very rugged. I also caught up on some letter writing for which I often used aerogramme.

As I walked through the streets of Kowloon one morning I happened to meet the owner of the company to whom we had delivered the wheat. I had met him on the ship and he turned out to be a very down-to-earth person. Although the owner of the company, he dressed more like some of the workers I had seen on the ship. He seemed surprised to see me in that context and invited me to have some lunch with him. Being a local Chinese native he knew the real authentic restaurants of the city. We entered one and he introduced me to *dim sum,* which is actually a manner of serving a great variety of food offerings. We had a pot of Chinese tea and every few minutes a waiter would come around with a covered platter of all delicious and intriguing kinds of dishes presented one at a time. Because the portions were small the customer could sample many different foods or have more of any given favorite. Dim sum became one of the items for which I later searched in any area where Chinese food was offered. Steamed bread turned out to be one of my personal favorites.

On April 1I visited the "Ellen Maersk" in a rainstorm to talk to the captain. He said he was willing to take me as a work-away to Japan but he needed permission of the company. I contacted my sponsor, Mr. Boyson, at the local office and asked if he could contact the company in Denmark for me. He said there would not be enough time, as the ship would leave the following day. Luckily this ship was owned by the A P Moller Company and was a sister-ship to the one that had brought me to Hong Kong. I talked him into sending a cable to the home office and left my telephone number at the YMCA. At 8:30 PM Mr. Boyson called to say that he had received the OK from the home office. I checked out and rushed to collect my $100 at the local office. I hurried to the dock to take the company launch out to the ship. The challenge came when the launch docked and I had to get my 270-pound scooter down a flight of concrete steps and over the side of the vessel gunwale. I talked a young Chinese into steering the scooter as I carried the back of it backwards down the steps to the launch level, At that point a couple of the seamen who were heading for the same ship helped me to get the scooter into the launch. I then collected the rest of my possessions and we were on our way. At the ship the other seaman helped me carry my baggage up the gangway ladder as I sought an officer to help me load the scooter. I returned to the launch with a good length of strong line and rigged the scooter for hoisting onto the ship. Once it was lifted I returned to the gangway and went aboard. It was midnight and I was soaking wet but greatly relieved to know that this ship would be my ticket to Japan.

Due to the rain they couldn't load stores for the ship on the usual schedule. So, we didn't leave until 3:30 PM the next day (April 2) which, made all the hectic rush of the prior day unnecessary. Once at sea I was changed from the pilot's cabin to a two-person cabin by myself with a private bathroom and shower. The crew consisted of 11 Danes and 25 Chinese who all worked very well together. Cooperation and moral were very high. The two Danish apprentices were Lau and Henrik. I was considered to be in their category of seamen and we got along very well. Immediately we had a guitar session in the officers' lounge and all entered into the entertainment with gusto. (Note: When entering or leaving a dining room on the ship the Danes say "Wel bekomen" as a greeting.)

As we headed for Taiwan we three washed down the ship, which is done after leaving any port. As usual the meals were great with the kitchen being open at all times for snacks . . . etc. On April 3 we arrived at Kaohsiung, the deep southern port of Taiwan at 5:00 PM. Here Chinese immigration is very strict especially with the Danes who deal with Communist China. Foreign money must be sealed aboard the ship. To go ashore a seaman's pass is required with a photo. We came alongside at noon the following day and I took the day off to explore a bit of this relatively new nation with Antonio from Hong Kong who was Portuguese and Spanish. He had been included as part of the Chinese crew. The local women were quite attractive and the little kids were cute trying to sell us chewing gum. Many of the adults spoke some Japanese, a legacy of WW II. I got a chance to try some of the Japanese I was still studying. (Note: 2.5 cents US was equal to $1 Taiwanese.)

# CHAPTER TWENTY-SIX

## The Rising Sun

The next day we left at 8:00 AM and headed through the Taiwan Straits (Straits of Quemoy) between Taiwan and the Communist mainland. Often shelling still takes place across these straits. The shells contain propaganda leaflets. As we passed the islands south of Japan the sea was getting quite rough as I started my job of painting various parts of the ship. I painted my way all the way to the port of Yokohama. We arrived at the Union Pier at 3:00 PM on April 9 and there was no problem with me being on a passenger list. The captain told me that there was no rush for me to leave, as the ship would be there for several more days. It turned out that there was no gate at the dock and we could come and go as we pleased. The following day I went into Yokohama by bus and had a tough time changing my Hong Kong money. I had missed the Hong Kong-Shanghai bank by 3 minutes. I checked for mail but there was none. I returned to the ship and we had a party until 4:30 AM. The next day I went into town again and changed my money and got a haircut in Yokohama's Chinatown by a young woman barber who was very good. It cost just 400 yen, which was quite cheap given that we got *360 yen for one US dollar*. This Chinatown is the most famous in Japan and a favorite destination for many Japanese after hours.

Lau Larsen, one of the apprentices and I had become very close and we decided to go out on the town one night. I had been studying my Japanese grammar book with some vocabulary. We decided we needed more words so we each bought a small English-Japanese dictionary. We did some shopping and saw some of the sites of the city. Later we went to a restaurant to have a drink and dinner. It was a bit out of the way and the staff members were not too used to foreigners but very hospitable. They were surprised that we ate with chopsticks although forks and spoons were offered. We got friendly with several of the female staff and they ended up closing the restaurant with us still in it. I used my Japanese a bit and we looked up words when needed. Everyone had a great, friendly time singing songs and making jokes.

Later as we waited in line for a taxi Lau dropped his almost-finished cigarette on the ground and said' "Get it". Unfortunately for him my strong right foot stomped down on the butt just a fraction of a second after his did. The result was Lau hopping around the area on one foot and yelling in Danish to my great amusement. Only a few of the Japanese in line seemed to enjoy the incident as much as we did. By this time Lau was also laughing. This turned out to be a very non-typical seaman's night ashore and Lau said he had never had so much fun. Together we had spent less than 1000 yen ($2.80 US) in 5 hours

On April 12 I drove the scooter to the city and bought a new tube for my tire and returned to the ship. At about 3:30 PM I left the ship after checking with the Custom's Officer. After he checked my visa he told me that I had to go to the central customs office four miles away on the main pier so I could have my baggage inspected. It seemed a bit ridiculous given that we had been in port for three days with no gate and I had visited the city several times. Had I wanted to smuggle any object into the country I could have left it anyplace on the way to the office and picked it up later. However, I had nothing of suspicion so I went to that office where they did not look at anything. They stated that I had to register my scooter in Japan and get a new international license all of which required mounds of paperwork, a doctor's certificate of good health, an eye test, a valid home license, 800 yen and a delay of at least a week. I was told I had to go to the Land Registration Office but nobody could tell me where it was located. I decided to pass on all of the above as it was not in my travel plans.

I drove to Tokyo and checked into the Ichigaya Youth Hostel for 200 yen. The next day I contacted Hiroshi Nishida whom I had met in Port Said, Egypt a year before. He was a medical student at Keio University and lived in a small apartment in Yotsuya Sanchome. We agreed to get together and I spent the rest of the day seeing some of the sights of Tokyo. It was a huge, hectic metropolis and the driving was a challenge. Often I parked my scooter and used the subway or streetcar. I quickly became accustomed to the very efficient subway system where everything was done in colors. If you looked at the multi-colored map of the city you could follow the color of the particular line from your present position to your destination including any changes. At the platform you would see the signs in English (romaji) and Japanese for the name of that station and the names of the next stations on both directions. If you wished to use the green line to the point where it intersected with the purple line, you would get off the green car at the appropriate station, look down at the floor, find the purple line and follow it. It would lead you to the purple line platform through tunnels and over steps if necessary. You would wait on the designated spaces and a purple train would come and take you to your next desired destination.

You had to be careful and aware if you traveled at rush hour because there were many more travelers than spaces in the cars. The unique solution to this challenge was to have "pushers" employed by the railway company who would force the waiting line into the cars when they appeared to be already full. Thus, you would be jammed up against all sorts of people you didn't know very well (until the ride was over). You would buy your tickets at machines and pass them through a scanner as you entered the platform. When you left the destination platform you would pass your ticket through another scanner and the amount of the fare would be deducted. It became obvious that the majority of city dwellers used public transportation for almost all their travel needs. Not many local people owned their own car. You were not allowed to purchase a car unless you proved that you had parking arrangements off the streets.

I toured the Olympic Stadium that had been used in 1964. I photographed the main buildings, which were truly Asian in design. As well, I visited the Meiji Jingu Shrine, which commemorates the era of enlightenment until 1912 when the short Taisho era commenced. It lasted only until 1925 when the current Emperor, Hirohito, ascended the thrown. In the Meiji era the Emperor had established the Diet (congress) and the prefectural system of land division. I caught a photo of a family bringing a new-born baby to the shrine in the same manner as a Western baptism. Dress-up occasions brought out the beautiful, traditional Japanese kimonos. However, day-to-day garb was much as in the West, especially for office workers.

One of the individuals I planned on meeting was Father Bill Ducey from Charlestown, Mass. He was a Sacred Heart Missionary priest who had been in Japan for 8 years. His sister, Mary Sullivan, lived in my home town, Wilmington, and worked in Grant's store with my mother. When she learned that I would travel around the world she gave me her brother's address in Japan and asked me to look him up when I got there. Of course, at that time I expected to travel for 8 months or possibly a year. Here I was 3 years later finally getting to his area. I called him on the phone and he invited me to visit him at the central church and retreat center in Tomobe that day. He gave me directions as regards which subways to use and which train to take north. I used my rudimentary Japanese to make sure I got on the right train from Ueno Station and found Father Ducey waiting for me at my destination. He said he was quite surprised to see me because he only realized after he had hung up the phone, that I only had about 35 minutes to make all the connections. We spent the afternoon chatting over lunch and he showed me the local pond where they were developing a recreation area including small rowboats.

Father Bill was a very gentle kind of guy, 40 years of age, and his manner endeared him to the locals whether Catholic or not. He had learned his Japanese, like most of the foreign priests, at the language school in Ropongi, Tokyo. Now after 8 years he was quite proficient although when I first heard him I made a note that he spoke Japanese with a Charlestown-Boston accent that was hard for me to miss. His height (over 6 feet) made him stand out physically and he made friends with ease. At the end of the day I returned to Tokyo with a promise to visit again as I later toured Japan.

When I got in touch with Hiroshi again he invited me to stay with him in his "*aparto*". I moved over to Yotsuya Sanchome and met his landlords, Mr. and Mrs. Hara. As was typical for a student, his room was very small at 3-4 tatamis. A tatami is a thick straw mat, which covers most interior Japanese floors. It is about 3.5 feet by 7 feet. It is a standard used to reference the size of any room. With no chairs everyone would sit on the floor on cushions, *zabutons*. The traditional position is known as *seiza*, sitting on your heals with you legs under you. I was told that the younger generation of Japanese was having problems using this position as many of the homes and restaurants now had western chairs and tables. Because space was at a premium in Japan, the rooms of an apartment or house were multi-functional. Hiroshi's small apartment had a low table and cushions for sitting during meals of chats. When it was time for sleeping the table would be set on end against a corner wall and the *futons* (thick mattress-like rolls) would be brought out and spread on the floor with appropriate linens and pillows. I would guess this was better for posture than the thick mattresses we used in the west.

There were several small apartments in the building and there was a common cooking area in the downstairs hallway. The toilet fixtures reminded me of those I had seen in parts of France, squatters in the floor. I had also found them in the mid-east. Hiroshi's school was within walking distance and the streetcar ran by the front of the building. I spent a little more than a week with Hiroshi as I prepared to make a significant journey all around

Japan. I actually found Chuo Motors, which was an agent for NSU scooters and bought a second hand brake light switch for 250 yen.

As might be suspected, I traveled with very little clothing. Generally I wore chino slacks that could easily be washed and casual shirts depending on the weather. When I had to face a more formal setting I would take out my best slacks (which had been bought for me by Matt Busby's family in England) or Uncle Hughie's suit, which had been my dress-up outfit during most of my trip. By the time I arrived in Japan those English slacks were still holding up beautifully being of fine quality and wrinkle free. However, the sole drawback was that the pockets had been progressively wearing out. Now I had difficulty keeping anything in them and almost lost some important items. For a low-budget traveler of Scottish descent it was natural for me to replace the pockets. To the dismay of many store clerks I went on a search for pockets. Finally I visited a tailor, explained my situation and asked if I might buy two pockets. He agreed and I walked out of the store clutching these all-important pieces of cotton. Back at Hiroshi's apartment I dug out my small sewing kit and sewed in the new pockets with very small stitches. Now I was ready to face the nation of Japan. How could I lose with new pockets?

One day Hiroshi introduced me to a visitor who was his brother, Shoji. However, he was also the son of his aunt and uncle which confused me a bit. He later explained that one Japanese custom was for a family with several children to give one of them to an aunt and uncle who could not have children. This had been the case with his family. So, although Shoji was a blood brother, he was being raised as a son by his aunt and uncle whom I also met later. Shoji was a student of engineering in Tokyo. Hiroshi's father, sister and brother-in-law were all doctors. His father lived in Hobara Machi (town) in Fukushima Ken (prefecture=state in the USA) north of Tokyo on the same large island, Honshu.

Tokyo was a very crowded city and apartments were very small. Few of them could have their own bath (o-furo). The common answer to this was the community public baths usually within a few blocks of each dwelling. Of course I went to the baths with Hiroshi and Shoji and managed to raise a few eyebrows when I partook of the total experience as a native. The two sides of the building were divided for male and female patrons. We paid our 28-yen at the desk located between the two sides and proceeded to the locker room with our small towels and soap. We undressed completely and put our belongings into the small locker and took the "key" with us on a cord along with the small towel and soap. The key was a piece of flat wood with several cuts of varying length into one end. This combination of cuts would fit, and open, only one locker door. We went into the next room, which had a series of wash stations along the walls for the guests. At each station would be a small stool, a bucket and brush. It was important to note that the Japanese bath is not intended to be cleansing but therapeutic and relaxing. Thus, the first step is to wash and rinse completely before entering the actual bath. I can imagine how I stood out with my red hairy body amongst the small Japanese men who have little body hair. I didn't notice any other redheads there. By this time in my travels I had learned to "Do as the Romans do, when in Rome". So, I went about my body washing as I sang a Japanese song I was learning. The older woman who came by to pick up soap wrappers . . . etc. didn't seem to be phased although she might have had an amusing story for her family by the time she got home that day.

When it was time to enter the community bath I noticed there were two large baths like swimming pools. We took our rinsed towels with us and entered what I thought must have been a pool in Dante's inferno. I later found out that this was the *cooler* bath. We would stay for about 10 minutes and when we got out I was like a lobster. I did not take up the challenge of the hotter bath. The first one was so hot that we would wring out our towels, wipe off our bodies with them and be dry by the time we got back out to the locker room. Outside of large cities private homes usually had there own bathtubs. They could be round or square and be about 3-4 feet deep. In later travels I used a number of different *o-furos* including other community public baths.

As was the case several times in my journey I had taken up smoking when I was hanging out with heavy smokers. In Japan I found cigarettes good and cheap at .20 a pack. The common brands were Hilite, Peace and Hope. I noticed that most older men smoked very heavily. One place where smoking was prevalent was in the "Pachinko" parlors. These arcades usually contained several hundred vertical pinball machines all of which seemed to be flashing lights and making ear-splitting noises at the same time. Devotees of the game would spend hours feeding the small steel balls into the colorful noisemakers. Those who were successful would be rewarded with prizes of goods as they finally left. I was convinced that pachinko was the number one national game in Japan. However, the number one team sport was *yakyu* (baseball), which is played with a rubber ball having different characteristics than the one used in the USA. They had leagues from Little League to professional levels and the fans were truly dedicated.

During my stay with Hiroshi I contacted and remet Shiro Kanda whom I had also met in the Port Said Youth Hostel in Egypt. He was from Shiga

Ken quite a distance to the west. He had finished his college degree and got a position with the Japanese Railways. As is the normal path, he was working as a conductor on a train because he was just starting with the company. He would experience all levels of employment with the firm before he would become part of management. This was the typical Japanese system. You had to learn from the bottom up. Shiro told me that his travel mate in Egypt, Norio Tokomitsu, was working in Okayama, which I would visit later in my journey. Shiro was with his very cute sister, Tomiko, and we caught up on our past as we all ate *tempura*, lightly deep-fried seafood, vegetables . . . etc. served with rice. This dish was a favorite with the Japanese as well as visitors. I was to hear that the process of deep-frying had been introduced by Portuguese missionaries many years before.

When I would enter a new country for the first time I would try to learn enough of the language so I could, at least, order foods that I found tasty and desirable. Usually my language background would allow me to make sense of most menus. However, in Japan the menus were in Japanese characters and I had no clue as to their meaning. No problem. The Japanese had a great system that eliminated any confusion. At the entry to the restaurant there was a large glass display case in which were realistic plastic replicas of all the dishes on the menu. The names were in Japanese but it was obvious what they contained in most cases. So for me, instead of going in and ordering from the waiter, I would pull him outside and point to the dish I wanted. Later as time went on I was able to order my favorites inside. The one dish, which became, and still is, my number one was *katsudomburi*. It's like a meal in a bowl. A lightly breaded pork cutlet is cooked in a frying pan or on a grill in a sauce of beaten eggs, onions and flavorings. When ready, it is sliced into strips and served over a deep bowl of steaming white rice through which all the juices would flow. Like many dishes it is usually served with a small portion of pickles (pickled *daikons* . . . etc). I was to order this dish all over Japan.

# CHAPTER TWENTY-SEVEN

## "On the road again"

On April 21 I said my good-bys and left to discover the culture of this diverse land. My route took me west through Hachiyoji and some beautiful mountain scenery on my way to the Mount Fuji area. April is the month of the cherry (*sakura*) blossoms and they were out in abundance along the mountain roads. I had been surprised that the Japanese drive on the left side of the road meaning that the driver sat on the right side. Of course I had had plenty of practice driving on the left in the British Isles, Sweden, Australia and Hong Kong. I found the roads to be very crowded and the drivers to be very daring. Most streets were quite narrow and the speed limits were very low, expressed in kilometers per hour. Most cars were like compacts but many trucks seemed to be of the size in the USA.

One of the customs that I really appreciated was a part of the welcoming at any restaurant or tavern. As soon as you were seated a waitress would approach you with a small steaming towel for each person. This *o-shibori* would be used to wash and refresh your hands and face. When I would stop for coffee or tea after many kilometers of scooter travel, I would almost take a facial bath with this towel. It was the perfect refresher.

I checked into the youth hostel at Lake Saiko. Saiko was one of the Fuji *goko* (five lakes that surround the base of the mountain). I found the Japanese Youth Hostel system quite well developed. There were many locations around the country and they had some unique characteristics. Usually they would be filled with youth groups from various schools who were on some kind of class trip. The available breakfast was almost always the same: a bowl of white steaming rice, a raw egg, small sheets of processed seaweed, a few Japanese pickles, hot green tea and a bowl of *miso shiro* soup. The raw egg is cracked

Reflection of Mt. Fuji

into a small dish, it is whipped with soy sauce and then poured over the bowl of very hot rice which somewhat cooks it. In any event I got quite used to it and ate this breakfast at every chance.

Of course, everywhere I went the guitar went with me and I found that young Japanese students love to have sing-a-longs. The one song from the US that I could always count on most people knowing was "You are my Sunshine". As well, many would know the traditional old time standards like Steven Foster's "Old Black Joe". In fact, that melody was used in a sad movie by the name of "The Harp of Burma". They often recognized many of the folk songs of the "Peter, Paul and Mary" era also.

The next day I was extremely lucky when I went outside and saw the full majesty of Fujisan. It was a very clear day and I took the opportunity to take several photos of its symmetrical grandeur. I happened to pass a puddle, which resulted from the rain the previous night. I used it to take mirror image of Fujisan over Lake Yamanaka. I didn't realize how lucky I was until much later when I met people who had visited Japan on several occasions and had never seen the top of the mountain. I worked my way through Hakone Park and continued west along what was referred to as the Tokaido Line,

Me as lord of Inuyama Castle

I stayed in Miho Hostel and the following day I raced to Shizuoka for Mass, which was said by a French priest. He invited me for coffee and a chat afterwards. He explained that this particular region was famous around Japan for the growing of the cherished green tea. As I would pass the fields and hills I would spot the rows of green tea bushes that looked like a bunch of green balls that had been pushed together to form a line. I was told that the first pick of the tender leaves is referred to as the "Emperor's pick". It is the most desired of the leaves.

I drove on the main highway through Nagoya and stopped for a visit in Inuyama. It was an historic town with an original castle and a shrine. The castle was the only one in Japan, which was still owned by the original family. I paid an entrance fee and climbed the several stories noting the degree of defense built into the construction. In the front of the building was a stand that had the uniform of a lord of the house. It was used by a local photographer for the many tourists who came to the site. A patron would put on the period hat, stand behind the costume and insert his arms through the back of the ample sleeves. He would then hold a folding fan in one hand with the other resting on the hilt of the sword. I decided to get recorded as a lord except that I had the photographer use my camera. With a squint of my eyes I was able to produce an image not unlike many of the Japanese. Years later I would still fool my friends when I would introduce them to the "Lord of Inuyama".

I also found another cultural treasure in this area. It was famous for cormorant fishing. The cormorant is a dark-colored goose-like bird that is bred and used for nighttime fishing. The fishermen take their boats out on the river and light a fire to attract the fish. The cormorants have a ring around their necks so they cannot swallow the fish that they catch. They are then reeled in by the attached line and the fish are taken from their mouths. This method dates back hundreds of years and is carried on by certain people of this area.

From Inuyama I drove to Otsu where I stayed in the largest youth hostel in Japan. Located near the shore of Biwako (one of the largest lakes in Japan) it is also the headquarters of the youth hostel system. From here the next day I visited Konancho where I was the daytime guest of the family of Shiro Kanda. His family ran a shoe shop as well as a coffee shop. One niece was a teacher of English at the local junior high school and I was obliged to visit and spend some time with the students. As was often the case, the poor embarrassed English teacher would have to demonstrate his/her English skills in front of a large group of curious and doubting students. However, we had a great time together and I was able to give them a geography lesson, as well, from my travels this being the 31st country of my journey. Shiro's sister, Tomiko, had come home for a visit and I got to re-meet her.

On my way back towards Otsu I stopped to take a photo of a typical Japanese house, which looked a bit weather-worn and plain on the outside. I had been told that the inside was a total contrast with clean and neat rooms very efficiently used by any family. I got to find this out in person as the young man who lived there came out and we got engaged in conversation. Shobu Sato was a physical education teacher at the Kyoto Technical University and he and his sister, Reiko, lived in this average Japanese house that features mostly space-saving sliding doors. He was a bit surprised at my journey and invited me to be their houseguest. Reiko was a college student who kept the house immaculate and was a great cook. Soon I learned that their father had died seven years before and their mother had passed away just the prior month. Both of them enjoyed music and we had some great times with them, their friends and the guitar. Reiko, who was studying music in Osaka, wrote the words for a mother's greeting song to a new baby, "Konnichi wa akachan". This was the first song in the start of my Japanese repertoire. For Shobu I wrote out the English words to "500 miles" which was very popular in Japan, as well as elsewhere. We had dinner one night with his friend, an insurance salesman, and later took a drive around the hills surrounding Kyoto also looking down on Biwako (Lake Biwa). His friend insisted on giving me a small transistor radio with an earplug. I was to find out later that I was able to listen to several stations as I traveled. The only one in English was the "Far East Network" offered primarily for the GI's who were there.

At Shobu's house I got a genuine introduction to a home style Japanese bath (o-furo). In the case of a home there was always a drained washing area and faucets within the enclosure where we would wash and rinse completely before entering the bath. In most cases these baths were about 20 degrees warmer than I would have preferred. However, if you used the slow approach you could ultimately immerse your whole body without screaming. Here, as in many locations in Japan, I was interviewed by the local press resulting in an article and photo. On some occasions I would meet school students who would recognize me from this publicity and want my autograph. This kind of notoriety almost went to my head. However, it was another chance to get a look at their culture from a different point of view.

On April 29 there was a national holiday due to its being the Emperor's Birthday. It seemed to me that there were many holidays for a variety of reasons. Golden week was set aside to honor senior citizens. On May 5 I noted that the speedometer on the scooter read 31,950 miles.

In Wilmington I had been a Junior Rotarian when I was in high school and members of the Wilmington Rotary Club suggested that I visit Rotary Clubs wherever I found them. I had carried with me the name of the Kyoto Rotary Club President, Mr. Kato, he being a friend of Harold Foley of Wilmington. I contacted Mr. Kato and was invited to attend the local Rotary Club meeting at a large hotel in the center of Kyoto. Here was one occasion where I knew dress-up was in order. So, I pressed my suit, shirt and tie and presented myself to Mr. Kato before the start of the meeting. I had no idea that I would get another lesson in Japanese culture at this time. We sat down in the lounge and I mentioned regards from Mr. Foley whom he acknowledged. However, he seemed quite disturbed that I had no formal letter of introduction from the Wilmington Rotary Club. The length and scope of my travel since leaving home did not seem to make any difference. I later deduced that this was an absolute necessity given that I was never invited into the meeting room and we had lunch together in the lounge. As I became aware of formal Japanese etiquette I understood this to be the norm. It was a surprising contrast to the small-town Wilmington Rotary Club where members attended in their work clothes including bib-overalls.

On Sunday I went to Mass in Otsu where a French priest presided. I also met Sister Regina, a Marynoll nun from Nebraska. I got caught up a bit as she was wearing the newer version of the habit, plain but similar to western clothing. As for the local religions I was learning that Shinto is almost like a national religion, which primarily is a relationship with nature. Every town and village seemed to have at least one Shinto shrine (*jinja*). The other main religion is Buddhism where you would find the temple (*otera*) to which was often attached a pagoda. It seemed that every Japanese person was a Shintoist regardless of what other religion he/she might practice. The culture allows for very specific areas in which the Shinto priest and the Buddhist monk play an integral role. The specifics of this division are a study in itself. I was to learn that St. Francis Xavier introduced Christianity into Japan at Nagasaki. Although there were many missionaries in most parts of the country, the number of Christians was only 1-2 percent of the population.

In this area I was interviewed again by some of the media including NHK (*Nippon Hoso Kyokai*) national radio and the Asahi newspaper(*shinbun*). The regimentation of the average person was made clear to me as I sat in the office of the newspaper and happened to be present at mid-morning. At some point a bell sounded and before I knew what was happening everyone in the office was lined up and doing exercises to the radio led by the manager. Of course I couldn't be left out and found myself joining the workout with gusto. The place and role of each person were well defined and understood and everyone acted as was expected by society. Thus, did the US have future industrial challenges trying to compete with "Japan, Incorporated".

One aspect of Japanese culture that had been grossly misunderstood in the West was the profession of the geisha. The true geisha was trained as a professional entertainer who could sing, dance, tell stories and provide pleasurable company for those who would patronize their locations. It was a very honorable profession. Many a geisha was a young girl from the countryside who was sold to the geisha master and schooled for many years in the required skills. Unfortunately our GI's who occupied after WW II got the impression that all geishas were prostitutes. At that time another class of young woman came into being, the bar hostess. They could be found in just about every bar and were more the answer to what the GI's were looking for. Today the geisha is a diminishing life style but there are may hostesses in all locations. I witnessed a great example of their talents when I attended the Kamagawa Odori in Kyoto. The presentation consisted of role-play, ensemble music and singing at a true professional level. All instruments were those that had been used for centuries. The staging was very elaborate with side stages that descended out of sight and reappeared with new musicians playing the song in progress. This presentation is considered a cultural treasure.

When I finally headed for Kyoto I was directed by one of the Konan cho teachers through a town known for ceramics. He hadn't informed me that it involved 16 kilometers of really bad road. The small wheel radius of the scooter amplified every bump just as it had on the cobble stone streets in Munich. When I arrived in Kyoto I headed for the Utano Youth Hostel to find that it was completely full. Remembering some advice I got from a Japanese friend I headed to the *koban*, the small police box at the railroad station. It was quite late and I was embarrassed when I realized that I had awakened the patrolman inside the two-room building. I asked him if he knew where I could get lodging at a reasonable price. He made several phone calls during which he asked if I would mind the traditional Japanese accommodations including sleeping on the floor on *futons*. I let him know that I was here to learn about Japan and those accommodations were just fine.

After a few more calls he said that he had found a place close by which would cost 700 yen ($1.95/day). I said that would be fine and he insisted on taking out his bicycle and leading me to the small Japanese hotel. My room there had a TV, radio, telephone and private tile bath and toilet. It turned out that the bed in the room was western style and I could not believe the number of complimentary (*sabisu* = service) items provided for me. They included a

Japanese robe (*yukata*), a comb, toothbrush, individual razor, shaving soap, hair cream and tissues. Periodically I would hear a knock on the door and the greeting "*sabisu*". The owner or another family member would come in with tea, coffee, cakes, cold drinks and many more welcomed items.

Mitsura Tanaka was a high school teacher who had visited Wilmington with one of his students, Kiyoshi Okuno. Mr. Tanaka had been a guest teacher in my classroom at Wilmington High School when I was a substitute teacher prior to my leaving home. I contacted Mr. Tanaka and was a guest teacher in his school, Saikyo Commercial High School, in Kyoto one day. In preparation for this I dragged out "Uncle Hughie's suit" and had to prepare it for the dress-up occasion. This was not a problem as "*sabisu*" took the suit and *O-baasan* (grandmother) pressed it beautifully with a small, neat iron and a very small ironing board which was at a level convenient to her as she sat in her usual position on a cushion (*zabuton*). After school I was asked to attend the meeting of the "English-speaking Society" where the members were prohibited from speaking anything but English. Later we had some refreshments with Kyoshi Okuno who was now graduated. It was interesting to re-meet them 9,000 miles, 30 countries and 3 years later.

I moved on to Osaka and looked up one of Hiroshi's fellow medical classmates, Yoshitani Tamai. His younger brother was also a medical student and the family was obviously very dedicated to education. Yoshitani had heard of me from Hiroshi and he was expecting me. He and his family were interested in being brought up-to-date on my wanderings in, and before, Japan. Again I was privileged to be included in the daily lives of an average family. While with them they gave me a fairly comprehensive introduction to *sushi,* which I learned to be a manner of serving all types of food items in conjunction with white rice. *Nigirizushi* is a small block of compacted rice which may have a great variety of toppings including, egg omelet, raw fish (of many kinds), eels . . . etc. The most popular raw fish sushi is *maguro,* which is red tuna. *Maki* rolls are made by rolling out white rice like a sheet and then covering it with layers of seaweed (*nori*), *surimi,* various vegetables . . . etc. It is then tightly rolled up and sliced across to create bite-sized portions. Thus, it is inaccurate to refer to *sushi* as eating raw fish or anything else raw. Raw fish may be part of a given *sushi* item, but it is not part of all *sushi*. Raw fish is called *sashimi*. Most of these *sushi* items are eaten with soy sauce and/or *wasabi* (truly potent green mustard).

While visiting with the Tamai family I was fascinated by the small garden that received such TLC from the mother of the family. She pointed out that the true Japanese garden had only rocks, water and trees. Any flowers were considered an extra. I took the opportunity to find a barber and got a "complete" haircut for 300 yen (.84 US). It was a middle-aged female barber who shared the shop with her husband. The process consisted of the usual cut plus the shaving of my ears, forehead and hairline. All areas of my skull were then massaged in full. I always loved to have any barber work on my head but this one almost put me in a trance. I remembered it for many years thereafter.

At times I used to wonder what the young people did for entertainment at night in Japan. I got a partial answer as I accompanied Yoshitani and his brother to bowling at a local alley. We were using the large balls with the slim pins (candle pins?) and I had not bowled for several years. Given that, I shocked myself as well as my hosts as I totaled a 209 in one of the three games we bowled. I had never bowled that high and I don't believe I ever did again given that, for me, bowling was only an occasional diversion when other options were not apparent.

It was about this time that I had been contemplating the wars that had taken place in various parts of the world and were seemingly on-going somewhere. I wondered in my notebook, "Many countries send troops all around the world for war. Why can't they send citizens to seek peace?" I was not aware of the efforts of the "Peace Corps" at that time but became familiar with them upon my return to the USA. It's too bad that many countries don't follow this idea and send "citizen ambassadors" around the world to let others know that peace is possible.

I finally left to head further west and went to Ashiya where I stayed in the youth hostel. There I met a group of college girls from Seishin University in Okayama and we had a great jam session in the evening. One of the girls was Kazuko Date and she was quite interested in my trip on the scooter. She mentioned that her father was the owner of Date Motors in Hiroshima where he sold and repaired cars and motorcycles. They asked me to look them up if I got into the area of their school. I promised to do so and the following day I headed through Kobe in the direction of Awaji Shima, a small island which was the stepping stone to entering Shikoku (four prefectures).

On my way through Kobe I had an amusing incident, which confirmed the image of westerners not trying to speak any other language. I was following route #5 which would lead me to the ferry dock to get to Awaji Shima (island). There was some road construction and a number of detours resulting in my losing my way. I was in the city and I spotted a lone, well-dressed, young man waiting for a bus. I pulled the scooter over to the curb and said; "*Gomen nasai. Koko kara, kokodoro go bame wa doko desuka?*" (Excuse me. Can you tell me where is route #5 from here?) Trying to be pleasant and helpful he looked directly into my Scottish countenance and said, "Solly, no speak Engrish". Once more I tried by saying. "*Sumimasen, watakushi wa kokodoro go bame o sagashite imasu. Doko desuka?*" (Pardon me. I am looking for route #5. Where is it?) Again he leaned close and said, "Solly, no Engrish". Finally I got his attention and broke his spell by saying, "*Tabun anata wa sukoshi Nihongo dekiru.*" (Maybe you speak a little Japanese). When it finally hit him he did an audible gasp and apologized profusely. He wanted to know how I learned Japanese and we ended up having a nice chat before he pointed me in the right direction to catch route #5. I made a mental note to encourage any youngsters from the USA to study a foreign language and open their world a bit wider.

I took the ferryboat to Awaji Shima and witnessed the reported whirlpools of the water around the island. It is like a steppingstone to Shikoku and sits in the middle of the Setonaiki (Inland Sea). The trip was only 350 yen for the scooter and me. A good road led to Naratsu where I took the second ferry to Tokushima, one of the largest cities in Shikoku. It was a mere 300 yen. On a great road (route #11) with little traffic, I continued to Takamatsu where I went to confession and communion at the local church. It was quite impressive and the bishop who had said the Mass came to talk to me afterwards. He was Japanese (rare) and had just returned from a trip to the USA. I went on to Okamoto-cho where I found another group of college students at the hostel. In speaking about this, the smallest of the four main islands of Japan, I was to learn that it was lagging behind in development as compared to Honshu. I was told that there were still steam trains running in the southern part of the island. That was a great contrast to the modern efficient trains I had seen and ridden up to this time. However, regardless of the equipment involved the Japanese trains were painfully punctual. You couldn't assume that because you would be five minutes late at the station that the train would still be there. You might catch a glimpse of it heading down the track.

The Japanese have a long love affair with gardens and I was able to view one of the most famous in Japan on the following day. It was Ritsurin Koen (park). The extensive development of every square foot of the area was truly eye-catching. One of my favorite views that I recorded with my Zeis Ikon was from a hill overlooking the large pond with a graceful Japanese style bridge across the middle. It was full of huge, colorful *koi* fish, which were being fed a type of breadcrumb by the visitors. They swarmed around as I contributed some food to their diet a bit later.

One of the most beautiful parks in Japan

Exquisite mountain scenery—Shikoku

I continued west on highway 11 and eventually was attracted to a beautiful country scene unfolding ahead on my left side. The entire area was terraced with rice fields leading to the valleys and mountains in the distance. Not far away were a house and a storage shed apparently made of straw. I would learn that these buildings were classic and very expensive to build in modern times. The talented artisans were decreasing in number. On the right in the distance was another more modern, 2-story, masonry building which I would later recognize as a a school. Aside from the school I was looking at a scene that had probably not changed in centuries.

As I walked up and down the road to get various angles on the shot I noticed a middle-aged man attaching a fairly large sign to a post. It was for the "Country House Motel". I was curious and, as usual, not bashful. So, I approached the man and asked about his business. He had a small motel not far up the highway and was a sort of "one man show" when it came to all the tasks involved in operating the business including advertising. He was a bit reluctant at first until he realized I was able to speak some recognizable Japanese. Then he became curious about my travels and soon invited me to be his guest at the motel. I followed him to the small building, which housed his home as well as the motel rooms. He introduced me to his wife and she immediately set out to prepare dinner for us. I became the celebrity guest and was treated royally. During the meal he explored my travels up to that point and was surprised that I could travel for so long by myself with no strings attached at home. In the evening he introduced me to the national sport of *sumo* wrestling on TV. This sport of giants goes back centuries and is a uniquely Japanese sport. The wrestlers are trained over many years and pushed to gain enormous weights giving them the solid platform for the action. This sport is accompanied by very colorful traditions and pomp. The object of the action is to push the opponent outside of the circular ring or to make him touch anything but his feet to the mat. A bout is over in a matter of seconds usually and there is a national elimination tournament resulting in the crowning of the *yokozuna* (top champion). I was surprised later to find out that a number of foreigners were taking up the sport as professionals. For a number of years the *yokozuna* was an Hawaiian. *Sumo* is probably the only sport that drew larger crowds in Japan than baseball at this time.

The following day I thanked my hosts, took their photo with my scooter and moved on to Dogu Onsen, one of the famous hot spring baths in Japan. These baths were always an object of extreme pleasure for the Japanese as they pursued the benefits of natural health resources. Although I did not take the time to patronize this spa I later regretted it as I covered the 23 kilometers of bad road on route 196 on the way to Imabari. Not only does this type of highway increase my travel time, but it also rattles my bones on the small-wheeled vehicle. This trip took me around the northwest corner of Shikoku ending up at the shore of Setonaiki (the inland sea). For only 650 yen my scooter and I were transported by ferry across this body of water through a number of beautiful islands to the small port of Onimich on Honshu.

# CHAPTER TWENTY-EIGHT

## Egypt recalled

I went on to Okayama and looked up Norio Tokumitsu and his family. I had met him with Shiro Kanda in Port Said, Egypt. Norio was quite surprised to see me inasmuch as Shiro had not been in touch with him. His mother was a typical, dedicated center of the family who managed most things about the house and family business. She taught the elegant tea ceremony. I should mention that skill at the tea ceremony and *ikebana* (flower arranging) were an assumed study for all young Japanese girls. His father was a chemist who had retired from Kurashiki Rayon Company. He was a good-natured scientific devotee. He was pleased to learn that I had a degree in Chemical Engineering. When we would talk and I would ask a question, the answer would come over a long period of time with the use of many sheets of paper with diagrams and symbols. He was always dedicated to making sure that his listener truly understood his explanations. I got used to the idea of calling him O-jisan. I had found that in Japan it was common for young people to refer to adults by the terms O-jisan (uncle) or O-basan (aunt). This extended to others who were referred to using forms of address as if they were related. For example, a young man might refer to a slightly older woman as O-nesan (older sister) even though no real family relationship existed. The language reflects the respect for age shown in Japan wherein there are different words for older brother or sister versus younger brother or sister. My small grammar book had taught me that—"san" was a suffix, which went on the end of any name except your own. It is an honorific and you never honor yourself. It can mean Miss, Mrs. or Mr. The child's version of it is "chan".

One incident that he described very accurately was the B-29 bombing of Okayama during WW II. He even described the maneuvers and two types of bombs used. Luckily we could speak about this type of subject with no emotional reactions. He related that the Japanese optimism was based on the belief that the many different nationalities in the USA would not work together for the defense of the country. Obviously the results of the war proved that not to be the case.

While I was staying with Norio's family we went to a ceremony at the new house that was being built for them. This was a Shinto rite in which the priest came to the house when the roof was finished and blessed it. The dedication took place on the roof with the priest and the father of the family with the contractor also present. The area was adorned with paper streamers and the priest did a number of incantations during which sake was poured on the four corners of the house. Then all toasted the occasion with sake. At the conclusion the contractor and the workers were given presents and lunch. I noted that the older houses have glass in the windows that rattled because there was no putty in them. As well, I noticed that when cement blocks were used for walls or foundations, they were stacked directly over each other instead of staggered as we do in the west. I believe it had to do with the aesthetics of the form. If the wall was over 3-4 feet high there were steel rods placed vertically inside for strength.

One day Norio took me along with his girlfriend, Masako, to Uno harbor where we went sailing with his university friend, Ishiisan. He was an engineering student and had built his own sailboat. The ride was smooth and we enjoyed the trip immensely. I got a great photo of the beautiful sunset with Masako in the foreground. Her friend, Yuriko, was from a family whose relative was a diplomat and had been stationed in Greece. So, surprisingly Yuriko could speak a little bit of Greek. We dated a few times but it was obvious that her father did not appreciate her spending any amount of time with an American from the USA.

One day I visited Seishin University and remet Kazuko Date who said she had spoken to her father about my travels on the scooter and he was interested to meet me if I passed through Hiroshima. We had another great jam session with the guitar and her friends. About this time I had a problem with the clutch and upon taking all apart I found that one of the parts was worn. I made a temporary repair noting that I would have to do something more permanent soon.

As usual my hosts would not consider taking anything monetary to compensate for my visit so I looked for things that might need repairing. I found two toasters, a heater and a bicycle all of which needed assistance to be put into useable form. While I was making these repairs Norio's mom and the lady next door were busy making me my first *yukata*, a light cotton kimono for casual wear. It was really comfortable especially after just coming from the scalding bath. In this house they had their own *o-furo* which was a heavy cast iron tub heated directly from below with a small wooden rack on which the bather would stand in order not to touch the surface of the tub. One night when the bath had been prepared for me I checked the temperature of the water before entering. It was scalding. I found that the only way to get used to it was to slowly and gently lower one leg at a time into the caldron and then slowly settle the rest of the body without making any waves or disturbance. I was pulling off this feat quite well until my bottom made contact with the fiery hot side of the tub. My physical reaction and muffled scream more than made waves in the vessel multiplying the heat shock I was feeling. Eventually I did lower myself totally into the very hot bath and learned to enjoy soaking in this breathtaking medium.

Finally the day came when I had to get on the road again and I said some sad farewells to the Tokumitsu's. I had to promise that I would drop in again if I came back this way from Kyushu. I continued west and arrived in the city of Hiroshima later the same day. I looked up Mr. Date at his motor sales company and he invited me to stay with his family. He had heard about my travels by scooter from his daughter, Kazuko, and wanted to know all the details. He was a very successful businessman and owned the entire 6-story building where his business was located on the first floor. The family home was on the 5th floor of the building. The other floors were rented out as office space. I met Mrs. Date, their younger daughter (Keiko, a university student at a local college) and the younger brother who was in high school. When I was later given a tour of the building we went to the roof where there was a large advertising sign for Lotte Gum, one of the more popular brands of chewing gum in Japan.

The Date's made me feel truly at home. Again this was a factor that made my entire journey so meaningful as I was hoping to learn about the common people of each country. Although I found this type of hospitality everywhere I traveled, I was to be amazed at the degree to which this happened in Japan. I was ushered into a room of my own and later the mother of the family got very busy preparing the many-course meal of the evening. I spent a large amount of time answering questions about my travels and specific queries from Mr. Date regarding the durability and reliability of my scooter. He was particularly interested in how I kept it operational when I traveled in many areas where spare parts would be unavailable and cycle repair shops rare. I related to him some of the adventures I had had such as the gear-stripping problem in Australia. He recognized that I had been blessed with some mechanical skills, which were augmented by my engineering studies in college. By way of example I explained that just a couple of days before I had detected that the clutch in the scooter was slipping. I had taken it apart and discovered an internal part that was worn to the point that there was no longer any possibility of adjusting it. He seemed to understand the situation, which I tried to clarify with a sketch of the unit.

Date family at Date Motors

The following day he introduced me to his niece, Nobuko, who had a very good command of the English language. She had volunteered to be my tour guide of Hiroshima for the day. I left my scooter at Date's garage and she drove us around this huge city. Of course, one of the places I wanted to visit was the peace park located on the site of the explosion of the atomic bomb on August 8, 1945. We strolled the flower-filled gardens of this memorial and viewed the Dome under which is a container holding the names of all those who perished on that sad day. At the far end is the museum, which Nobuko understandably declined to enter. She had been there several times and the vividness of the photos and displays were hard on the peace of soul. I toured the building and easily understood her reluctance to view the contents more than once.

She related to me that her father was a policeman and the family was visiting in the countryside staying with relatives. When the bomb went off he was on his way to visit them. He immediately tried to return to the city. It took him two days to get to his old police station area passing hundreds of bodies in the streets. Many of the bridges were totally ruined which also made travel difficult. When he arrived at his precinct there was nothing left of the building and all of his fellow officers had been killed. He felt guilty that he was the only survivor. With the commitment and resignation of the typical Japanese official he found a battered old desk and set it up on the corner of the street and started to organize the chaos of the aftermath of this catastrophe. It was a bit unnerving to listen to a local person who had experienced that horrific bombing even though she was very young at the time.

We also drove out to her family home and went hiking up her favorite mountain nearby. The view was terrific and the scenery so peaceful. We later returned to the Date home and I learned that Mr. Date had taken my scooter clutch assembly apart and was having a brand new part machined for me. I re-assembled the clutch and all was like new. As well, he didn't think much of the spare tire I had and had replaced it with a new one. My feeling had always been that I didn't care how much the spare tire was worn as long as it would get me to a place to repair a flat on a decent tire.

That evening Kazuko returned for a home visit and we had a great time with all the family together. After dinner I was asked to teach the girls some of the western dances. We did some Latin dances such as the cha-cha and added some line dances like the bunny-hop. They were very enthusiastic and their parents got a big kick out of our comical attempts. When I mentioned that I would be leaving the following day, Mr. Date insisted on giving me some souvenirs. One was a beautiful gold sake cup (*kinpai*), which came in a typical neat wooden box. On the outside of the box he wrote in Japanese "Visit Commemoration—Date—Japan" and on the inside, "1967/5/30—Showa 42". He enclosed a 100 yen Olympic coin in the same wooden box. He also presented two miniature defense devices (*jutte* = ten hands). These had been used by police for sword defense in the days of *samurai*. I was a bit at a loss in this situation considering that I was usually able to show my appreciation by repairing or making useful items for the family. However, in this case the family had everything in working order thanks to having a mechanic as a father. We took quite a few photos with my camera and others. The following morning I took some additional photos and thanked my hosts prolifically as I headed further west towards Kyushu.

Along the very scenic coast I would come across the famous Kintaibashi Bridge with its 5 spans. It is so revered that it is restricted to foot traffic only. Not far away I looked offshore at an island and saw the well-known Torii (gate) at Miyajima. People throughout Japan would relate to both of these sites even though they may not have had the opportunity to see them. This was the area of Iwakuni where there was a sizeable U.S. military base. Many of the programs I would hear on my little transistor radio were broadcast from Iwakuni on the Far East Network.

When I came to Shimonoseki I found the only connector at that time linking the four main islands of Japan. All of the other crossings had to be done by boat or airplane. This was a tunnel that ran under the sea to Kyushu. I drove the 1.8 kils. distance and arrived in Kitakyushu and continued through Fukuoka. I ended my long day of travel at Kurume where I got a Japanese room for 500 yen. I was really ready for the hot bath, as I had driven 192 miles (310 kils.) from Hiroshima on my reconditioned scooter. While bathing that night I reflected on the inordinate pressure put on students in this country of conformity. Many of the youngest students put in a full day in class and the attend "*juku*" tutoring sessions in the evening. Often the education plan for the child starts before kindergarten so that entrance will be gained to the right primary school, which will lead to the right junior and senior high schools resulting in acceptance to the "right" college. There are usually entrance exams for every step of this process and the student is put under extreme stress to do well. Once the student has entered college, the pressure is off (unless a specific discipline like medicine) and the degree will come with not too much effort. Thus, there were a great number of employees working in jobs for which they were significantly over-qualified.

The next day I traveled to Nagasaki where I checked into the Youth Hostel. That evening I got a taste of writing Japanese (at my level) when I wrote a very brief letter in *katakana*. It required one and a half hours. Normally all Japanese correspondence is written in a combination of *katakana, hiragana* and *kanji*. However, I had only learned *katakana*, which is written as it sounds like *hiragana. Kanji* characters are picture-words, which came from China and have the same meaning although pronounced differently in the two languages.

The next day I found the peace park, which is smaller than the one in Hiroshima. The 32-foot statue is a male figure with one hand pointing to the sky from which the bomb came on August 9, 1945. The other hand is extended in a horizontal position in a gesture of peace. Not far from this location I visited the Church of the 26 Martyrs named after the 26 religious who were slain in 1596 in a clamp down on foreign religions. The group included six foreigners as was explained to me by a Belgian priest I met on the grounds. He had been there for many years.

In Nagasaki I had to attend to some logistical matters as I cashed my last $20 traveler's check. That gave me 7,200 yen to make it all the way back to Kyoto where I expected a letter from my mother with an international money order in it. As well, I had to apply for an Alien Registration Card, a requirement if you stay beyond the initial 2-month visitor's visa. With this taken care of I headed south and caught the ferryboat from Shimabara to Misumi. Some of my fellow passengers were young school students who were on a field trip. Apparently one of them had seen one of my TV interviews and started to ask me about my world trip. Soon I was giving a geography lesson to the whole group, which led to many requests for autographs by the enthusiastic youngsters.

Once on shore I continued to the city of Kagoshima where I received my 2-month extension of my visa in my Alien Registration Card. It cost me 1,000 yen that substantially reduced my travel budget for the trip back to Kyoto. At this point I had 3,900 yen ($11). As I passed Sakurajima (active volcano) I noticed that smoke was streaming up from its cone. I later learned that it had erupted just 3 hours before I arrived. Its activity was evidenced by the lava rocks that filled the surrounding vistas.

That night I stayed over in the youth hostel in Miyazaki and went to the local mission church for Mass the following day. It was staffed by Italian priests with whom I had coffee after Mass and talked about my time in Italy. I even had a chance to practice my Italian. After hearing about my journey to that point one priest took a liking to me and insisted on giving me 300 yen to help me along, a small (but welcome) increase in my travel funds. I continued on to Beppu and stayed at the Aso Youth Hostel named for the nearby mountain, which is so well known throughout Japan. It is also an active volcano. It had not erupted in some time so we were allowed to climb to the top. There you could smell the sulfur and see some of the steam coming up from the crater. I walked down a bit inside and could feel the heat through my shoes. I took a photo of the inside and then decided not to risk my luck while I backed away from the edge of this national monument. I would be told that a perfectly symmetrical mountain near Asosan is often mistaken for it.

My route thereafter took me along the east coast heading north until I got back to the tunnel leading to Honshu. When I had traversed this 1.8 kilometers I arrived back in Shimonoseki. I took the opportunity to speak to a school crossing guard asking him about the condition of the roads around the west and northwest shores of the island. He assured me that they were very bad and almost impossible for the scooter to use. There were 200-300 kilometers of unpaved road. As we discussed the general conditions of the roads in Japan he invited me to his home for tea. As the subjects of chat went

Feeling the heat inside Mt. Aso volcano

to things of the USA to my travels he and his wife invited me to stay for the night. This led to meeting the neighbors, the local school children and the rest of his family. They all couldn't have been more friendly and hospitable. Together we all took a walk to see a beautiful sunset and in the evening we rode in his car to the surrounding hills where we got a gorgeous view of the straits with many nightlights. The next morning, after interviews with NHK TV and a newspaper I left to head east with 1,400 yen ($3.89) left. I arrived late in the day in Hiroshima and made the promised stop with the Date family. That evening's dinner was punctuated with the many questions about what I had experienced since I left them.

I should note that Japanese life was so ordered that they couldn't conceive of my mode of travel nor the length of my journey. Even in the USA this trip was considered unusual as most people have other major life commitments, which prohibit traveling for any long period. In my case I was able to take advantage of one of those life-style breaks between my military duty and getting locked into a career-type job.

I saw Nobuko Date the following morning before I drove the 168 kilometers to Okayama and surprised the Tokumitsu family. Again it was like I had come home to a place where I was known and welcome. It would later surprise me as to how often this occurred in Japan. Norio's father brought me up-to-date on the progress of their new home and we discussed many of the areas I had visited. They had also traveled extensively within Japan and were very helpful in giving me tips.

As I drove towards Kyoto I passed through the city of Kobe where my world travels almost came to a screeching halt. The traffic was very heavy as is usually the case in any large city. It consists of many passenger cars, busses and a great variety of trucks in three lanes. As I proceeded in the left line of vehicles I ended up directly behind a delivery truck with a tarpaulin over the top. It was held in place by a hemp rope that had come loose in several places. When we stopped for a traffic light I didn't notice that the rope had become entangled in the rear view mirror of my scooter on the right side. As the truck pulled away at the change of lights it yanked the scooter ahead at a wild angle and my legs went out for balance. I felt like I was on a bucking bronco. I turned the steering to the opposite side in order not to be dragged off balance. For what seemed like several minutes (probably seconds) I flailed around trying to get my right foot onto the break. When I finally did so I pressed with all my might and the rope broke. I pulled over to the side to let my nerves settle and continued on to Kyoto where I arrived with 100 yen (.28) left.

# CHAPTER TWENTY-NINE

## The "Scottish stretch"

I headed directly for the post office in Kyoto and went to the general delivery counter. I presented my passport and asked the young clerk if there was any mail for me. He returned with a bundle and started to go through it. He pulled out 19 letters and 4 postcards for me and gave a slight grin after I asked him in Japanese, "*Sore dake?*" (Is that all?). One of the letters was from my mother. She informed me that the funds I had been counting on had been forwarded to the Mitsui Bank. It was too late to go to the bank so I returned to Otsu and the house of my friend, Shobu. The next day I went to the bank and had no problem getting the $250 and having them issued as traveler's checks. I noted that the last time I had received $250 from home was when I had arrived at Tipper's house in Melbourne, Australia on last July 24th. It was now June 9th of the following year. Thus, I had journeyed almost 11 months in four countries on $250 of my own funds. This shows the very real impact of the friendliness of people all over the world. Obviously I had started this far-flung trip with a huge confidence in the goodness of my fellow beings. The above showed the proof of just such a belief. My fellow citizens had contributed immensely to my ability to visit them and gain the treasures of their knowledge and acquaintanceship.

Now as I prepared to carry on in my Japan sojourn, I had to spend some time repairing the horn switch and a couple of leaks on the scooter. At the same time I repaired the automatic toaster for Shobu. I made inquiries about the condition of the roads on the "*Ura Nippon*" (backside) coast. I was told that they were very bad and would be impossible with the scooter. I decided that I would drive up the west side of Biwako (largest lake in Japan) and follow the coastal roads as far as I could. Then I would cross over to Fukushima to visit Hiroshi's family and return to Tokyo.

I left Hiroshi's address at the post office for forwarding and attended Mass. There I re-met Sister Regina with whom I caught up on news, which included the heating up of the Arab-Israel problems in the Mid-east. I drove past Biwako and continued along the coast facing the Sea of Japan. When stopping at a police station to get directions I was asked many questions about my travels by the young officer. He insisted on contributing 1,000 yen to my resources. I found that many people wanted to somehow participate in this trip, which would be an impossibility for them.

I drove through Niigata and on to Akita and Aomori over a 3-day period with a total of only 6-7 kilometers of bad road. Unfortunately some of the worst road pavement was inside the tunnels that I had to pass through along the way. In these cases I could not see very well as I first entered the tunnel and I had to struggle at times when I hit huge potholes. I noted that in this area the women working in the fields have a unique uniform, which includes a slotted face covering for protection from the sun. As in most parts of Japan I could see very high mountains close to the sea each day and some of them were snow-capped.

Rare sod roof quality—northern Honshu

I had passed a beautiful, sod-roofed house just before getting to Aomori. It was in great condition and was quite unique at this time in Japan. I took a photo for my later memories. I was too late to catch the ferry to Hokkaido so I checked into the local youth hostel that was in the upper floors of a kindergarten. The next day I got a kick out of the reactions of the kindergarten kids when they saw my scooter and all my packs. The ferryboat to Hakodate cost 1,500 yen and took 4 hours. I was starting to feel in my climatic element as the local latitude was just about the same as my hometown. I was surprised to find an abbey of the Trappist Nuns not far from this port.

Kindergarten tots at Aomori youth hostel

I went on to Sapporo where the Winter Olympics were to take place in 1972. The sites of the ski jumping and other events were taking shape on the surrounding mountains. This area had the feel of a Yukon town with square grid layouts of the streets and mostly non-traditional buildings. This made my navigation of the cities much easier as the system had *cho's* and *jo's* very much like the streets and avenues in New York City. Many of the buildings had metal roofs, which had been introduced by the Americans. Of course, I had to remind myself that this was the last part of Japan to be developed and, therefore, more modern systems were being initiated here.

I stayed in the youth hostel and met a Japanese friend named Kunihiko. With him I went to the local public bath and enjoyed Genghis Kahn, the mutton strips you cook yourself over a battle helmet-shaped domed grill from which the dish gets its name. It was quite affordable at 200 yen (.56). As a foreigner I could get away with pouring the drippings over the bowl of rice, which always accompanied the meal. The Japanese are generally purists when it comes to eating rice, their revered staple. On another occasion we ate *sukiyaki* together and I enjoyed the cooking at the table of beef, vegetables and noodles in a broth. These types of meals lend themselves to sharing as they entail a certain amount of tableside preparation during which all participants socialize.

The next day I went to church where the clergy were all Japanese Franciscans (St. Francis Xavier had introduced Christianity to Japan). After the Mass I chatted with several of the monks and learned about the influence of my alma mater here. In 1886-87 Dr. William Smith Clark, Professor at Massachusetts Agricultural College, taught at the newly established Sapporo Agricultural College (now Hokkaido University). He introduced many methods and ideas that helped to develop the massive agricultural business of this northern island. He is remembered throughout Japan by his admonition to his students of "Boys, be ambitious". Mass. "Aggies" later became the University of Massachusetts at Amherst where I received my degree in Chemical Engineering.

When I had time on my hands in this area I used much of it to answer the deluge of mail I had received in Kyoto. As I did this I was comfortably established in the Shio-kari Onsen youth hostel where I proudly received a complement on my Japanese from the warden there. He said that he seldom met a foreigner who had any useful degree of skill in his language. As one might suspect this led to a much greater degree of interaction with local citizens, which was the true aim of my entire trip. I never wanted my conversations to be limited to just those who spoke my language even though there were always English-speaking locals to be found.

At this hostel I also had to deal with some mechanics. I could tell that the throttle cable on the scooter was in bad shape and would have to be repaired. I found that I had to force the unit along, as I was not able to find a cable that I could use for the purpose. I finally decided I could use a thinner cable temporarily and I happened to have one in my bag from Australia. People have always been amazed at my reluctance to get rid of something that had a potential use some time in the future. Luckily this time it had paid off. Before heading north to Wakkanai I asked about the road in that area. I was told that I would run into about 8 kils. of bad road. That 5 miles would not have been too bad except that it turned out to be 25 kils. of unpaved highway.

Long before I arrived in Wakkanai it announced itself by the smell of fish drying in racks outside in the sun. If you were downwind it would clean out all your sinuses within a couple of miles. I found a US Air Station there as well as a small contingent of US soldiers. I met several of the GI's and had a chat about life in the most northern city in Japan. Being on the coast the scenery was quite spectacular. I photo'd the Rishiri Islands off the west coast and some unique fishing boats tied up on the beach. I climbed to a high hill where I visited a local cemetery. From there I viewed Sakhalin Island to the north. It had been turned over to Russia after WW II. Japan had been lobbying for its return for a long time.

The following day I headed south again along the partly paved road and developed a problem with the main ignition switch along the way. As I worked on it at the side of the road a local truck driver stopped to lend a hand. It was a one-man job but I appreciated his friendliness. He was Shigechi Yamada who owned his own truck and worked 16-hour days to support his wife and three young daughters. He invited me to visit them in Nayoro and I later dropped by when I knew he had returned. His wife was quite lively and ambitious and welcomed me enthusiastically. As expected his children were a bit shy with this foreign stranger in the house. However, they later loosened up and especially when in the company of their grandfather who also lived there. He would give them "*onbu*" (piggyback) rides and they loved it. At night we had a great sing-along with the guitar. I was able to sing a couple of the children songs by this time and they delighted at our being able to sing together.

The following day I had an opportunity to properly repair the ignition switch. I needed a spring to fix the switch cover and I was able to do that with an old clock spring. While at the house I was approached by a visiting American bible preacher who thought that Billy Graham was a hypocrite. Knowing that the Japanese are dedicated to non-confrontation and being polite to everyone, I gave the couple a few tips on dealing with those foreigners who become "pushy" at times regarding their own agenda. After taking a few photos of the children with their grandfather I thanked this dear family for their hospitality to a total stranger. I drove that day through the huge forests of the area and went on to Asahikawa and Sounkyo where I stayed at the hostel having just beaten the rain; it was the rainy season. It was also a hotel with an *onsen* and the hostelers were allowed to share the scalding baths with those who were paying substantially more for their privacy. All seemed to enjoy each other's company regardless of perceived status. All sang along with the guitar that evening including the staff members who were very friendly.

The following day I continued a bit further to the east to take in the beauty of this national park, Daisetsuzan. I recorded the vistas with my Zeiss Ikon and noted that the surroundings reminded me of parts of Maine where I had

worked prior to entering the USAF. The road brought me back to Sapporo
where I met Usuisan and stayed in his room where we shared a meal and
long talks about other parts of the world and the Japanese culture. I went to
church here and prepared to return to Honshu the following day. On that
day I dropped by Chitosei Air Force Base, which I had known as a USAF
base. However, by this time it had been turned over to the Japanese Defense
Force. I stopped and chatted with the guard about the Defense Force and
its mission. Oddly I felt some commonality with this airman even though it
had been four years since my discharge. I briefly visited the village of Shiraoi,
which was an historic village of the *ainu* natives (the Japanese white race).
They had been the original settlers of Japan and had been pushed northward
by the developing civilization in the same manner as the native Indians in
the USA as they were pushed further west

   I raced to Muroran to try to catch the ferry and luckily it left 30 minutes
late. The ticket cost 1800 yen ($5) for me and the scooter for the 7-hour
trip to Aomori. The sea was fairly calm and it was a smooth trip. In an area
much like an open dorm with raised tatami mats the passengers could curl
up and get some sleep. I was able to do so for part of the trip. By the time
we arrived at the port I had to let myself into the same youth hostel above
the kindergarten. It was a great feeling to realize that the honor system was
still intact in some places. After the traditional breakfast I headed south and
took a poorly maintained Route 102 to Tawadako (Lake Towada) over 60
kilometers of unpaved highway. The disappointment in the surface condition
was over-shadowed by the beauty of the lake and its surrounding hills. On
this day I ended up at a youth hostel 26 kils. north of Morioka and it was
quite unusual. Hostelers had private rooms and meals were served to them
in their rooms. This was hard to beat at a usual cost of 200-250 yen. I could
have easily stayed here for a number of days but went on the next day to
Hobara town in Fukushima Prefecture arriving at the home of Hiroshi's father,
a medical doctor. This was to be a very significant visit.

Dr. Nishida & assistants—Hobara, Fukushima

# CHAPTER THIRTY

## Dr. Nishida's "hostel"

Dr. Nishida was a kind and concerned person as well as a highly regarded doctor. His house was huge and had a large living area as well as his offices and treatment facilities. There seemed to be a great number of people coming and going at all times and I had a bit of difficulty in separating the family from others. One local lady was in charge of the kitchen; another did the driving and another most of the housework. An elderly gentleman was assigned to answer the many phone calls that came in at all hours. The doctor also had two nurses who assisted him. My confusion was relieved a bit when I talked to Hiroshi by phone. He let me know that his brother, Shoji, had been adopted to his aunt and uncle. His oldest sister was married, the next one was a doctor and the third a teacher. His youngest sister had been adopted to his family. To some degree the house reminded me of a dormitory with people arriving and leaving on various schedules. I was shown to a room, which I had to myself and got quite comfortable in a short time. I was also shone the third floor of the house that was typically up a set of extremely steep steps.

I used my first day there in getting acquainted and repairing the headlight and switch that had been giving me problems for a while on the road to Hobara. As well, I found that the coil wire had been wearing through and was shorting out on the flywheel housing. With these repairs finished I was ready for the road again. That evening I was invited to dinner at the home of a newspaper reporter. He was intrigued by the length of my journey and the attempts I had made to accommodate to local customs, language . . . etc. I really surprised him by eating the offered *nutto* (sticky, pungent fermented beans) along with everything else on the menu. His news story included the fact that this strange foreigner even ate *nutto*. I must admit I wouldn't go out of my way to have it again but my iron gut had held up once again.

One of the local scenic attractions was the Bandai Skyline, a well-paved and curving drive through the local mountain (Bandai). Indeed the scenery was spectacular as I made the drive on the scooter, again feeling more of a part of what I traveled through because of this mode of transportation. I stopped for lunch at the top and bought a souvenir for Dr. Nishida. After a number of photos I returned to Hobara and presented the doctor with the small present from which he got quite a "kick". I guess it really was like "coals to Newcastle" but he thanked me profusely.

Much of the activity I was witnessing around the house was preparation for a "farewell dinner" for the doctor who would soon head for a medical convention in Czechoslovakia and other parts of Europe. I was invited to attend this grand event with 20-25 people seated along a huge table in his house. As well, I was asked if I could entertain the guests with the guitar. By this time I had learned several Japanese songs and I added others, which were quite well known around the world. As a result my photo was in the newspaper the following day with the story of the doctor's coming journey. A charming neighbor I met at that time was a very young-looking 72-year old lady who invited me to drink tea at her home the next day. Due to her concern for my continued good health she served both of us raw birds eggs to drink with some flavoring like soy sauce, I had no problem and she informed me that they were good for your stomach and avoiding indigestion.

Finally on July 3rd I said a round of sad good-by's, took several photos and headed for the main highway (route #6). I couldn't get away from the doctor without accepting 2,000 yen to insure I got along OK. It was as though I was leaving my own family again. I had been made to feel like one of this large and welcoming group. I pondered this experience as I bounced the 60 kilometers of bad road to the highway. Thereafter the going was fine. I headed south and when I got to Mito I turned west and re-visited Fr. Ducey at Tomobe. As I stayed there for several days I met several Irish priests who were studying at the language school in Tokyo. As well, I met a number of priests from the USA who would gather in Tomobe from their small local parishes and socialize once a week. With Fr. Ducey, Fr. Conley, Fr. Margraff and Brother Nakazawa I went to their favorite restaurant in Mito where the specialty of the house was Genghis Khan, now one of my preferred dishes.

Tomobe re-union with Fr. Ducey

While with Fr. Ducey I was able to catch up on the Arab-Israel 6-day war thanks to the Time magazine he had. In our discussions I noted that the missionary's job was unique in Japan as the ordinary citizens were quite prosperous. More often the missionary priests offer the locals some relief from starvation and/or living conditions not applicable here. One way of attracting locals to the parish was to teach English. The Japanese are dedicated to learning a foreign language. It is mandated in grade schools as well. English is apparently recognized as the most international language. So, any native speaker can easily find some part-time work teaching it. We, from the USA, have a slight edge as many Japanese make a point of wanting to learn "American" English as compared to the British version.

As these other priests became familiar with my travels they all asked me to visit their little parishes and meet the local parishioners. As I was so far behind in my journey I passed on most of them. However, Fr. Coleman Conley (of Beverly, Mass.) was located at a church with a kindergarten in Tsuchiura on my way back to Tokyo. I stopped there and was introduced to the cook, teachers and educational director. During the several days I visited I shared the local routine with Fr. Coleman. I visited the 120 youngsters at the kindergarten with my Arabic Ouqual headdress and had a great songfest with them and the guitar. They had been taught 5 English songs by Brother Nakazawa and belted out the words with gusto.

One evening Fr. Coleman decided to put on a real BBQ for the staff and I was invited to join them. They really lit up as we sang many songs around the fire. The Japanese are very group-oriented and relax easily when there are a significant number of them together. Individuality is frowned upon which produces the saying, "He who stands out will be knocked down". Again I became a bit better acquainted with several of the staff including the janitor. This stop on my journey would play a unique role in my future.

Fr. Coleman & kindergarten kids—Tsuchiura

One night Fr. Coleman and I visited one of the few local Japanese Catholic families, the Sakurai's. They had 5 children (really Catholic) and the mother was a sweet, warm source of the family emotion. Each child was made to feel important and special. This was a model home for all that it is supposed to mean. Several of the children were studying music and we had a great time for hours. I was able to sing 6 or 7 Japanese songs by this time and they were delighted. They had a score of questions about my travels and my family back at home. The father of the family was a very solid provider and a talented amateur archer. He was practicing for a big competition that was just a week away. Again, this experience would broaden my awareness of the typical family life in Japan.

Soon I was on my way back to Tokyo where I noted my speedometer reading as 36,146 miles. This meant that I had driven almost 8,000 kilometers (about 4,800 miles) in Japan. At Hiroshi's apartment I had 12 letters waiting along with one set of my slides. It was not often that I could predict my schedule well enough to have the slides returned to a forwarding address. I was always relieved when this was possible so I could check the quality of the photos.

While staying with Hiroshi I became much more adapted to the daily life in the city. One day I was asked to do an interview for Radio Japan (short-wave broadcast) known as "Hello America". It played in two parts and I was paid 4,000 yen (slightly over $11), which added significantly to my cash available. Later I was interviewed on the Far East Network at Drake AFB. This is the countrywide English-speaking station listened to by most American GI's and me on my little transistor when I could get the reception. With my host here, Bill White, I started to investigate the possibility of flying across the Pacific with the US. Air Force. Although I was a USAF reservist (non-active) there was no way that I could get a hitch back to the States. I would have to turn to the old reliable "work-away" on a ship.

On another occasion I was invited by Mrs. Hara to go to the Bon festival. At this time the members of a family will go to the family cemetery and invite the spirits of their deceased to come home and celebrate the season with them. At night there is a *Bon Odori* which is like a community line dance around a raised platform decorated for the occasion. After watching the repetitive steps of the dance I was able to mimic the others and do a decent version of their favorite to a number of rounds of applause. That's hardly the way to get a proud Leo to end his crazy impersonations of a real dancer. It was all great fun and we ended the night with a good portion of *kori-mizu* (flavored shaved ice), another O-bon tradition.

During the many weeks I spent in Tokyo I remet Yoriko and had several dates with her. From her chats I could tell that her father was really totally intolerant of foreigners. That really frustrated her, as she was an attractive young Japanese woman whose social life was greatly dictated by her father. Finally one evening, as we were about to part into different subway stations, she suggested that we not meet any more. Her rationale was that she was growing serious about a future with me but she knew that it would be impossible with her father's prejudice. Although I had taken a distinct liking to her, I could understand her conclusion especially since I had no intention of entering a bonded relationship at this point in my travels. I sympathized with her given the trap she lived in. There was sadness for both of us as we turned in opposite directions. I did remember that at one time her brother was stationed in Greece in the Foreign Service and she had visited him there.

It was like a different world being away from her father's dominance. And so I saw that this type of family discontent was not limited to the USA.

On the day that Hiroshi and his student friends finished 5 examinations, they decided to go out at night and celebrate. One of their favorite local beer gardens was on the roof of a multi-story building and it had a Spanish motif. Of course there was a band playing and encouraging anyone in the audience to sing a song. My beer-drinking buddies talked me into doing a song and when the band learned that I would sing in Spanish, they insisted that I do another. I sang a second song in Spanish and the result was that all my buddies got free beer. Of course, the joke was on me, as I had never acquired a taste for beer. Thanks to my European travels I enjoyed a glass of wine. The common wines were not that good in Japan at that time. However, we managed to toast far into the night.

Some of the unique things I found in Japan included the *furoshiki* which is a square cloth used to carry all sorts of things in a bundle. Many have beautiful patterns and are common for shopping. When I would change money at any bank I was surprised to see that every clerk would calculate the transaction on a calculator and then check it on a *soroban,* the ever-present abacus.

In pursuing a way of getting back to the USA I started making a long series of trips to Yokohama to check on ships. As before, I was able to locate a copy of the shipping news in English and would visit the port whenever there was a possible ship tied up there. I knew that the best bet for working on a ship was with a Scandinavian vessel. However, none of the Scandinavian ships went to Hawaii, which was my next hopeful port of call. As a possibility, I applied for a US Coast Guard waiver at the US Consul's office. This would theoretically allow me to join the union ($60) and have a chance to work on a ship registered in the USA. I later received the waiver but it never amounted to any positive result. One very kindly young man whom I got to know fairly well was a Mr. Onishi of the US "States Line". He would contact me if there were ships coming with which I had a chance. I would always check in with him when I was in Yokohama and he would give my spirits a lift with his kindness. I had learned that there was no hope in working on a Japanese ship.

On July 25 I decided to give myself a birthday present as I went to Odakyu Department store to take the first test for wearing contact lenses. I was amazed to learn that most department stores had a complete optician's department with all the professionals and equipment. After a preliminary exam I was checked for tolerances by wearing plain lenses for two hours. The results were OK so, I was told when my own lenses would be ready.

These were what would later be referred to as hard lenses, quite thick and heavy. When I picked them up they gave me lessons on how to put them in and take them out and then I was on my own. The total cost for the lenses was $29.40 including the testing and the application kit. I was instructed to use them for a few hours per day at first and then increase the time slowly. Ultimately I got up to 10-11 hours at a time but I was greatly relieved when I was able to take them out.

On one occasion I put them in at Hiroshi's apartment and started walking down the street at night to the streetcar station. At some point I blinked and thought that one had come out. I stopped dead in my tracks and made everyone walk around me as I sized up the situation. I checked my suspicions by covering one eye and then the other. I found to my dismay that one was not there. I slowly re-traced my steps back to the apartment bending low to see if I could catch the shine from the lens. I stopped by the local convenience store that I had visited and soon the whole neighborhood was trying to locate the elusive lens. Not finding it, I decided to go back to the room and take out the other one in order not to chance losing it also. As I used my small mirror to remove the lens I took the opportunity to look at the inflammation in the other eye. As I pulled the eyelid up I found the lost lens which had tucked itself totally up under it. I called off all the neighbors and decided that I would give my eyes a rest for a couple of days.

Hiroshi and some of his friends decided to go camping at Kawaguchiko, one of the five lakes at the base of Mt. Fuji. I had some appointments that day so I followed them by train the next day. They had found a nice spot and pitched a couple of small tents. Because most of them were music majors I was instructed to bring the guitar. This resulted in a number of "jam sessions" and solos by each in their own disciplines. One of Hiroshi's fellow med students was Osamu who had driven his car to the area. However, he was having some trouble getting it started. With a few adjustments we got him going just in time to avoid a downpour. We had quickly dug gullies around the two tents and all squeezed in for more songs while keeping dry. Later the skies cleared beautifully and there were fireworks over the lake. The water was very clear, as we had found out earlier when we swam. We made the trek up Mt.Fuji, mostly by car, to see the sunrise and it was gorgeous. This was a very traditional rite for any Japanese and foreigners who got into it. On the way back to Tokyo we stopped at Shiraito no taki, a restaurant that was mostly surrounded by a waterfall. I recorded the group's image here as they sucked up ramen noodles.

Hiroshi & friends at Kawaguchiko

By this time I had to apply for another visa extension. As time went on I became very frustrated, as I had seen all of Japan that I had intended and was ready to move on. However, I could not connect with the means of doing so. I made many trips to Yokohama and Mr. Onishi had told me that, if I were able to find a job on a ship from his line, they would take care of the fee to join the union. Some of my frustration was lessened by the friendliness of this young man who had never before met me. Our chats were to have a unique relationship in my future.

One of the current hit love songs in Japan was "*Shiritakunai*", "I really don't want to know" which was a western style song in the USA. Hiroshi had the recording of it and wrote out the Japanese words for me. Over some days I learned it and added it to my international repertoire. One evening I went to a rooftop restaurant with Fr. Sean, a priest of the Sacred Heart. There was a singing contest with the orchestra and I tried it and won first prize. I brought the prize back to Mrs. Hara who was quite pleased.

# CHAPTER THIRTY-ONE

## "Hello Brother", the poem

In respect to my intention to visit Hawaii I started reading James Michener's "Hawaii" which I found fascinating. The following of the various ethnic groups to this land of opportunity was a history lesson within itself. I could relate much easier to the customs of the Japanese who immigrated there as I had become aware of some of their background during the prior 5 months. I guess it was this novel and other sources that prompted me to try to sum up the incredible sojourn I had been living for the past 3 years among citizens of 31 countries. As I mulled it over in my mind I ended up jotting down the thoughts, which came to me. On August 19th I finished the poem that I named "Hello, brother". It summed up my feelings regarding the diverse and informative mass of humankind I had the privilege of meeting along the path around the world. It is directed at all people everywhere regardless of gender. "Hello, brother" is found at the end of this book.

One evening I went to the local grocery store and got into a conversation with the owner and his friend who were both interested in international conversation. They explained to me that one humorous aspect of WW II was that the English terms which had been used for many years in baseball were prohibited by any announcers and in common speech. That meant that they had to fabricate Japanese terms for the baseball jargon. For example a "home run" would be reported as something like a "trot to your house". They would imitate the announcers and go into fits of laughter at the manner in which the games were reported. They were happy that they were again allowed to use such expressions as *"sutoraiku wan"* (strike one).

During a week or so I was alone in Hiroshi's apartment as he was in Fukushima with his family. On August 22 he returned to get ready for the re-start of the school year after the summer vacation. In Japan the school year starts in March and ends in February. After the summer break the students return to the same school year. The grade schools up to high school levels are run by the local municipalities. However, the high schools are run by the prefecture (state) and teachers are transferred quite often to areas that are far from their homes. (Note: Until this time in Japan I had taken up smoking again but decided that I could do without it and quit.)

On September 5th I surprised Hiroshi with his first birthday cake. He was 25 years old and we celebrated with some of his friends. Shortly thereafter I started to develop a bronchial cough. It seemed to get deeper into my system as the days carried on. It would really cause me to cough when I lay down at night. I was sure I was shaking the whole building when I coughed. It seemed like it was coming from my toes. Finally, after almost a week, I went to the clinic at Hiroshi's medical college, Keio. It cost 1,000 yen for the first consultation and 2,050 yen for x-rays. The prescription I was given was a powder, which I was supposed to swallow with a small glass of water. It was like trying to chug-a-lug powdered lime. I think my system recovered when it got the message that it would have to put up with this medicine for the near future. After I recovered I offered the medicine to Mr. Hara who took it with pleasure.

I had been waiting for two months for the Kollbjorg, which was going to Hawaii. However, when I approached the captain he said I could not go with them because they had a Chinese crew. This was odd as I had worked with a Chinese crew on another Scandinavian ship. At this point I had to make a change in plans. Time was marching on and I wanted to visit Hawaii, San Francisco and Seattle before heading for home. So I decided that I would try to go directly to the US west coast and possibly fly to Hawaii and back for a visit.

On September 21 I checked with the M/S Queensville, which was heading for Seattle but I had no luck. I also checked with the M/S Granville where there seemed to be a possibility. The ship was heading for Long Beach and then to the San Francisco Bay area. I noted for the Captain that I had worked on three other Scandinavian ships and had a letter of recommendation from the first Captain. The Captain said he didn't know the K-line company's position on a work-away. I checked with a Mr. Yoshida at Daito Co. and he said that they had no say in the matter. Later as I made a final contact my opportunity was confirmed by the Captain. I quickly wrote letters to my mother and others and called Fr. Ducey and Nobuko in Hiroshima to say farewell. With Hiroshi and the Hara's we ate a final supper together and I brought in some fancy pastries for all. The neighbors came by with too many souvenirs and wished me well in my return to home. The next day I packed, took photos of all in the *genkan* area and said a sad good-by to all including the flower shop man next door and his daughter, Yumiko. I headed south to Yokohama by way of the toll road tunnel. It was a quick trip except that there was a fork in the middle of the tunnel and all the signs were in Japanese only. Given that I was on a relatively narrow scooter I could pull over to the no-traffic area and pull out my map. Knowing where Yokohama was on the map I could check the *kanji* characters and decided that the right fork was probably the correct one. Luckily I was on target and I arrived there by mid-day. I met Mr. Yoshida from the company and he assisted me in processing the scooter and myself through customs and immigration by just signing forms in the office. I thought that I might have a problem with the scooter but all went smoothly.

Farewell to Hiroshi, Shoji, Hara's & neighbors

I boarded the ship, reported to the Captain and was assigned to a cabin. The scooter was put in a gear locker forward and would stay there for the whole voyage. It turned out that the ship was not going to sail until the next day. I contacted Yuriko and she came down to spend some more time together before I left this enchanting land. The next day, September 24th we departed at 0700 and I watched the shoreline of Japan disappear as we sailed east. Because it was Sunday we had the day off. That gave me plenty of time to ponder the incredible five and a half months I had spent throughout the Land of the Rising Sun.

I had been received in every country with warm hospitality and kindness, but there seemed to be something special about Japan. When I later had time I checked my diary and learned that I had spent 165 days in this fascinating country and of those I spent 140 days in the private homes of newfound friends I had never met before starting my journey. This was the essence of the cultural education I had derived from my trip. Staying with a family in any country is a privilege one would pay for but it is not allowed. These gracious citizens had allowed me to get an in-depth look at a uniquely different culture from the inside. These lessons were invaluable and I would treasure them for the rest of my life. As expressed, I was very much impressed with the gentle citizens of Japan but I had no idea what a huge part of my future would involve this land where the culture was so drastically different from my Scottish heritage.

Our first few days at sea were pretty rough and I was getting a bit queasy. However, I didn't feel bad when a veteran sailor mentioned that it always takes him a few days to get his "sea legs" once he's been ashore for any number of days. During this time I had learned to sleep in the hospital room, which was amidships where the effects of the pitching and rolling were minimized. Captain Ovesen's crew consisted of all Norwegians except for the Chinese laundryman. Norwegians go to sea by tradition and for good pay. This ship was 451 feet in length and it used 31 tons of heavy oil in the internal combustion engine to travel about 400 kilometers per day. We would not follow the great circle route (point-to-point on a 3-dimensional globe) increasing the miles to be sailed but it would result in staying further south and having much better weather. The ship had a water evaporation system that produced 21 tons of drinking water per day.

As we traveled east we had to advance the clock one half hour per day in order to make up for the direction of the sun's travel. Every place we were heading for had already passed the time on our clocks before us. Thus, by making this adjustment we would roughly keep up to the sequential changing time zones we were passing through. As a result, on Friday, Sept. 29th, at 8:00 AM we passed the International Date Line. In order to keep in time with the rest of the western hemisphere tomorrow would also be Friday, the 29th. We jokingly referred to it as the "2nd Friday of the week". Had it been a Sunday we would have had two days off duty.

I quickly formed a close friendship with Niels who was a great guy. We hung out lot and talked for hours about each other's home surroundings and lifestyle. I had the occasion to repair his radio a couple of times. We worked together a lot as the whole crew scraped, washed and painted the entire ship during the crossing. I noticed again that being in a humid setting near the water the nerve pain in my right knee was almost constant. We passed a lot of time having jam sessions with the guitar. I noticed that the majority of Norwegians were partial to country western music although they joined in any song they knew (the more beer the louder).

On October 1 we had a party for all with a great session. I noted that the swells were particularly high. It used to be unnerving at first to walk out on the deck and look up to the level of the water, which was 10-15 feet higher than the ship. Of course, we were in the bottom of a swell and I got used to it in time. I was also amazed by the birds that would follow us across the ocean. At some mid point other birds from the far shore would take over and accompany us to the land. Of course, they were well rewarded for their escort with the volume of food that was thrown over the side as I mentioned before.

On October 5th I caught sight of the land of the USA for the first time in more than three and a half years. It was the islands of Santa Cruz and Santa Rosa as we headed into Long Beach. For days I had been trying to organize my emotions about this last leg of my "dream sojourn". On one hand I was happy to be heading for home and my family but reluctant to see the end of this educational journey. So much had happened in those years and thousands of miles with so many incredible people of various cultures. It would take some time before I could try to put it all together. I hoped that the comprehensive diary I had kept would allow me to document this treasured adventure in a book some day. I had no idea how long it would take to make that happen.

On October 6th we docked and I went through immigration with no problems. We were to stay in port for 2-3 days and then continue to the San Francisco area. I walked into Long Beach, cashed a traveler's check and got a haircut. I must have still been in my "low-budget mode" as I got the haircut at a barber school for .75 compared to the usual $2.00. As I passed one busy park area I noticed on the concession stand a sign for hot pastrami sandwiches. This is one item I had not experienced in my entire journey. I'm sure it must have been available in some other lands, but I had not had the chance there. I was probably too interested in trying the local products. When I mentioned to the waiter that I hadn't had a pastrami sandwich in 3.5 years during my world journey he heaped the bun to overflowing and I took a long time to down this reminder that I was, indeed, back in the USA.

I took a local bus to my Aunt Mae's (Larkin) house and remet her and my cousins, Kathy (21) and Tommy (12). They had grown considerably since I had last seen them seven years before. It was their late father's (Uncle Hughie's) suit, which their mom had given me when I was in the area during my Air Force training. It had become my best "dress up" clothes during my trip especially when I was entertaining in a formal setting. It was still packed in my belongings.

Being my mother's youngest sister, Aunt Mae and I had long talks about my visiting their hometown in Scotland. She had a very vivid memory of most of the places I had seen. I was able to show her some of the slides of my trip in other areas while I visited. The slides of Scotland had long before been sent home. The following day we took a trip to "Disney Land" which was the only one of its kind in the world at that time. I was particularly interested in the A T and T display of "America the Beautiful" which was a filmed presentation in surrounding images having been recorded with 9 cameras simultaneously. I was truly surprised when the film was panning the famous areas of Washington, DC and it included a young man at a corner waiting for the traffic to pass so he could cross the street. The young man was me and I could remember the truck with the multi cameras mounted which passed by me as I waited. This was during the trip I made to Florida prior to starting my world tour.

On the way back to town we stopped at the ship so I could show the Larkins around. As I introduced them to the captain he was being visited by Howard and Gini Swift who were prominent in the Masquer's Club where Johnnie Carson had just been feted the night before. The captain asked me to entertain them a bit and we had a real long session. Apparently they were greatly impressed as they asked me if I could stick around the area and entertain at the Masquer's Club. As well, they were sure that they could get me on the Johnnie Carson show. I thanked them but had to pass, as I was anxious to get across the country before the bad weather came in.

I called my mother from there and she was disappointed that I was considering going to Hawaii before going home. She thought I'd be home in 2 weeks or so. She told me that she had to go to the hospital for a minor operation soon. The next day I went to church with the Larkins, took some photos, gave them some souvenirs and returned to the ship. It took the whole next day to sail to San Francisco where we docked in Alameda on October 10 at 8:15 AM. As I was paying off the ship at this point I had to be cleared by the Customs agent who came aboard. It hit me as humorous that here was the only place where my possessions were actually inspected although I had visited 31 countries and crossed international borders more than 40 times. The inspector was quite friendly and helpful. On my declaration form I had listed a total of $243 of goods being brought into the USA, the scooter being the largest part of that. However, he cut the value of all by the age of each unit and I ended up paying just $5.00 in import duty.

# CHAPTER THIRTY-TWO

## "Re-entry"

I said good-by to the captain and my shipmates and left the ship at about noon. I first crossed the Oakland Bay Bridge and started across the Golden Gate Bridge heading for George Frochen's parents house in Corte Madeira. I hadn't crossed the bridge when I was pulled over by the highway patrol. After checking my documents, the officer informed me that I could not use the scooter on any highways in California due to its low power. Of course I could use this bridge but had to take the first exit off the highway on the north side of the bridge. In any event I was soon having a joyous re-union with Mel and Marian Frochen. George was married and was in Texas going to DC—8 school for Delta Airlines. We had been stationed at Mather AFB in Sacramento together and we spent many weekends here at his super parents' home. It was truly ironic that George would become at Delta Airlines pilot as he had been eliminated from flying in the Air Force when it had been learned that he took an iodine pill for a minor thyroid condition.

As we talked through many pleasant hours we remembered the days when George and I (considered #2 son by "Mom" Frochen) would camp here on weekends as we toured his favorite spots in San Francisco. I had been unaware of Mel's line of work and was surprised to find out that he worked in an administrative position for the States Lines Shipping Company. He very well knew Mr. Onishi who had been so friendly to me in Yokohama. He said if he had known about my attempts there he probably could have gotten me on a ship from his company.

Gerry Monier had served with me in Bangor Maine at Dow AFB and it was through his wife, Eileen, that I had met and later visited Aunt Mai and her family in Ireland. He was now stationed at Merced and I looked up his phone number and made the call. I was shocked to be talking to Aunt Mai, herself, who was visiting the Monier's again. I drove the scooter there with some evident problems and had a great re-union with all of them. Their two daughters, Marlene and Jean had grown significantly and were truly beautiful and talented young ladies. After discussing all that had happened from the last time I had seen Aunt Mai, I had her pose for a photo as she pointed to the ""BIE 265" number plate (County Clair) of the scooter which she had witnessed starting its world journey with me from her house over three years prior.

Aunt Mai & scooter—three years later

After doing some repair work on the scooter I left Merced for the 120-mile drive to Sacramento where I would re-meet the Marcarelli family, close friends from my time at Mather AFB. John had sold me my first life insurance policy and I had become somewhat adopted by the family. I had kept in touch periodically as I traveled and had promised that I would visit if I got close to them as I returned home. John and his wife, Mary, had a great family with Pat, John, Jean, Tita and Lori (my little sweetheart). I was given a royal welcome and they couldn't believe all the places I had visited in the past 3 plus years. Immediately John arranged for an interview with the local press, which included a photo of him and me as he held my helmet. After dinner with this special family I headed out to the Rancho Cordova where many of us bachelors (including George Frochen) had rented apartments when we were going through training there. I had kept in touch with the Cavileer's who were the caretakers with whom we dealt for all needs. They had retired and were extremely happy that I had not forgotten them. Unfortunately Mr. Cavileer was in significant stages of Parkinson's disease. We had a nice visit and I headed back to Frochen's house.

By this time I had decided that I would forego the trip to Hawaii in the interest of getting home before the bad weather. I had intended to visit my Uncle Alex and Aunt Helen in Seattle before going east and I started investigating how I might make that journey. I became aware of "drive-away" agencies, which customers contract to deliver their vehicles when they want to fly to their destination but have the vehicle available there. After many calls and waiting I lined up a 1966 Chevrolet wagon from Allstate Driveaway Agency to be delivered to Seattle. On my part I would have to pay for the gas and oil and leave a $35 deposit. When I considered the possibility of driving the scooter there using only secondary roads, I decided that this wagon was the best possibility.

Mel and "Mom" were planning a vacation drive to the north and were prepared to take me with them if I had not been able to line up a way of departing. So, on October 21, Mel helped me load the wagon with my scooter and baggage and we said our sad farewells as we headed in bad weather to the north by two different highways. I drove almost without stopping and ultimately ended up at my Uncle Alex's door. The fuel and oil would cost me about $28 for 1,000 miles. After I had settled a bit we unloaded the wagon and I delivered it to the local dealer and retrieved my $35 deposit. I spent a few days with Alex and Helen to catch up on family history. Their son, Bobby, was also there and had traveled extensively in the Far East. Uncle Alex had retired from Boeing Aircraft and proudly showed me the country retreat he had on 10 acres of land, which had a 410-foot frontage on the river. He had a small camping trailer parked there and it was his "dream get-away" place.

While I was in the area I also looked up the family of Bob McKean who had flown refueling tankers at Dow AFB in Maine. I visited them in Yakima which is known as the "nation's fruit-bowl". They were a very solid family and I had dated their sweet daughter, Judy, a few times in Maine. There had been some possible scenarios where Judy and I might make a fine couple. However, she had found the love of her life and I wished her the best. He would be a very lucky guy.

At Mt. Rushmore—truly back in the USA

Back at Uncle Alex's home I was trying to find a way to get across the country to the East Coast. I checked on the train and it would cost me $30 for the scooter and $109 for me. However, I would arrive 3 days ahead of the scooter. I found that unacceptable; I would finish the journey with the mighty "steed" that had taken me so far in so many surroundings. Finally after checking with many drive-away agencies I got a 1966 Chevrolet wagon with three bicycles and 8 cases of canned goods inside. It was to be delivered to Ardmore just outside of Philadelphia. In this case I had to leave a $50 deposit. Uncle Alex insisted on loaning me another $50 to make sure I had enough money for gas, oil and tolls.

On November 17th, Uncle Alex and I used all our ingenuity to pack the scooter into this wagon with all the items that had been there when I picked it up. I called my sister Margaret and she told me that there was a bad snowstorm in the east and that my mother had gone to the hospital for the small operation and all was well. I left at 7:45 AM on route #90 heading for Spokane. I had purchased a jar of peanut butter, a jar of cheese spread and a loaf of bread. These would be my travel foods with whatever drinks I picked up as I refueled. I got so adept at it that I could make sandwiches as I drove.

Progress was somewhat slow as I ran into 1.5 hours of dense fog in Idaho and Montana. I had just entered Wyoming at 3:30 AM when I finally stopped to catch four hours of sleep in the car. I had covered 1,015 miles since leaving Seattle. I continued on to South Dakota and decided to drive an hour out of my way to view a true icon of the USA at Mt. Rushmore where Washington, Teddy Roosevelt, Lincoln and Jefferson looked down from their 5659-foot perch. I continued on to Paullina, Iowa to visit my brother-in-law, Bill's, family. Gwen (his sister) and Dale ran a typical local corn farm which I had visited as a teenager years before. I arrived at their door at 10:50 PM having driven 1,804 miles. We had a wonderful talk and jam session with their son who played drums. They insisted that we take a trip to the local newspaper office for an interview, which was later published there. I caught a few hours sleep and left at 4:10 AM for Cedar Falls to re-meet their daughter, son and son-in-law. Julie had been a pig-tailed youngster when I first met here but was now a beautiful young lady who was studying Spanish and was happy to have someone with whom to use that language. We had a great breakfast and I had to get on the road again.

As I drove through Iowa and Illinois there was quite a bit of snow around and the going was slower than I had hoped. With 2 hours sleep in the car I drove the rest of the way to Philadelphia. I parked in a downtown garage to try to find how I would get the scooter home from here. I tried the railway again but I would have to crate the scooter and go through a long process. With no obvious way to arrive with my scooter at home I decided that I would drive the wagon home as I was two days ahead of the normal delivery date and I was paying for the gas and tolls.

With that decision I was happy to leave Philadelphia and get on the road. I called my Aunt Margaret in Conn. and arranged to stop over at her house. When I arrived there I had driven just over 1,500 miles. This was my mother's older sister who was also anxious to relate to the visit I had made to their hometown. I was pleasantly reminded of how great a cook she was after eating sandwiches for days. I found out that my mother would be coming home from the hospital the next day.

WILMINGTON, MASS.    NOVEMBER 23, 1967

*The Last Half Mile . .*

Arriving home as promised to Bedouins*
*Photo courtesy of Wilmington Town Crier

For a long time I had planned my re-entry into my hometown by wearing my *ouqual* (Arab headdress) on my scooter. I had promised this to my Bedouin friends In Jordan. In order to do this I contacted the Enos family who had been great friends for a long time. The oldest daughter, Rose Marie, had been in my class in high school and I later worked with Dee, the loving and extremely funny mother. I would stop by their house the next day, get the scooter ready for the road, make my entrance as promised and return later for the wagon.

So it was on November 22, 1967 that I visited the Enos family and had a very difficult time getting the scooter running. It was slightly drizzling rain so I added my flowing poncho to my ouqual for the image. I then drove down the main street of Wilmington and entered the plaza where my mother had worked at Grant's store. I was waving and greeting everyone in Arabic and making a great deal of it. By this time my sister, Alice, had piled the kids into the car and had caught up to me. They followed as an escort. As I approached the traffic lights at the Silver Lake section I noticed Larz Neilson, Editor of the weekly Town Crier, press the crossing button resulting in my stopping there. He then recorded the scene with his faithful camera. He had been tipped off re: my return and it was to his office that I had sent accounts of my entire journey on a regular basis.

I finally continued to 23 Marjorie Road from which I had departed 3.5 years prior to find that my mother had just returned from the hospital 30 minutes earlier. There was also a reporter from the daily Lowell Sun newspaper who took a photo and interview. I was home at last with a treasure trove of experiences behind me. The rest of that day was a whirlwind of re-unions and a million questions. The following day was Thanksgiving and my mother and I celebrated it with my sister, Margaret Hansen, her husband, Bill, and their four daughters. In the evening I headed for Philadelphia and delivered the station wagon to the family there. They gave me a ride to the airport and Bill picked me up in Boston. Thus, I completed all the obligations incurred in getting home.

The following months were spent in trying to put this treasured experience into some lifetime context. I had spent three and a half years traveling through thirty-one countries and had absorbed an education of human interaction, which I could not have gotten in the most prestigious ivy-league university. I had started out with about $4,000 in my bank account and when I arrived home I still had $1,500 in it. This is not only a testament to my Scottish roots, but more so, to the inhabitants of the lands I visited. Their open hospitality provided a lesson I would have paid for, but wasn't allowed to. They had conveyed to me the universality of humanity in a very down-to-earth, common way. I kept in touch with many of them for long periods of time starting with my "arrived home" message that I enclosed in 128 Christmas cards, which I wrote in 6 languages and sent to 18 countries.

In summary of my dream sojourn among other common people I would reflect on the following poem, which I wrote in Hiroshi's apartment in Tokyo while I waited to find a means of crossing the Pacific back to the USA. Certainly my use of the term "brother" is meant in the biblical sense to include all peoples of all genders and races.

# HELLO BROTHER

We go through life complacent, and seldom stop to think; Of those whose
    lives are spent in quest of merely food and drink

God made us in equality, but yet by chance alone; Our lots extremely
    differ, like a precious gem from stone

From the arid desert wasteland to the modern life we know; From the
    towering new metropolis to the igloo in the snow

He blessed us each with dignity, a common bond for all; But how we
    force the level of this trait, in some, to fall

Too often we find the poorer man must hide it deep within; And bow to
    those above lest he, commit the social sin

His wish is opportunity to work with zeal and pride; And be accepted
    by all men, his freedom not denied

I've seen him in the desert, I've met him in the street, And spoken as a
    brother he never thought to meet

Upon my recognition of him, a fellow man; The blossoming of dignity
    within his soul began

The difference in our native tongues was little problem here; As contact
    and expression made our message clear

Mine was. "I came to meet you as a stranger from afar; To reconfirm to
    you and me, the kind of being you are"

His was, "I've often wondered if those who pass could know; How much
    I wished to greet them, mere brotherhood to show

But from my lowly place in life, I could not chance this urge; Until today,
    as if by fate, you happened to emerge

Your message was for my poor ears, indeed the sweetest song; I've longed
    to hear it many times—oh God I've waited long

We swapped ideas as neighbors do, but soon we had to part; Each felt a
    slightly different man, with warmth within his heart

So many times in other lands the scene occurred again; And now I know
    a closer bond of friendship with all men

I understand them better now, the message will not fade; A greeting,
    "Hello brother" was the meager price I paid.

Jerry Rooney, A Traveler

# *EPILOGUE*

During the winter of 1967-68 I worked as a substitute schoolteacher in order to have a flexible schedule and to be able to earn some income. In the spring I was contacted by Father Coleman Conley who had been re-assigned to the USA after 10 years in Japan and was working with multi-lingual, poor children in the south end of New Bedford, Mass. He convinced me to come to the Regina Pacis (Queen of Peace) Center to work with him after having last seen him at the church/kindergarten he ran in Tsuchiura, Japan. On the first Sunday I used the guitar for a folk Mass and later went downstairs to join the small congregation for coffee and donuts. As I entered the room a well-groomed lady got my attention and said, "You must be Gerry. I understand you speak Japanese. I'd like you to meet Ayako who is studying at the university in Dartmouth and living with my family". She was Lillian Corre, Ayako's American mother.

A year later we were married, had two children and have two grandchildren at this writing. Her plan to get a degree and return to Japan was interrupted by this Scottish troubadour with his guitar. She had been brought to the USA to study through the Sacred Heart priests who had many small churches in her area of Japan including one around the corner from her house. It was coincidental that Father Coleman and her sponsor, Fr. Albert Evans, had brought us together. As we later compared notes, Ayako had taught at that same kindergarten that I had visited with Father Coleman and, thus, knew the same head teacher, janitor, cook . . . etc that I had met.

In 1987 the neighboring town of Fairhaven (with the city of New Bedford) signed a Sister City Agreement with Tosashimizu, the hometown of the first Japanese person who ever lived in the USA. He, Manjiro Nakahama, lived with the whaling captain (William Whitfield) who had rescued him from a Pacific Island. Ayako was immediately involved with the Sister City Committee, which ultimately involved this first generation Scot who (to defy odds and/or logic) has been the Chairman of the committee for 18 plus years. Thus, Japan has played a major role in my life not only through my in-laws and friends who live in Japan but also through the Sister City agreement and the continual bonds that it nurtures.

I worked with Father Coleman until I got married and then was hired to an administrative position in Onboard, the New Bedford poverty program agency formed to deal with Pres. Johnson's "War on Poverty". I later moved to the manpower division of the agency and continued in various positions in other human services programs. I became the Executive Director of the "Opportunity Center", a sheltered workshop for mentally challenged adults, in 1983 and retired from that position in 2001. Thus, I spent 35 years in human services administration, which might sound a bit odd given that I received my degree as a Bachelor of Chemical Engineering. At one point this was put into an observant perspective by Jean (the charming wife of my good friend Mike Riccardi) when she observed, "I think you found your chemistry in people."

Many of those I met in my journey have lost contact but the experience still stands out in my personal history. One person with whom I kept an on-going contact was Hiroshi Nishida. When he finished medical school he came to New Jersey to do an internship. He was at the head table at our wedding. Later he did a residency in Maryland and we attended his wedding. We had a daughter, Monica, and they had one, Hanako. We had a son, Mark, and they had one, Kenchi. They had two more but we stopped. When Hanako was in junior high school she spent a year living with us and going to school with Monica. When Hanako graduated from college she went to Clarion University in Penn. and got an advanced degree in Library Sciences. Her wish was to spend a little time working in the USA and ended up as the Children's Librarian in the Watertown, Mass public library. At this point she became like another member of our family and a wonderful extra "auntie" to Monica's two children, Haley and Jack. In 2006 she finally returned to Japan to continue here education and career.

Hiroshi has made a great career as a neonatologist in Japan and was, in fact, pediatrician to several of the Emperor's grandchildren. He was well known for his campaign against SIDS (sudden infant death syndrome). He also expressed his dedication to children by running the "Silk Road" from Rome to Nara, Japan. The entire theme of the event was for the loving care of the children of the world. He did this in sections and he is to run the last section to Nara soon. Needless to say whenever we are close to him or vice versa, we enjoy each other's company and keep in close touch.

On a regular basis at holiday time I keep up the contact with Marie Needham in Ireland, Bunny Newton's daughter, Wendy, who now lives in Spain and George Macaratesi in Argentina. Bruno Schneiderbauer's two daughters, Elizabeth and Marion, each spent a summer with us as they got a good look at the seacoast as compared to their Alpine setting in Austria. Bruno and Piti also stopped by for a one-day visit when they had a stopover in Boston. Antal Ritzl finished his education and worked for the Swedish telephone company all over the world. When he was returning from Columbia, South America he stopped to see us with his wife, Lubica, and their young baby. For many years I kept in touch with Matt Busby and my other relatives in Scotland whom I had met during my journey. Later they passed and the contact was lost.

One other person with whom I have had constant contact is Jack Wong Sue who was an outstanding WW II hero in Australia. When Jack kept hearing the "armchair warriors" in Sydney expound on the life in the jungles in the war he got fed up and decided to write a real account. He was initially hampered by the loss of his diaries, but they were found by one of his mates. However, before he could write he suffered a stroke, which left half of his body useless. He spent the next 3.5 years writing 131,000 words with one finger of his left hand resulting in "Blood on Borneo" which became a best seller in Australia. His son, Barry, handles the business end of the publishing of this and other books by his dad. At one point "Blood on Borneo" outsold "Harry Potter". Despite his restrictions Jack is always a "can do" kind of guy and he is certainly one of the true heroes from my entire journey.

After living in a mobile home for the first year of our married life while Ayako finished her senior year of college, we bought our first home in New Bedford just after the birth of Monica. It was a home in need of a great amount of TLC but we determined to make it our dream house. However, in 1979 we decided we needed more space as we now had two growing children; Mark had joined Monica. We moved to a 250-year-old farmhouse at the end of a dead-end country lane in the adjacent town of Acushnet. My hometown of Wilmington was about the same size and I felt quite at home in our two acres with the brook running through. Ayako brought all of her artistic ability to the task of fixing up the gardens and interior decor as I dealt with the restoration of the building. We have worked over the years to make a home for our family and friends, which is a home to "live in". As for the "Irish Rover", it's still in my garage waiting for the next time I will tune it up and put it back on the road. Even when not running, it stands as a constant reminder of a magical time of my life.

We have been extremely fortunate with great neighbors, John and Arlene Pombo, and Arlene's sister, Charlotte Stone. As I assess the blessings of our surroundings I often reflect on those I met so long ago and so far away. They help me put my life into perspective. I'm always looking for an opportunity to say, "Hello, brother" to someone new.

Printed in the United States
141664LV00003B/59/P

9 781436 379014